Worldchangers

Worldchangers by Shandi Stevenson is an energetic and impressive compilation of short biographies of great Christians from all over the world and different eras. Each chapter is a stand alone, and each chapter is meticulously researched and documented. The book is a treasure. Stevenson is able to come across as erudite, but not stuffy. She is a fine story teller as well as an impressive academic, and *Worldchangers* is a fine read that I heartily recommend to anyone interested in getting to know several of the great saints of the faith.

John Carenen
Author of *Keeping to Himself, The Nick O'Shea* trilogy, and *Son-up, Son-Down*

The footsteps that Miss Stevenson chronicles in this first volume of her series *Footsteps Worth Following* are footsteps most of us would never know about and could not possibly imagine without masterfully and lovingly curated mini-biographies like these. Miss Stevenson artfully condenses the lifetimes of faithful and wildly diverse men and women who have gone before us to enliven our imaginations to what the Lord might do with our own lifetimes as we give ourselves over to Him in His personal and almighty work!

Reba Collins
Reading Tutor

I am really, really enjoying learning about these world changers! I find myself wanting to keep reading from paragraph to paragraph.

Lydia Griffin
Retired teacher and missionary

Worldchangers

SHANDI STEVENSON

Ambassador International
GREENVILLE, SOUTH CAROLINA & BELFAST, NORTHERN IRELAND

www.ambassador-international.com

Worldchangers
Footsteps Worth Following, Volume 1
©2023 by Shandi Stevenson

ISBN: 978-1-64960-581-8, hardcover
ISBN: 978-1-64960-340-1, paperback
eISBN: 978-1-64960-358-6

Scripture taken from the King James Version. Public Domain.

Cover Design by Hannah Linder Designs
Interior Typesetting by Dentelle Design

AMBASSADOR INTERNATIONAL
Emerald House
411 University Ridge, Suite B14
Greenville, SC 29601, USA
www.ambassador-international.com

AMBASSADOR BOOKS
The Mount
2 Woodstock Link
Belfast, BT6 8DD, Northern Ireland, UK
www.ambassadormedia.co.uk

The colophon is a trademark of Ambassador, a Christian publishing company.

Table of Contents

Introduction

In John Bunyan's classic allegory *Pilgrim's Progress*, Christian must find his way through the dark and terrible Valley of the Shadow. The valley is filled with confusing and distracting sounds of fear and pain, and Christian is threatened on both sides of the narrow, twisting path by yawning pits, traps, quicksand, and prowling enemies. As he feels his way through the shadows, Christian hears the voice of an unknown fellow traveler somewhere ahead of him, singing the praises of God. The voice ahead of him in the valley assures Christian that there is a way through and that he is still on the right path.

The stories of men and women who have walked with God and seen His faithfulness, who have navigated a dark and broken world with courage and integrity, are like that voice in the valley. They give strength, hope, and clarity to those who follow them. In his book *The Will of God as a Way of Life*, Gerald Sittser writes of the sadness he feels for Christians who live as spiritual orphans despite two thousand years of church history—history rich in stories of men and women who have experienced and shared the truth of the gospel in an endless variety of circumstances. Without the voice ahead of us on the road, it is easy to become disoriented or discouraged, lose our way, or simply lose sight of what is possible.

Worldchangers, the first volume in the *Footsteps Worth Following* series, is simply an introduction to a few of the true stories that have strengthened the faith and fired the imagination of Christians for decades—in some cases for centuries. The list of those included and the individual stories are alike in being far too short—barely a glance at a much larger, richer subject. My hope is that many who read this book will use it as an introduction to people with whom they want to spend much more time and to subjects and stories they will want to learn more about.

CHAPTER 1

William Tyndale

"A GREATER AND MORE PRECIOUS THING"

The walls and towers of the ancient castle were cold and forbidding, stark against the pale autumn morning sky. Only the robes and emblems of office worn by the assembled local dignitaries splashed color against the chilly stones. Some representing the church and others the state, they offered a solemn display of unity as they took their seats in the courtyard. All eyes followed the prisoner being led toward the center of the courtyard.

There was a familiar ritual to these ceremonies at the overlap of church and state, a ritual sending powerful messages about the foundational ideals of both. First, in a crucial part of the process, the prisoner was offered an opportunity to recant. By simply acknowledging that what he had done violated the laws of God and man and by promising repentance, the man might save his life even at the last minute. As expected, however, the prisoner refused to acknowledge that he had done wrong and refused to promise that his illegal activities would cease. He had probably known, ever since his betrayal by a trusted friend months before, what the end would be. He must have recognized almost immediately that the trap into which he had been drawn had closed behind him and would not open again. There was no decision left for him to make. This morning may even have come as a kind of relief after the long months of privation and bitter cold in a prison cell, awaiting the inevitable.

The man was now bound tightly to the cross in the center of the square, and bundles of wood were piled at his feet. Then a guard stepped behind the prisoner, for this convict was one of the lucky ones. He was to be strangled before being burned at the stake. It was a far easier death than many faced.

It is said that his last words, spoken in this foreign land, were "Lord, open the King of England's eyes." Then the rope tightened, there were a few terrible moments of struggle, and the dead body slumped against the cross. As the assembled spectators watched, flames were set to the wood, and the lifeless body was consumed by fire—the very fate so many of his books had met.

Just five months later, the dying man's prayer would be answered. His name was William Tyndale.

Early Life and Education

He was born in a village in Gloucestershire, in rural England, around the year 1494. Very little is known of his family or parents, but they must have had sufficient means and social standing to provide their son with the best education his age had to offer. He attended Magdalen College, Oxford (the same college where C.S. Lewis would be a professor centuries later), graduating in 1512, and in 1515 he received a Master of Arts degree from the equally prestigious Cambridge University.

Tyndale was a brilliant student, and his ability with languages was especially remarkable. All university students studied Latin and Greek, but Tyndale continued to study several additional languages after completing his degree and ultimately became fluent in Italian, Spanish, French, and German. He also mastered Greek so thoroughly that he was appointed professor of the language at Cambridge while he continued his studies in theology and languages. This meant not only that Tyndale could fluently read, write, and speak the major languages of Europe, but also that he intensively studied the works on which all of European culture and European Christianity were based, from the ancient fathers of the church, to the great Bible commentators, medieval philosophers, and major historians.

Most of all, however, Tyndale loved to study the Bible. He could imagine nothing more precious, nothing more astonishing, than the extraordinary privilege of studying the Bible in languages he understood deeply, intimately, and instinctively. Thus, at a very young age, Tyndale was struck by the contrast between his experience of the Bible and that of most English men and women. He pictured them, faithfully attending church week after week to hear the Bible read to them in Latin—a language few of them studied—and explained to them, in many cases, by priests whose Latin was so minimal that they, too, had never read the Bible. How different this experience of the Bible was from Tyndale's transformative personal adventure. He could compare a verse in several languages, mentally translating it in several possible ways. He could turn each word to the light like a many-faceted diamond, following themes and ideas and questions wherever they led, through all sixty-six books. The Scriptures, which so many churchgoers experienced as a remote and mysterious text in an opaque language, sprang to life and leaped off the page for Tyndale. For him the Scriptures became a rich reservoir of truth that nourished his mind and soul. It was a source of endless awe, of incredulous delight, that he could fill his mind and heart with the very words of the living God, waiting for no one else to grant him access. He did not believe that his experience of the Bible should be for the privileged few. He believed it was for everyone.

The words Tyndale would write decades later in his preface to the Book of Romans capture something of the growing urgency he felt as a young scholar:

> I think it meet that every christian man not only know it, by rote and without the book, but also exercise himself therein evermore continually, as with the daily bread of the soul. No man verily can read it too oft, or study it too well; for the more it is studied, the easier it is; the more it is chewed, the pleasanter it is; and the more groundly it is searched, the preciouser things are found in it, so great treasure of spiritual things lieth hid therein.[1]

For Tyndale, the Word of God should not be something outside the Christian, something on the periphery of his imagination, something punctuating the duties and dilemmas and experiences of his life. It should be inside—deep, deep inside where thoughts and ideas and feelings flow together. The Christian should know the Bible as a fish knows the water, or a bird the air, or a plant the soil that feeds its roots. It should be not the outer skin, but the bones and blood of the Christian's life. It should be a best friend, an advisor, a confidante.

"To William Tyndale," writes biographer David Teems,

> the Word of God is a living thing. It has both warmth and intellect. It has discretion, generosity, subtlety, movement, authority. It has a heart and a pulse . . . It enchants and it soothes. It argues and it forgives. It defends and it reasons. It intoxicates and it restores. It weeps and it exults. It thunders but never roars. It calls but never begs. And it always loves.[2]

From the beginning, Tyndale felt so strongly about every Christian's right to know the Word of God that—as a critic would complain much later when his passion had cost him his home and way of life—he was "always singing one note." At university he

---

1   Tyndale, William. "A Prologue Upon the Epistle of Saint Paul to the Romans." Trans.   M i c h a e l D. Marlowe. "Bible Research"; English Versions; Tyndale; Preface to Romans. Luminarium. Bible Researcher. Michael D. Marlowe. 2001-2012. Accessed May 30, 2022. www.bible-researcher.com/romansprologue.html.

2   Teems, David. *Tyndale: The Man Who Gave God an English Voice*. Nashville, Thomas Nelson. 2012. Page xvii.

formed groups of other students who shared his interest and joined him to study and discuss the Bible at informal meetings. Increasingly restless and outspoken, Tyndale the theology student grew highly critical of the standard practice requiring future leaders and shepherds of the church to study so long in so many other fields before being allowed to begin their study of the Bible itself. The explosive text was kept walled off, at the end of a long, winding trail of study. Only when they had mastered countless tools and ideas, and grounded themselves thoroughly in the teachers of the church, were students trusted with the perilous and privileged opportunity of "setting foot," as it were, on the sacred ground of the Scriptural text itself. Many of them, less motivated than Tyndale, never arrived, or if they did never got around to spending much time there.

Something about this seemed backward to Tyndale. Of course the teachings of the church were supposed to be rooted in and grow out of the Bible, but didn't the traditional training of theology students imply that it was the other way around? For his teachers, Bible study was like an ornamental dessert; for Tyndale, it was like the bread that sustained the life of a farmer's family. For the learned men of the church, it seemed like an optional, extra area of interest for exceptionally proficient students to tack onto their studies. To Tyndale, it was the highest priority—the one thing that should never be crowded out by anything else. It was only the Word of God, Tyndale believed, that could transform the individual and the church:

> There must first be in the heart of a man before he do any good works, a greater and more precious thing than all the good works in the world . . . That precious thing which must be in the heart, ere a man can work any good work, is the word of God . . . Therefore it is called the word of life, the word of grace, the word of health, the word of redemption, the word of forgiveness, and the word of peace . . . [3]

Joining the Controversy

It is not surprising that Tyndale became an increasingly vocal and well-known proponent of church reform, wading into the turbulent and rising waters of theological debate. A growing chorus of voices was being raised against both the moral laxity and corruption and the low standard of theological and Biblical literacy many saw in the late medieval church. On the continent, Martin Luther had already touched off an intellectual, cultural, and political earthquake by nailing his ninety-five theses to the

---

3   Ibid. 114–115.

door of the Wittenberg cathedral, and Luther was one of many who had long been offering many of the same arguments. Luther only made popularly accessible the same kinds of concerns that churchmen had been raising for centuries among themselves. All of Europe knew—had known for a long time—that the church was overdue for reform, especially after some of the more scandalous Renaissance popes. The church was too political, too financially and morally corrupt, and much too hypocritical.

For the past several centuries, there had been room in the Catholic church for many schools of thought, including those that made virtually all the same arguments Luther would later be excommunicated for making. England, in particular, had already been irrevocably transformed by its reform movement, led by John Wycliffe—sometimes called "The Morning Star of the Reformation." Wycliffe and his followers, derisively known as Lollards, argued for the priority of Biblical over papal authority, and for the importance of transforming the church from the bottom up by equipping lay men and women to study the Bible. Wycliffe had even translated part of the New Testament from Latin into English.

But now, like two nations stumbling into a war neither side wants, Luther and the Pope had drawn lines in the sand, and Europe was choosing sides. Positions were hardening too rapidly to allow for compromise. The window of time during which it had been possible for men of goodwill to engage in learned discussions about church reform, and for those of different points of view to unite in prayer for the future of the church, was closing. In the polarized intellectual climate created by the Protestant Reformation, as the Catholic Church did too little too late to stand against the tidal wave of change, people increasingly felt they had to choose. The Bible, or the authority of the church? The local congregation, or the centralized hierarchy? The Bible in the hands of the people, or the Bible jealously guarded by a corrupt elite? Even Wycliffe was dug up some years after his death and his bones burned, along with copies of his writings, as the new, more divided and more dangerous religious and political climate put his ideas too far outside the mainstream. His legacy now seemed less of a joke and more of a threat.

When William Tyndale began to argue for church reform, especially for the translation of the New Testament into English, he was in distinguished company—but he was also joining the conversation at precisely the wrong political moment. The church was steadily hardening its position against every hint of protest or dissent. It was also beginning to dawn on European heads of state that the explosive clash of ideas sparked by

Luther's Reformation was at least as dangerous politically as it was theologically. (Indeed, a century of bloody religious wars would decimate Europe in its wake.)

Tyndale, the passionate and outspoken young Bible scholar, was destined to attract suspicion and controversy. In 1521 he at last left Cambridge, after spending the previous fifteen years in the heady world of the universities. Even there, it was becoming dangerous and unpopular to speak against the Church's position on any issue. Perhaps Tyndale did not realize that what might be tolerated in a world where learned men debated as equals, trying on ideas for size, would be entirely unacceptable in a world where the local priest was the face of and spokesman for the church, expected to toe the party line at least in front of the laity. In any event, Tyndale began his career in the church by spending weekdays as the private tutor and household chaplain of an aristocratic landowner, Sir John Walsh, and by preaching and serving as priest for the local parish church. The position was supposed to be the beginning of his life's work in the English church—but it would only last two years.

By 1523, just two years into his first appointment, Tyndale had already attracted a dangerous amount of unfavorable attention from his fellow churchmen for his radical views on reform and particularly for his belief that English laypeople should be able to study the Bible in their own language. It was an idea that carried all kinds of dangerous connotations, implying as it did that the authority of the church was secondary to that of the Bible and that those without the years of education which, as Tyndale had discovered to his dismay, were considered necessary, might actually be competent to study the Bible without harming themselves or others.

Yet Tyndale might still have been allowed to enjoy his private beliefs in peace, had he not insisted on seeking to persuade others of his views. More and more he was raising his voice for reform within the church hierarchy, urging his fellow churchmen with both the written and the spoken word to consider his arguments. Even this might have been tolerated, however, had he not taken the additional far more controversial step of incorporating such incendiary ideas into his weekly sermons to his rural congregation. A united front before the laity was the least the church required. Tyndale was attracting too much attention, and he was going too far. There was not going to be room in the English church for him much longer—not if he couldn't keep his head down and stop stirring up trouble.

Tyndale was soon accused of heresy and summoned before a church council, where he was forbidden to preach in public any longer—a prohibition he seems to have disregarded entirely. A fellow priest visited Tyndale and debated with him. The priest insisted that if they had to choose, Christians would be better off without the law of God than without the Pope's. Tyndale is supposed to have replied with the famous words that would become his challenge to his own time and his legacy to ours: "I defy the Pope and all his laws . . . If God spare my life ere many years, I will cause a boy that driveth the plow, shall know more of the Scripture than thou dost."[4]

From Pastor To Translator

It was clear that Tyndale's time in the English church was ending, one way or the other. So Tyndale left his first and only clerical assignment and set off for London. But this was far from a surrender—in fact, it was the opposite. Tyndale headed for London with the express purpose of translating the Bible into English. The pushback he had encountered only solidified Tyndale's conviction that this was the great need of the English church in his time. And if no one else was going to do it, Tyndale, with his strong background in languages, theology, and Bible, was one of the men in England most capable of attempting it.

Nevertheless, the task Tyndale had set himself was a monumental challenge. Unlike Wycliffe, who had created a translation of a translation (basing his English New Testament on the Latin Vulgate instead of the original Greek), Tyndale planned to translate the New Testament directly from Greek into English. By translating from the original text into his native language, Tyndale hoped to achieve a translation that was both more accurate and more readable.

The task of translating all twenty-seven New Testament books would have been a daunting task—the task of a lifetime—even if Tyndale had found all the support and resources he needed freely available to him. Translation is a task ideally attempted by a committee, preferably with assistants to run errands to the library and copy notes and buy more paper.

Instead—as very quickly became clear after Tyndale's attempts to find patronage and support in London failed completely—Tyndale would be working in secret, and on the run. If his work, which was illegal, became widely known, he could lose not only his work, but also his life. The same was true for anyone who helped him with his clandestine project. The country chaplain had become an outlaw—a man apart, a man with a deadly secret that would dominate the rest of his life. "Tyndale's is a life lived as a project," writes one biographer, and another, "His commitment is final and all consuming."[5]

---

4   Foxe, John. "The Life and Story of the True Servant and Martyr of God, William Tyndale." Quoted in "Bible Research." Michael D. Marlowe. 2001–2012. Web. Accessed February 1, 2019.
5   Teems, 39.

The danger Tyndale had no doubt expected came quickly, and in 1524, the year after his arrival in London, a group of sympathetic London merchants smuggled Tyndale out of England. He escaped to Germany with his in-process translation, seeking refuge in Wittenberg with Martin Luther—himself the author of a revolutionary translation of the New Testament into modern German. Here, Tyndale hoped for the safety and the support to complete and distribute his New Testament.

He worked with a speed fueled by his passion and focus. For Tyndale, as one biographer has written, it was "an act of affection and rapture" to translate the New Testament. Tyndale himself described the Greek word "evangelion," translated by the English "gospel," as a term that "signifieth good, merry, glad, and joyful tidings, that maketh a man's heart glad and maketh him sing, dance, and leap for joy."[6] Tyndale was driven by eagerness to share the "good, merry, glad and joyful tidings" with his countrymen, and just a year after his arrival in Germany, in 1525, the translation was finished. It was printed in the magnificent German city of Cologne, and from there, the contraband books flowed back into England through countless underground channels—mostly hidden, like drugs or black-market merchandise, in the shipments of merchants sympathetic to the cause.

The Manhunt Begins

Its infiltration of England, and its creator's location, were concealed from the authorities, but the existence of Tyndale's New Testament was itself no secret. King Henry VIII learned of its publication almost at once, and he gave orders that every copy that could be bought, intercepted, or confiscated should be burned—a development which caused Tyndale to remark cheerfully that the king was funding the further printing of the New Testament by increasing the demand for it.

Meanwhile, Sir Thomas More, King Henry's Lord High Chancellor, engaged in a published debate with Tyndale, his fellow clergyman. They were well-matched as scholars and wordsmiths, but their real audience was not so much one another as the British church. They debated the dangers of an English Bible translation, the authority of the Pope, the practice of prayer to the saints, the sacraments of the church—every issue that was cutting a fissure through the European church. Always wiser than his master the king (who would ultimately have him executed), More recognized that you don't turn back the tides of history by burning books and sending people into exile. He knew that

6   Moynahan, Brian. *God's Bestseller*. NY, St. Martin's Press. 2002. Page 35.

the reformers were raising important questions the church was going to have to answer—that it was in the marketplace of ideas that the church would have to prevail.

The "letters"—really more like articles or essays—that More and Tyndale exchanged are among the great documents of the Reformation, but they were only part of a steady stream of tracts, pamphlets, and articles Tyndale wrote during his time of exile. He had a unique gift for writing that was accessible and compelling both to his fellow scholars and laymen—a gift that reflected his vision of every Christian's capacity to study and grasp truths that many believed could be safely handled only by highly educated specialists. As David Teems writes, "He writes with tenderness, with paternal authority and warmth . . . His text has a . . . kind of desperate charm that is both intense and weightless at the same time."[7] Tyndale's greatest work was certainly his Bible translation, but he was also an articulate writer of devotional and argumentative Christian texts, in addition to his many important letters to leading figures of his day. He even addressed the new and complicated political issues raised by the Reformation, writing about the duties of Christian subjects to church, state, Scripture, and conscience. Ironically, Tyndale's groundbreaking argument for the duty of Christians to obey the state in secular matters prepared the way very handily for Henry VIII's defiance of papal authority—a defiance which would bring the Reformation to England in a few more years and would cause Henry to view Tyndale and his New Testament in a very different light.

For now, however, Henry bitterly resented the fact that Tyndale had crossed swords with More—not only a high-ranking royal official, but also one who had helped the king himself draft a challenge to Martin Luther earlier in the Reformation. To Henry VIII, always very sensitive to opposition, Tyndale's defiance seemed almost personal—not simply the breaking of a law, but a dangerous shot fired at the authority of the king himself. The king's sophisticated network of spies, informers, and back-channel contacts kept track of Tyndale's activities throughout Tyndale's time on the Continent.

Despite this animosity, however, Henry's opposition to Tyndale was—for a man who executed two of his wives and two of his most trusted advisors— comparatively restrained. Henry actually sought to bring Tyndale home and welcome him back into the fold. It would probably have been a significant public relations coup for Henry to achieve this. Not only this, but Henry knew he was failing to staunch the flow of English New Testaments from the Continent, and he may have realized that it was time to try a new approach. Still, from Henry's perspective the offer he made Tyndale—a self-confessed lawbreaker who had fled

---

7   Teems, xvi.

the king's authority—must have seemed remarkably generous. He even deputed an English merchant to find Tyndale and personally convey the king's invitation, assuring Tyndale that the king was inclined toward "mercy, pity, and compassion."[8] If Tyndale would just promise never to publish or circulate either Bible translation or other writings in the future, the king would guarantee his right to return in safety.

Despite his many friends in Europe, and despite the contacts he was able to maintain with some in England, the life of a hunted exile is always a lonely one. Tyndale seems sometimes to have been poignantly homesick. He was reportedly moved to tears in speaking with the king's messenger—perhaps overcome with visions of the green English countryside, the faces of those he missed, the memories of living freely and openly among friends, the pleasure of seeing those ploughboys he had talked about reading the New Testament in their language. Yet, as the messenger reported back to the king's advisor, Tyndale insisted on "always singing one note." He would love to return to England, and he would give his promise never to write another book as long as he lived— on one condition. Would the king consent to authorize an English New Testament and permit its publication and distribution?

Vaughn, the king's messenger, reported Tyndale's words to the king and his advisors:

> I assure you, if it would stand with the King's most gracious pleasure to grant only a bare text of the Scripture [that is, without explanatory notes] to be put forth among his people, like as is put forth among the subjects of the emperor in these parts, and of other Christian princes, be it of the translation of what person soever shall please his Majesty, I shall immediately make faithful promise never to write more, not abide two days in these parts after the same: but immediately to repair unto his realm, and there most humbly submit myself at the feet of his royal majesty, offering my body to suffer what pain or torture, yea, what death his grace will, so this [translation] be obtained. Until that time, I will abide the asperity of all chances, whatsoever shall come, and endure my life in as many pains as it is able to bear and suffer.[9]

Exile, and the Old Testament

Tyndale seems never to have given up all hope of returning to England, but after this plea was rejected by the King, he must have known how likely it was that he would die in exile. It was time to focus on his next project.

---

8   Piper, John. "Always Singing One Note: A Vernacular Bible." DesiringGod.org. John Piper. Web. Accessed November 16, 2019.
9   Ibid.

As he looked to the future, Tyndale dreamed of completing an entire English Bible and seeing it in the hands of men, women, and children all over England. Already he had begun to work on translating the Old Testament from Hebrew. The work was going well, and the heady atmosphere of Reformation Germany was the ideal sanctuary in which to make progress on his task. Even as Tyndale knew there was a price on his head and he would probably never see his native land again, he knew that he was connected to England as never before by the gift he had given it. All over England, Tyndale's New Testament was transforming men and women, families and churches. The spark had touched off a fire that was already burning too hot and spreading too fast for Henry VIII to have any hope of containing it. Tyndale might never be able to speak face to face with those whose lives were changed, whose minds were fired, whose souls were fed by his translation, but it was enough to know that it was happening—that, in this one little corner of the world, the very Word of God had been set free.

The greater the impact of the forbidden New Testament, however, the greater was Tyndale's personal danger, even in the far more welcoming climate of Germany. Soon he was denounced for heresy again. No longer safe, even in Germany, Tyndale went into hiding to continue his ambitious task. To have any hope of completing his translation of the Old Testament before his enemies closed in, Tyndale would need to disappear—and, somehow, he did. Henry VIII's right-hand man, Cardinal Wolsey, was a powerful man who had eyes everywhere, but all the efforts of his impressive spy network were in vain. Tyndale's hiding place was such a good one that its location remains unknown to this day.

Meanwhile, the winds of change were blowing through England. Increasingly impatient, not with Catholic doctrine but with the inability of his queen to bear him a son, Henry VIII became interested in any theology that would allow him to legally divorce his faithful wife of many years and marry the latest in a long series of mistresses—or rather, in this case, a woman who courageously refused to become the mistress of a married man, king or no king. Anne Boleyn, with whom he was head over heels in love, seemed like the answer to all Henry's problems. Unable to persuade the pope that his marriage should be annulled, Henry VIII solved his problem another way. Deciding that he should ride the convenient wave of Protestant zeal breaking over Europe after all, Henry broke with Rome entirely, declaring himself head of the Church of England. Having thrown in his lot with the challengers of papal authority, and having married Anne Boleyn (who had been influenced by Wycliffe's teachings and was a reader of Tyndale's New Testament), Henry began to reconsider his stance on several theological issues. It didn't hurt when it dawned on him that confiscating the land and money of monasteries all over England would pour unimaginable wealth into the royal coffers.

Tyndale must have dared to hope that the end was in sight—that the Protestant Reformation, and with it the English Bible and its translator, would soon be welcomed to England. It seems clear that Tyndale believed his danger had diminished, because he took the bold step of emerging from hiding in Germany and moving openly to Antwerp in the Low Countries (modern Belgium). Here he lived and worked, cautiously but openly, making progress on the Old Testament translation and savoring his newfound freedom to move about the streets or share a meal with friends.

It was a welcome relief. Tyndale's life must often have been a deeply lonely one. First a young scholar consumed by his work and then a man on the run, Tyndale never married, even though he shared Martin Luther's rejection of the doctrine of clerical celibacy and wrote of marriage with a respect and tenderness which suggest that giving up his chance of family life may have been one of the greatest sacrifices he made. His friends in England might never see him again, and now he was, to some extent, isolated also from those he had made in Germany. Now, during his time in Antwerp, Tyndale made a point of connecting with the growing community of religious refugees there. After so long in hiding, he seems to have been eager to be part of a community once again. Despite the many difficulties of his situation, Tyndale guarded against a tendency to hole up with his books and fail to participate in the life of the church or to live out the Scriptural truths he valued so highly. As a biographer writes:

> During these years, Tyndale also gave himself methodically to good works because, as he said, "My part be not in Christ if mine heart be not to follow and live according as I teach." On Mondays he visited other religious refugees from England. On Saturdays he walked Antwerp's streets, seeking to minister to the poor. On Sundays he dined in merchants' homes, reading Scripture before and after dinner. The rest of the week he devoted to writing tracts and books and translating the Bible.[10]

---

10 "William Tyndale: Translator of the First English New Testament." ChristianityToday.com. Christian History. Web. Accessed February 1, 2019.

The Friend

In so many ways, then, Antwerp seemed like a new beginning. The New Testament was flowing into England through every port, the political situation in England looked more promising every day, and Tyndale was savoring something like a normal life. The Old Testament was progressing well. And then something wonderful happened. Tyndale was befriended by a young Englishman who became a comrade, a partner, a supporter, a protégé —something between an apprentice and the son Tyndale had never had. It looked as if Tyndale would not have to finish his Old Testament translation alone but would finally have another English speaker to run errands for him, to help with the work, to discuss the translation, and to cheer him on toward the finish line. Henry Phillips, a fellow Oxford graduate, struck Tyndale as a man of both integrity and intelligence who shared his love of languages and literature.

We now know that Henry Phillips was a dubious character with a lot to hide. He had fled England under a legal and financial cloud, accused of robbing his father and impoverishing himself through gambling. He was an unscrupulous man desperate for money. He fitted perfectly the profile of the shifty character in search of a bargaining chip he could trade with the authorities to solve his own problems.

Perhaps Phillips was a natural con artist, gifted at being whomever his mark wanted him to be. Perhaps Tyndale, after so many years of caution and secrecy, got careless and let his guard down. Probably the truth is somewhere in between. In any case, the two Englishmen, meeting in a foreign city and taking a liking to one another, were soon close friends. Week after week, Phillips dined at Tyndale's house and met Tyndale's friends. He must have shown great respect and enthusiasm for Tyndale's work because the two conversed by the hour. One can imagine the delight Tyndale took in speaking English with another educated man, who seemed to share so many of his beliefs, and who seemed to understand and even to share Tyndale's passion for Bible translation. Soon Phillips was one of the very few trusted friends who had almost complete access to Tyndale's books and papers.

And all the time, as we now know, Phillips had sought Tyndale out to betray him to the authorities. So much of Tyndale's life in exile remains shrouded in mystery that to this day it is not certain who was paying Phillips. Perhaps the English authorities who had pursued Tyndale so long, perhaps some European power, perhaps some less reputable source. Only one thing is clear: the young friend Tyndale had been so delighted to find was in Antwerp with one mission—to find William Tyndale, draw him out, and betray him to his enemies.

Betrayal

Phillips sprang his trap on May 21, 1535. Arriving at Tyndale's lodgings and learning from the landlady that Tyndale was at work in his study, Phillips entered. With typical opportunism, he is said to have asked Tyndale for a loan, and Tyndale—always notoriously generous with money, unhesitatingly gave it to him. Phillips then asked Tyndale to dinner, but Tyndale quickly assured Phillips that he already had an invitation to dine out and that Phillips should go with him as his guest. The two men left the house together. To reach the street, they had to traverse a narrow entryway, which could only be negotiated single-file. Tyndale motioned for Phillips to go first, but Phillips, with a show of courtesy and respect to his older friend, insisted that Tyndale walk ahead of him. As Tyndale stepped into the street, the taller Phillips who stood behind him could easily point down at his friend to signal the soldiers Phillips had already arranged should meet him there. Tyndale was so bewildered and stunned that the soldiers later told Tyndale's host they "pitied to see his simplicity" when they arrested him.[11] Betrayal had done what all the king's spies had failed to do, and the elusive exile was in custody at last. He was charged with heresy, and imprisoned in the Castle of Vilvoorde, a massive medieval structure modeled on the infamous Bastille in France, and at this time the main state prison for the entire Low Countries. Phillips would ultimately be lost to history, but only after several more daring feats of theft, fraud, and treachery.

Tyndale's imprisonment at Vilvoorde would last the rest of his life—a little more than a year. Heresy trials in the Low Country were conducted by special officials from the Holy Roman Empire who were not always available, and prisoners might be held many months waiting on the slow pace of travel and correspondence, as well as the inevitable legal delays. As summer dwindled into autumn and the cold, damp Belgian winter seeped into his cell, Tyndale endured many months of cold and deprivation, waiting on the slow advance of all but inevitable death.

The only surviving letter from Tyndale's imprisonment, written to an official he hoped might be able to help him, vividly captures the harshness of these months of imprisonment, as well as his priorities during the last year of his life:

11   Moynahan, 328.

I believe, right worshipful, that you are not ignorant of what has been determined concerning me. Therefore, I entreat your Lordship, and that by the Lord Jesus, that if I am to remain here during the winter, you will request the Procurer to be kind enough to send me from my goods, which he has in his possession, a warmer cap, for I suffer extremely from cold in the head, being afflicted with a perpetual catarrh [inflammation in the nose or throat], which is considerably increased in the cell. A warmer coat also, for that which I have is very thin; also a piece of cloth to patch my leggings: my overcoat is worn out; my shirts are also worn out. He has a woolen shirt of mine, if he will be kind enough to send it. I have also, with him, leggings of thicker cloth, for putting on above; he has also warmer caps for wearing at night. I wish also his permission to have a candle in the evening, for it is wearisome to sit alone in the dark. But above all, I entreat and beseech your clemency to be urgent with the Procurer that he would kindly permit me to have my Hebrew Bible, Hebrew Grammar, and Hebrew Dictionary, that I may spend my time with that study. And in return, may you obtain your dearest wish, provided it is always consistent with the salvation of your soul. But if any other resolutions have been come to concerning me, before the close of the winter, I shall be patient, abiding the will of God to the glory of the grace of my Lord Jesus Christ, whose spirit, I pray, may ever direct your heart. Amen.[12]

Like the Apostle Paul writing to Timothy during his last imprisonment centuries before, Tyndale longed for a cloak to keep warm and materials to continue his study and writing. His "dearest wish," however, for himself as for others, was always for the Word of God.

Tyndale had lived for years with the very real prospect of imprisonment and death always at his elbow and had lost at least one close friend to execution in England for sharing Tyndale's Protestant views. In his famous tract, "The Obedience of the Christian Man," Tyndale seems to grapple in advance with any temptation to hatred, bitterness, and resentment in response to unjust treatment by secular authorities:

Christ is the cause why I love thee, why I am ready to do the uttermost of my power for thee, and why I pray for thee . . . .Do therefore the worst thou canst unto me, take away my goods, take away my good name; yet as long as Christ remaineth in my heart, so long I love thee not a whit less, and so long art thou as dear unto me as mine own soul, and so long am I ready to do thee good for thine evil and so long I pray for thee with all my heart: for Christ desireth it of me, and hath deserved it of me. Thine unkindness compared unto his kindness

---

12   Anderson, James Maxwell. *Daily Life During the Reformation*. Google. Books. Page 82. Accessed November 16, 2019.

is nothing at all; yea, it is swallowed up as a little smoke of a mighty wind, and is no more seen or thought upon. More[o]ver that evil which thou doest to me, I receive not of thine hand but of the hand of God, and as God's scourge to teach me patience and to nurture me. And therefore have no cause to be angry with thee . . . .Thus is Christ all and the whole cause why I love thee, and to all can nought be added.[13]

Tyndale's trial came at last in August of 1536, and, as expected, he was convicted of heresy, degraded from the priesthood, and handed over to the secular authorities for prosecution and punishment. Now, at last, the process moved quickly, and Tyndale was sentenced to death, then executed on October sixth. Those who witnessed his execution in the courtyard of the castle said that he was calm, maintained his innocence till the end, and called God as his witness that he had never intentionally altered even a single word of the Holy Scriptures.

The impact of Tyndale's New Testament on his native land cannot possibly be overestimated. Just months after his death, Henry VIII legalized the English Bible, and ploughboys across the land did, indeed, begin to read and study it as Tyndale had dreamed they would. Tyndale's translation influenced not only the Protestant Reformation and its emphasis on vernacular translations of Scripture, but also future translations such as the Geneva Bible and the King James Bible, which would transform the language, literature, and culture of Great Britain and be carried from it around the world. To some it might seem a tragic irony that Tyndale gave his life to provide something for his people that would become officially sanctioned and freely available just decades after his death. But the truth is that Tyndale's translation did more than speed the English Bible into the hands and hearts of readers. Without the scholarly standard his translation set and the appetite for English Bibles he helped to create as well as to feed, those who followed him might have found the road far harder.

David Teems points out that many of the most beloved phrases from the English Bible originate with Tyndale, "And while old and well rehearsed to you and me, to the English believers in 1526 they were astonishingly new." Among the examples Teems highlights are: "Behold the Lamb of God"; "I am the way, the truth, and the life"; "For thine is the kingdom and the power and the glory"; "Seek, and ye shall find"; "With God all things are possible"; "Looking unto Jesus, the author and finisher of our faith"; "Behold, I stand at

---

13 Tyndale, William. *The Obedience of a Christian Man. The Works of the English Reformers, Vol. I.* Ed. Thomas Russel. Page 69. Richard-22872.net. William Gross, "OntheWing.org." 2011. Accessed February 6, 2020. Web. https://www.richard-2782.net/obediencechristianman.pdf.

the door and knock"; "For my yoke is easy and my burden is light"; "Fight the good fight"; "I am the light of the world"; "Take, eat, this is my body"; "Blessed are the poor in spirit"; "Christ in you the hope of glory"; "A man after God's own heart"; and "Death, where is thy sting?"[14]

It seems certain that Tyndale would not, for a moment, have regretted the sacrifices he made. Because of his work, countless men, women, and children read and heard the Word of God who might otherwise never have heard a single word of it in their own language. It was the great desire of Tyndale's life, and it was granted.

---

14   Teems, xx; 60–61.

CHAPTER 2

Roger Williams

"HAVING BOUGHT TRUTH DEAR"

A January day in New England, in the year 1636, was no time for a seriously sick man to be facing the wilderness alone. Beyond the fringes of the English settlements, with their houses huddled together as if against the bitter wind, the wild forests of the New World lay silent, mile after mile under the snow. When the sun went down, the cold would cut like a whetted knife through even the warmest clothes. And the man who hurried alone from under the eaves of his house, his breath etching the frigid air and his face drawn with illness and grief, was unprepared for the unwelcome adventure before him. He had barely had time to throw on all his warmest clothes and to stuff his pockets with food before saying goodbye to the home he would never see again and the wife and children he was leaving to survive the winter without him as best they might. And he was stunned and grieved by the betrayal of men he had trusted, who, despite having given him until the spring to leave their settlement (because of his severe illness and the harshness of the winter) had changed their minds and were planning to have him secretly arrested. It was only because one of them still valued his friendship so highly, despite their many disagreements, that he had received enough warning to vanish into the wilderness just ahead of that fateful knock at the door. Roger Williams, who, like so many, had already fled his homeland in search of freedom of conscience, now found himself an exile once more. He turned his back on the lighted windows and smoking chimneys of the town, faced the vast, still forest, and began to walk.

It was not the first time Roger Williams had found himself driven by his keen mind and exacting conscience to part ways with men he valued and respected. It was not the first time he had found himself outside yet another circle, forced to break a new trail. Indeed, the line of footprints in the New England snow, heading away from the community he hoped to belong to and toward the wilderness, represent something fundamental to the nature of Williams' mind and personality, as well as to the shape of his life. Again and again it would happen: some question would arise of great importance both to Williams himself and to men with whom he shared the overwhelming majority of his convictions. As both sides studied and discussed the question, their opinions would diverge. The importance of the issue to both sides would prevent compromise, despite, in some cases, lifelong mutual respect and affection. And then, once again, despite his naturally social temperament, his lifelong desire for fellowship and community, his broad sympathies, and the depth of his roots in the rich and crowded cultural and religious tradition to which he was indebted, Roger Williams would find himself on the outside looking in, regarded with suspicion and resentment as a troublemaker, and walking a road on which no one else could follow him. And yet, in the end, the gifts Williams bequeathed to the community and the tradition, to which he was always an outsider, were invaluable both to its survival and to the rich legacy it has left to us.

Early Life, Education, and a Mentor

Roger Williams was born in London, probably in 1603, although the exact date is unknown. Beyond the names of his parents and siblings, his father's profession as a merchant and trader, and the area of London in which he grew up, little is known of Williams' childhood before the momentous encounter that would shape the rest of his life: his meeting with Sir Edward Coke.[1]

Sir Edward Coke, one of the greatest legal minds England has ever produced, was in his sixties when he saw Williams, then around thirteen, taking shorthand—a skill increasingly in demand at the time. Coke not only hired Williams as a clerk but also took the bright, determined young man under his wing. It seems he invested in his eager pupil the hope and care he might have wished to spend on his children. As spectacularly bad a husband and father as he was a great lawyer and scholar, Coke had lived to be disappointed by or estranged from all his children to varying degrees. In return, the young Williams—whose relationship with his father seems to have been distant and difficult—saw in the brilliant and abrasive lawyer the intelligence, the courage, and the heroic commitment to truth and justice that Coke's less appealing qualities hid from so many.[2] Williams was blessed to absorb and to shape his life around these most admirable qualities in his mentor, while gradually outgrowing and overcoming the harshness and

1   "Roger Williams...A Brief Biography." Roger Williams Family Association. Copyright 1997-2019. Accessed February 6th 2020. http://www.rogerwilliams.org/biography.htm.
2   Barry, John M. *Roger Williams and the Creation of the American Soul*. NY: Viking. 2012. Pages 42-46.

arrogance that made Coke even more combative in private life than he was in the great legal contests of his day.

During his years with Coke, the teenage Williams, sitting by unnoticed, always recording the proceedings in shorthand, found himself with an extraordinary front-row seat at some of the most crucial defining moments in British legal history—moments that would shape the future not only of Britain but also perhaps still more of the infant colonies across the Atlantic. The balance of power between the king and the Parliament, the integrity of the Constitution, the often explosive interplay of political and ecclesiastical power, the effect of great religious debates on politics and political debates on religion—all of this, and Coke's courageous championship of law, logic, and truth as he navigated these stormy seas, were the backdrop against which the young Williams' mind and character developed.

Coke gave his young protégé yet another great gift when he arranged for, and subsidized, his education, first at Charterhouse School and then at Pembroke College. Coke was assisted in his provision for Williams' future by Williams winning a scholarship for his mastery of Hebrew, Latin, and Greek—an early sign of Williams' keen intelligence and his gift for languages.[3] Williams graduated as an ordained minister and received a paid position right away. Despite gathering clouds on the national horizon, Williams' future must have looked bright when, in 1629, he married his wife, Mary.

It demonstrates the magnitude of the storm breaking over England that scarcely a year later, in 1620, the young couple would set sail for North America—not at all the place where they had planned to establish their home together, or the life they had planned to lead.[4] It was also an early indication that a stable or predictable life was to elude Roger Williams and his courageous wife for the rest of their lives. "I desire not to sleep in security and dream of a nest which no hand can reach," Williams would write six years later when danger and exile had pursued him to the New World. "I cannot but expect changes, and the change of the last enemy, death."[5]

Controversy and Persecution in England

What, then, was the rising tide of danger and dissension by which the young Williamses, like so many others, found themselves swept up and carried along? Roger

---

3   Ibid. 57-58.
4   Gaustad, Edwin. *Roger Williams*. Oxford UP. 2005. Lives and Legacies series. Page 13.
5   Quoted In Warren, James A. *God, War, and Providence: The Epic Struggle of Roger Williams and the Narragansett Indians against the Puritans of New England*. New York: Scribner. 2018. Page 58.

Williams had been born into a tumultuous century for England. During the seventeenth century, tensions between church and state, king and parliament, "high church" and "low church," would ultimately erupt into a Civil War that would tear England apart and claim the head of a king. Long before the coming of war, however, many would flee to Holland or to North America in search of the freedom to organize their churches and raise their children away from the increasingly severe persecution of Puritans under the influential Archbishop Laud. Laud, with the backing of the King, sought to achieve much greater uniformity of doctrine and practice in the Church of England, and in particular to purge the church entirely of the dangerously independent Puritans.

In this increasingly tense and suspicious atmosphere, the young Roger Williams was one of many who confronted an uncertain future and a difficult decision about whether to stay in England and weather the storm or establish new communities abroad. Indeed, England was growing more and more hostile to Puritans and other dissenters just when Williams was beginning his adult life and developing his own radically Puritan convictions. Both Puritans—so called for their desire to "purify" the doctrine and practice of the Church of England, and to seek that same purity in their own lives, families, and congregations—and "Separatists"—named for their belief that the Church of England had become irremediably corrupt and that congregations of sincere Christians must now separate from it in order to worship Biblically—struggled to understand the tides of history and to discern their duty as Christians and citizens.

A small but serious minority of British Protestants of this era sincerely believed that they stood on the threshold of a new era, an era which would usher in the Kingdom of God on earth. A much larger group did not go this far but still considered the advance of morality, justice, and truth in society an important part of the church's responsibility. And, increasingly, all Puritans were forced to consider their survival, as individuals and as a community. As the laws of England began to restrict and penalize more and more severely any departure from the approved Anglican doctrines and practices, and as ministers and congregations were brought more and more under the supervision and regulation of the state, not only Puritans but Baptists, Quakers, Catholics, and others found themselves facing an uncertain future.

Most Puritans identified deeply with England and the heritage of the British Reformation, and they felt responsible for and to their native country. But some began to see the new English territories of the New World as their opportunity to create a better version of England, an England that was true to its best self, an England that would protect British Protestantism against the dangerous incursions of unscrupulous men upon the rights and responsibilities of its citizens. As Edwin Gaustad puts it:

> Far from England's intruding and persecuting bishops, protected from the nation's nosy and arresting sheriffs, the Puritans, taking only the New Testament as their pattern and guide, could fashion a pure, nonpolitical, uncorrupted, noncompromised church . . . .Leave England in one sense, but go to England's new lands across the Atlantic, so that they could still be part of their nation and of its church . . . a light, a beacon, an instructor and guide, showing their homeland the path to true Christianity . . . .In New England, they would not forsake their nation: They would redeem it.[6]

Williams himself was slow to embrace the vision of the Puritan New World, deeply reluctant to turn his back on England. He was determined to stay as long as he could live, speak, and write freely. But as pressure on Puritans increased with the ferocious determination of Archbishop Laud to root out their influence, more and more found themselves imprisoned, and others were forced to flee to Holland or America to escape a choice between perjury and prison. The net was closing around all Puritans, and Williams saw the relative safety and anonymity of his early life evaporating. It seemed clear that if he did not leave England immediately, his arrest was virtually certain. So, with his new wife, Williams made his first—but not his last—nick-of-time escape from arrest and imprisonment. Unable to delay, he and Mary braved the hazardous winter crossing of the Atlantic—the perils and hardships of which, with storms, malnutrition, disease, parasites, and other horrors almost unimaginable today, were a daunting prospect.

Arrival in the New World

When the young couple arrived in Boston, they were at first welcomed warmly into the Puritan establishment of New England. It must have seemed as if a richly rewarding life of fellowship, community, and ministry was opening to them after all—just not quite where they had expected.

But Williams was a man whose passionate, unhesitating commitment to truth inevitably led him to rough and lonely places, where few had the courage to follow. There is no question that Williams was sometimes—perhaps often—mistaken in his views. There is also no doubt that Williams' integrity and courage were at times, especially as a precocious and cocky young man accustomed to the heady company of older and more

---

6   Gaustad 13.

experienced men, disfigured by arrogance and impatience. Williams' desire for fellowship and reconciliation with the larger body of Puritans was sincere and seems to have grown throughout his life, but there were probably times when greater gentleness and patience might have achieved the understanding that Williams always hoped could be attained through frank discussion and closely reasoned argument. Yet the final testament to Williams' integrity is surely that, as his life progressed and as he was disciplined by loneliness and suffering, his conscience gradually grew more and more costly to himself while weighing more gently on others.

In any case, the young Williams wasted no time in alienating the Puritan establishment that had been so ready to welcome him, and he soon found that even in New England, few Puritans were as dedicated as he was himself to renouncing every vestige of corruption in the church. Upon his arrival in Boston, Williams was welcomed warmly and was promptly offered the position of minister in a church there—surely a great compliment to the reputation of so young a man and so new an arrival. But because the congregation had not fully and officially severed all ties with the Church of England, a step Williams had come to believe was necessary, he declined the appointment, creating, at least in some quarters, a resentment he would never be able to overcome. Instead of settling in Boston, he lived and preached first at Salem, then at Plymouth, then at Salem again, managing to stir up controversy and to alienate authority wherever he went. Williams was building a reputation as a troublemaker even as he earned respect and affection from many.

The Three Points of Disagreement

Williams' disagreements with other Puritans in both England and New England involved several matters, from the role of women in the church, to the use of the Book of Common Prayer, to the flag flown in New England settlements. But these, however contentious, were ultimately matters on which Puritans were not unanimous and on which differences could be respected and tolerated. Williams' staunch refusal to compromise on such questions would have narrowed the circle of those who trusted and admired him, and might have limited the progress of his career, but would probably never have put him outside the larger community. It was three much more fundamental issues that would ultimately drive a wedge between Williams and both the Puritans and Separatists.

The first of these seemed to many to strike at the authority of the King himself. Williams challenged the charter granted by Charles I to the Massachusetts Bay Colony, not so much on legal grounds as on the moral grounds that the land might not have been the King's to bestow, because it was not clear that it had been honorably and fairly purchased from its Native American owners. While some English settlements had negotiated their own purchases of land from Native American tribes fairly and honestly, Williams felt strongly that in other cases it was very likely the settlers had cheated and misled the tribal authorities in ways they would never have dared with another European. And the presumption inherent in the idea that the King of England had the right to give Indian lands to anyone he chose troubled Williams. In an age when few questioned prevailing attitudes toward the Native American Indians, and even Christian missions among them often reflected a patronizing condescension, Williams was a bright exception. Not only did he take very seriously the widely professed Puritan conviction that a great—perhaps the very greatest—priority in settling New England was to take the Gospel to the Native Americans and translate it into their languages, but Williams also met the New England Indians as friends and equals, devoting himself with genuine respect and rare patience to learning (and publishing an important book on) their language, and to understanding them as human beings. "His understanding of the Indians, particularly the Narragansetts, was illuminated by a willingness to engage and observe the natives on their own terms, on their own ground," writes James Warren.

> Dealing with them as he did, day by day and one-on-one, he came to value their friendship and the skills that ensured their survival in a wilderness that could be as brutal as it was unforgiving. Williams found much in the way the Indians lived admirable. Indeed, their interpersonal ethics often seemed to him superior to those of Christian Europeans. As he would later write in *A Key*, "I could never discern that excess of scandalous sins amongst them, which Europe aboundeth with. Drunkeness and gluttony, generally they know not what sins they be; and although they have not so much to restrain them (both in respect of knowledge of God and laws of men) as the English have, yet a man shall never hear of such crimes among them of robberies, murders, adulteries, etc, as amongst the English."[7]

In short, Williams shared with his Puritan neighbors a desire that the natives of New England should come to know the true gospel of Christ, but it was characteristic of the differences between Williams and his fellow English Christians that Williams should consider it vitally important to guard against coercing or tricking the Indians into accepting Christianity. The first step, in Williams' view, was to maintain a consistent

---

7   Warren 46-47.

Christian testimony by treating them with fairness and respect. "Christ had called upon him to love and treat his new neighbors with dignity and respect," writes Warren. Williams was concerned with "learning all he could about the Indians' spiritual and temporal world, and exposing the Indians to what he knew of the Christian faith—but not imposing Christian beliefs or English culture upon them against their will."[8] Ultimately, as historian James Kloppenberg notes, "Since all people—Puritans as well as Wampanoag or Narragansett—are sinners, he urged the English to adopt an attitude of greater humility in their encounters with the native people of America."[9]

In his later years, Williams would be a tireless diplomatist, throwing himself into the breach again and again to try to bring reconciliation, peace, and justice out of the complicated and troubled relations of the English settlers and the competing tribes of the area. Indeed, when in his old age Williams' property was destroyed in a Narragansett raid, plunging him into poverty for the remainder of his life, Williams spoke in his last surviving letter not with bitterness but with loyalty and thankfulness of the Narragansetts who, when Williams was eventually banished in the dead of winter from the Puritan settlement, befriended and sheltered him and his family until they established their new home.[10] Not only his respect for the Native Americans but also his scholar's mind, his apprenticeship under such a great legal mind as Coke, and his personal integrity drove Williams' concern that the great Puritan experiment in godliness, liberty, and truth should be established on an unassailable foundation.

One can imagine, however, the indignation and consternation of the colony's leaders when Williams' expressed his concerns about the charter. It was received not only as an attack on the colony's legal existence (despite Williams' repeated attempts to clarify that he was trying to raise a moral, not a legal question), but also as a very serious accusation of hypocrisy that undermined the "city on a hill" the Puritans were trying to establish in New England. Williams agreed not to repeat his concerns publicly, but he continued to discuss them with friends, and some of the Puritan leaders saw this as proof that he could not be trusted, having gone back on his word. Williams, who seems to have naively assumed that his fellow believers and fellow scholars would be grateful and eager to enter into an evaluation of an important question, anxious only to be certain they were doing the right thing, does not seem to have realized how much this dispute undermined his standing in New England. He had become a man who had to be watched.

---

8   Ibid. 46-47.
9   Quoted in Warren 48.
10   Quoted in Barry 387.

The second and third issues that fueled the flames of controversy between Williams and the Puritan leaders were related to one another and were rooted in the same more fundamental disagreement. One was the question of requiring all citizens to take Christian oaths, whether or not they belonged to the church or were even professing Christians, and one was the question of mandatory church attendance for all. Of course, both these disagreements hinged on different understandings of the relationship between church and state. Many Puritans believed that in New England they were creating a theocracy, in which the secular authorities and church leadership would work together to create a unified way of life and community modeled upon Biblical truth. As part of this enterprise, many Puritans believed that secular authorities were appointed by God to enforce both tables of the Ten Commandments—the "first table," as they called it, which governs man's duty to God, as well as the "second table," which deals with man's duty to his fellow citizens. Williams belonged to a very small minority who believed that secular government had no role in enforcing the first table—in other words, that church government functioned within the church and secular government outside the church. Only the second table, which governed the way human beings treated one another, was in Williams' view the province of secular government.

It is important to remind a postmodern society that Williams' plea for freedom of conscience sprang not from the tacit assumption that religious beliefs are unimportant or private or purely personal, but from his conviction that they are so important that we dare allow no intervening influence to come between them and the individual soul. Unlike many modern proponents of religious toleration, Williams believed that objective truth exists and may be known, and that men are responsible to respond to that truth. Williams writes in his most important book, *The Bloody Tenent*, words that might have served as his epitaph: "[H]aving bought truth dear, we must not sell it cheap, not the least grain of it for the whole world, no not for the saving of souls, though our own most precious." Rather than asserting a right to dissent from revealed truth, Williams—in a head-on dispute with Quaker George Fox in which Williams, for a change, took the solidly orthodox side—called the Bible "the outward and external Light, Lantern, Judge, Guide, Rule, by which God witnesseth Himself and His Truth in the world."[11] In his battle of words with the Puritans, Williams appealed again and again to truths which he and they both professed to hold sacred, submitting their controversy to an authority beyond

---

11   Williams, Roger. *George Fox Digg'd Out of His Burrows*. Early English Books. Online. Page 141. Accessed May 30, 2022.https://quod.lib.umich.edu/e/eebo/A66448.0001.001?rgn=main;view=fulltext.

their own opinions. The state, Williams believed, must not be allowed to usurp the place which belonged only to the Word of God.

Williams was jealous not only for the freedom of the individual to respond to God alone but also for the authenticity and purity of Christianity. This authenticity, Williams believed, is possible only when commitment to Christianity and Christian worship and service are voluntary. In *The Bloody Tenent*, Williams writes, "[W]hatever worship, ministry, ministration, the best and purest are practiced without faith and true persuasion that they are the true instruments of God, they are sin, sinful worships, ministries, etc."[12] Williams viewed this as one of the most important reasons why neither the church nor the state has the right to coerce religious profession or observance. Perez Zagorin writes in *How the Idea of Religious Toleration Came to the West*:

> Williams stands out in his life and work as a deeply religious and even prophetic personality whose greatest care was for God's people and conformity with Christ . . . his theory of toleration, developed chiefly in the interests of religion and the truly spiritual Christian . . . [paradoxically] issued in . . . a completely secularized conception of the political order."[13]

The story of the growing rift between Williams and the Puritan leadership in Salem and Boston—the letters back and forth, the many discussions, the appearances to defend his conduct—is a long and complicated one. Neither party was hasty, and both struggled for some compromise or reconciliation. But in the end, the authorities viewed Williams' continuing to discuss privately his concerns about the charter as both the last straw and perhaps also as the excuse they needed. Williams was to be banished from the colony. It was only because during these final proceedings, Williams was seriously ill—indeed, he was unable to appear at all of them—that he was granted the indulgence of staying in Salem until spring lifted the threat of the ferocious New England winter. Then, he would have to find a new home. But so seriously did the Puritan leaders take the threat they believed Williams posed to their community that, when opportunity offered, they changed their minds and decided to send him back to England on a ship that would soon be departing. In England, Williams would almost certainly have been imprisoned immediately if, in his condition, he survived the voyage. The journey and the prospect of prison were, to a man in his condition, a virtual death sentence. That the leading figures

---

12   Williams, Roger. "The Bloody Tenent of Persecution, for Cause of Conscience, in a Conference Between Truth and Peace." *The Norton Anthology of American Literature*, 6th ed., edited by Baym, et al. Volume A. New York: Norton, 2002. Pages 235-237.

13   Zagorin, Perez. How the Idea of Religious Toleration Came to the West. Princeton UP. 2003. Page 206.

of the Massachusetts Bay Colony were not unanimous in this decision is evident from the remarkable fact that it was founder John Winthrop himself who warned Williams in time for him to escape at the last minute, sick, and stuffing his pockets with corn paste.[14] Turning his back on the home he would never see again, Williams plunged into the frozen wilderness.

Into the Wilderness

He was fortunate to survive his first winter, and the Narragansett Indians almost certainly saved his life by taking in the sick man and providing him with food and shelter. Even so, his survival is amazing. Williams, a rugged and athletic man who rowed and walked through the wilderness well into his seventies and had no patience with complaining about physical exertion or hardship, would write thirty-five years later that he could still feel the ferocious cold and snow of that winter, and that for fourteen weeks he didn't know what Bed or Bread meant.[15] Not only his physical sufferings but also his loneliness, the separation from wife, children, and friends, and the sense of betrayal and rejection by men he never ceased to respect, made that winter a bitter one for Williams.

But it was also to prove the beginning of an extraordinary chapter in the British settlement of New England. Williams purchased land from the Narragansetts, not only to build a new home for himself and his family but also to welcome others. He named his new settlement Providence, to honor the guidance and protection of God. So it was that Williams passed into history as the founder of Rhode Island, a new settlement in the New England wilderness, where Baptists, Quakers, and other ostracized groups found the freedom of conscience they had sought in vain for so long, and where he became the first to establish the religious liberty which the newborn United States would one day embrace.

In a revolutionary experiment, Williams and the other signatories created a community in which the secular would be divided from the religious—church attendance and the profession of faith would be viewed as the province of church leadership, not that of the new colony's government. Williams never ceased to defend and seek to spread his own beliefs and what he believed to be Biblical Christianity—indeed, the famous champion of religious liberty undertook in his old age an arduous river journey to a settlement of

---

14   Barry, John. "God, Government, and Roger Williams' Big Idea." Smithsonian Magazine. January 2012 Issue. Accessed May 30, http://www.smithsonianmag.com/history/god-government-and-roger-williams-big-idea-6291280.
15   Ibid.

Quakers whom he sought to persuade to abandon what he considered the unbiblical aspects of their beliefs. But he never ceased to believe passionately that requiring individuals to profess certain doctrines or conform to certain practices only polluted the purity and sincerity of the church and led to hypocrisy and falseness that was anything but pleasing to God.

Legacy and Writings

For the rest of his life, Williams would defend his colony and his ideas. He found himself, in a sense, fighting on two fronts—defending his ideas about religious liberty to the Puritans while also defending the importance of civil law and government to the predictably contentious ragtag group of outcasts and utopians that gathered in Providence. Williams also found himself caught between the English and the Indians, pouring his time and his energy into diplomacy and the effort to prevent injustice and violence. Indeed, in an ironic but fitting turn of events, Williams was to find himself trusted by and aligned with the Puritan settlements in a new way, and promoting their interests as well as those of the Native Americans.

Williams would make two trips to England during his life to defend the legal interests of his new settlement. He made enemies there, but he also made important friends, including Oliver Cromwell and the British poet John Milton whose masterpiece *Paradise Lost* is considered by some to be the greatest work in the English language. Williams would also become arguably one of the most important and influential early American writers, producing his controversial four-hundred-page landmark book *On the Bloody Tenent of Persecution, for Cause of Conscience, Discussed, in a Conference Between Truth and Peace* which presented to other Christians his Biblical case for religious liberty. The book was shockingly divisive and controversial in an age when the duty of the church to influence the state, and vice versa, was taken for granted by almost everyone, but it also became Williams' great legacy to the future United States.

Williams undoubtedly carried his ideas too far toward the end of his life, ultimately ending his days unconnected with any organized church, often worshipping with his family in his own home. Few would defend this as being consistent with Williams' own beliefs and arguments throughout his life. Yet even Williams' harshest critics in his own time never challenged his courageous integrity, and those who knew him best recognized the humility that underlay his commitment to truth, his sense of obligation to follow the truth wherever it led and to submit his views to constant revision in its light. In the end, at least from his own point of view, the things that united Williams to his lifelong rivals and critics in the Puritan community were more important to him than the things which divided them. As he wrote to his old friend John Winthrop, with whom he disagreed passionately by letter on more and more issues throughout their lives without damaging their mutual esteem and affection, "as you Say you doe, I also seeke Jesus who was nayled to the Gallowes."[16] Williams had also reminded his friend that lies, confusion, and "private interests" prevailed among both Englishmen and Indians, but "these things you may and must do: First, kiss the truth where you . . . see it. 2. Advance justice, through a child's eyes. 3. Seek and make peace, if possible, with all men."[17]

Williams spent his final years in Providence, impoverished after the destruction of his house by fire in an Indian raid and in poor health—and despite his having been invited to return to Massachusetts so long as he would promise not to air his dissenting opinions. To the end, Williams was often difficult and sometimes mistaken, but never lost the very rare degree of courage and honesty that enables a man to live his whole life as if he really believes what he says he believes.

In a book of reflections to his wife, which reveals a very tender and gentle side of his personality, Williams reminded the woman who, as a young bride, had turned her back on everything she had ever known to dare a treacherous winter crossing of the Atlantic, that Christians are in this world like passengers on a ship. Whatever is lost and suffered on the way, their final destination is in heaven, where they will reap "a neverending harvest of inconceivable joys."[18] Roger Williams, who never had his portrait made, died around the age of eighty, on a date unremembered by history. But it was probably not his earthly legacy but that neverending harvest of inconceivable joys that was on his mind.

---

16   Barry 385.
17   Warren 253-254.
18   Gaustad 108.

CHAPTER 3
John Woolman
RADICAL AUTHENTICITY

The young man was nervous. He hesitated and fumbled as he explained his situation. Always, he found it too easy to be afraid of offending others—especially those who might think he had no right to challenge them. Why did he feel so strongly about something when others he respected didn't see any problem with it? Why did that keep happening to him, over and over? Would he seem arrogant? Judgmental? Just plain odd? Why couldn't he pacify his conscience with the same explanations that satisfied others so much older and wiser than he? He wasn't any good at this.

But he had made up his mind, and he had no choice but to explain as best he could, both to his employer and to his friend and would-be-customer. He couldn't do it, he said—could never do it again. He offered reasons, and he tried to explain his thinking. When it was over, he wasn't sure he had succeeded. But he knew the bottom line, at least, was clear: the client would have to find someone else for this job. For him, the page was turned, and there could be no going back.

The young man's name was John Woolman. He was beginning his career as a clerk—one who worked in a shop but was also paid to draft legal documents—and he had just refused the job of writing a receipt for a slave. The enslaved woman had already been given as a gift to the wife of a friend—and not only a friend, but a fellow member of Woolman's Quaker congregation. Woolman knew that his refusal to write the receipt would change nothing. The woman would remain enslaved, her owner's mind would remain unchanged, and the receipt would simply be written by someone else. But his hand would not touch it. Woolman had decided, after a similar request had taken him by surprise some months before, that he could not bring himself to draft another instrument of slavery. As famous poet and fellow Quaker John Greenleaf Whittier would write in his introduction to Woolman's *Journal*, "God's voice against the desecration of His image spoke in his soul."[1]

This was the first test of Woolman's resolution. It represented a memorable victory for an unassuming young man, who, although raised in his Quaker faith, had only recently become a Christian believer himself, and had begun to grow in his new life after a wild and unhappy adolescence. It was also only the first of many times when John Woolman would feel called upon to stand out, and to stand alone.

Early Life

John Woolman was born in 1720 to a devout Quaker family in colonial New Jersey. Their Quaker faith was an essential part of young Woolman's upbringing, and he could remember what he called "the operations of Divine Love" seeming real to him even before the age of seven. He also remembered being troubled and puzzled at a very young age by the hypocrisy he recognized all around him—by the gap between the principles his parents taught him and the daily life of so many Christians:

> From what I had read and heard, I believed there had been, in past ages, people who walked in uprightness before God in a degree exceeding any that I knew or heard of now living: and the apprehension of there being less steadiness and firmness amongst people in the present age often troubled me while I was a child.[2]

It would continue to trouble him all his life—a life which would be largely spent grappling with the challenges of living a life of integrity that reflected what he claimed to believe.

The young Woolman had a precocious sensitivity not only to hypocrisy but also to cruelty and selfishness—and especially his own. One pivotal incident in his childhood, which Woolman would later record in his published *Journal*, revealed the early roots of that ability to consider the effects of his choices on others which would become so characteristic of him as an adult:

> On going to a neighbour's house, I saw on the way a robin sitting on her nest, and as I came near she went off; but having young ones, she flew about, and with many cries expressed her concern for them. I stood and threw stones at her, and one striking her, she fell down dead. At first I was pleased with the exploit, but

---

1   Woolman, John. Page 8 *Journal of John Woolman*. Christian Classics Ethereal Library. Accessed May 30, 2022. https://ccel.org/w/woolman/journal/cache/journal.pdf.

2   Ibid. 27.

after a few minutes was seized with horror, at having, in a sportive way, killed an innocent creature while she was careful for her young. I beheld her lying dead, and thought those young ones, for which she was so careful, must now perish for want of their dam to nourish them . . . .and for some hours [I] could think of little else but the cruelties I had committed, and was much troubled.[3]

The importance of this memory in Woolman's life reflects his capacity for empathy with the perpetrators and victims of greed, selfishness, and cruelty. All his life, he would show an unusual humility and compassion toward those whose hypocrisy and unkindness he challenged and exposed, identifying with and feeling for them rather than vilifying them.

It was not without a struggle that Woolman moved beyond mirroring his parents' faith and found his own confidence in Christ. As a teenager, he rebelled against many of the practices and expectations his parents had taught him and developed an appetite for company and habits he himself believed, all the while, to be wrong and destructive. "Having attained the age of sixteen years, I began to love wanton company," Woolman wrote. He often felt shame and regret when he considered the choices he was making and would resolve to turn over a new leaf, but he failed again and again. Like so many others, he would realize his need for the saving work of Christ only when he had repeatedly tried hard and failed spectacularly to live rightly through grit and willpower. "Upon the whole, my mind became more and more alienated from the truth, and I hastened toward destruction," he would write years later. "I knew I was going from the flock of Christ and had no resolution to return, hence serious reflections were uneasy to me, and youthful vanities and diversions were my greatest pleasure. In this road I found many like myself, and we associated in that which is adverse to true friendship."[4]

Woolman's experiences during these years would shape his future perspective and distinctive voice as both a speaker and a writer. He would always have a rare insight into the restless hunger for distraction, the loneliness, and the gnawing guilt that drive people to activities or indulgences that seem to offer, not happiness or peace, but some temporary escape from seeing clearly the choices they are making. In the future, Woolman would be noted for his mistrust of many of the pastimes and pleasures which he knew had been simply a way of drowning out the voice of his restless and dissatisfied heart. He also learned from these years to value honesty as the bedrock of any truly caring relationship and to see selfishness, rather than friendship, in the false sense of community that uses

---

3   Ibid. 27-28.
4   Ibid. 28.

others to ease our boredom or guilt. Much of Woolman's courage later in life to challenge even his own close-knit community must have come from reflections on this experience of sacrificing everything to fit in, and of prioritizing relationships that weakened rather than strengthened his own character.

It was a life-threatening illness that began to shift the course of Woolman's life. Knowing that, young as he was, he might well be about to die, Woolman felt deep guilt and regret about the ways he had knowingly wasted his time and energy, and he felt fear and sadness as he thought of passing into eternity. After his eventual recovery, he was determined once again to change his ways—and for a while, he did. But as the memory of his illness receded, he slipped back into his old ways and again spent less time thinking about eternal things. He continued to read the Bible and to study the lives of his parents and others he admired, but he despaired of being able to make his own life like theirs. Again and again, he embarked upon a period of self-reformation, and again and again, he returned to his old ways. Gradually, shame and despair replaced his rebellion—he wanted, now, to be a different man but found it impossible. As Woolman would later write, he was "not low enough to find true peace," but failure and desperation were beginning to wear him down. "At length," Woolman would write, "through the merciful continuance of heavenly visitations, I was made to bow down in spirit before the Lord." After years of failed resolutions and doomed self-reliance, he began to see "the power of Christ prevail over selfish desires."[5] Woolman loved to speak of God as of a Shepherd, and he never forgot how patiently and persistently God had pursued him. This memory was another source of Woolman's unusual depth of patience with others in later life.

Adult Life and Keeping the Store

Until Woolman was twenty-one, he lived and worked on his parents' farm. His adult life began when he moved several miles away into town to become the clerk and bookkeeper of a shop—seemingly a sort of general store such as would have been common on the colonial frontier. After his conversion, Woolman seems to have recognized that the structure, simplicity, and comparative isolation of life on his parents' farm greatly helped him in his efforts to distance himself from the wild friends whose influence he now feared, and to develop the habits and disciplines that would strengthen his growing faith. So as he prepared to move into town and a much more "public" life, Woolman recognized the importance of the transition and took seriously the new responsibilities

---

5   Ibid. 29.

and new temptations ahead of him. While it might seem easy to laugh at the idea of worldly temptations lurking in a little town in colonial New Jersey, Woolman mistrusted not so much the recognized vices of drinking, gambling, and sexual temptation but the subtler temptations of busyness, ambition, greed, and peer pressure—the constant, wearing, low-level clamor of other voices to which a Christian might listen instead of what Woolman called "the voice of the true Shepherd." To Woolman, it was always an important principle that not merely "professional" Christian leaders, such as ministers or missionaries, but all Christians should live lives that portrayed the truth of the gospel, however they made their livings. Their attention should not be distracted, their time wasted, or their priorities disarranged. So he took his new job in the store seriously as a calling from God, writing that he hoped to "serve Him, my gracious Redeemer, in . . . humility and self-denial,"[6] in his new job.

At first, Woolman found, it was indeed difficult to encounter the distractions and temptations of his new life, and in particular, the one thing he feared most: the proximity and increased pressure of his former friends, who no doubt assumed that now he was in town and living on his own he would be ready to rejoin the old crowd and spend his evenings with them again. But Woolman had already begun to learn that the strength he had sought in vain in his own repeatedly broken resolutions and fragile willpower was to be found in his "true Shepherd." "At these times I cried to the Lord in secret for wisdom and strength," writes Woolman of these early encounters. "I found my Heavenly Father to be merciful to me beyond what I can express. By day I was much amongst people, and had many trials to go through; but in the evenings I was mostly alone, and I may with thankfulness acknowledge . . . [that I] felt my strength renewed."[7] Characteristically, Woolman's growing insight into the moral bankruptcy of his friends' lifestyle and his struggle against the pressure they put on him prompted not a harsh or superior attitude, but a deep compassion and concern for those who were still entangled in a trap from which he felt he had been rescued, through no merit of his own. "And now," he wrote,

> as I had experienced the love of God through Jesus Christ, to redeem me from many pollutions, and to be a succor to me through a sea of conflicts, with which no person was fully acquainted . . . I felt a tender compassion for the youth who remained entangled in snares like those which had entangled me. This love and tenderness increased . . . [8]

6   Ibid. 31.
7   Ibid. 31.
8   Ibid. 31.

Although John Woolman is remembered today as a writer and speaker whose ministry carried him far beyond his hometown, his years clerking in the store were foundational to his character and convictions, placing him, as biographer Geoffrey Plank notes, at the crossroads of the British Empire of trade and commerce. Here Woolman began to think through his understanding of business, profit, trade, money, and time, and to develop his perspectives on which kinds of lifestyles and occupations were conducive to a Christian life and witness and which were not. Not what is possible but what is beneficial, and not what is normal but what is clearly in keeping with the gospel, was the standard Woolman sought as he waited on customers, stocked shelves, kept his meticulous accounts, or sat alone in the evenings reading, praying, and thinking. "[B]eing clearly convinced in my judgment that to place my whole trust in God was best for me," wrote Woolman of his twenty-three-year-old self, "I felt renewed engagements that in all things I might act on an inward principle of virtue, and pursue worldly business no further than as Truth opened my way . . . ."[9] Instead of assuming that the goal of work was always to earn more money—even if there is already enough to live on—or assuming that the goal of running a business is always to grow more profitable—even if it already consumes too much time—Woolman felt that Christians must weigh the values of the emerging consumer economy against Christian values, and economic priorities against eternal ones. Woolman's desire grew that, however he might make a living and whatever life he might end up leading, he would pursue not profit, comfort, popularity, or pleasure but the love of God and the service of others.

These early reflections are essential to understanding Woolman's later impact as a powerful voice against both slavery and the exploitation of Native Americans. He saw with a clarity others did not how spiritual and moral truths—as well as millions of human beings—were being sacrificed to the quest for financial security and a higher standard of living. Many of the hand-wringing excuses offered in defense of the slave trade boiled down to economics, as did many of the rationalizations Woolman would hear from his fellow Quakers who owned or traded in slaves. The moral simplicity of Woolman's later arguments against slavery would reflect his belief, developed during these early years as a shopkeeper, that Christians, while engaging in hard work and honest trade for the support of their families and the good of others, must always guard against unreflective, whole-hearted participation in the race to accumulate wealth. For Woolman, it was not an empty platitude but an obvious and profound truth that the love of money is the root of all kinds of evils.

---

9   Ibid. 32.

But if his own conscience was growing both strong and tender during his years in the shop, one final piece of Woolman's future ministry and legacy was still missing: his voice. Perhaps surprisingly given his later reputation as a speaker and writer, Woolman faced a tremendous struggle with fear and shyness when he first began to realize that sometimes making the right choice oneself is not enough—sometimes one must speak out to others. The first time Woolman's convictions on slavery were tested, as we shall see, he felt deeply conflicted and even spoke of his concern, but he ultimately lacked the confidence to oppose two men older than himself whom he trusted and respected. Woolman would later vividly recall another formative occasion on which he first struggled, like an animal in a trap, to escape the conviction that he ought to challenge the conduct of an older man:

> About the time called Christmas I observed many people, both in town and from the country, resorting to public-houses, and spending their time in drinking and vain sports, tending to corrupt one another; on which account I was much troubled. At one house in particular there was much disorder; and I believed it was a duty incumbent on me to speak to the master of that house. I considered I was young, and that several elderly friends in town had opportunity to see these things; but though I would gladly have been excused, yet I could not feel my mind clear.
>
> The exercise was heavy; and as I was reading what the Almighty said to Ezekiel, respecting his duty as a watchman, the matter was set home more clearly. With prayers and tears I besought the Lord for His assistance, and He in loving-kindness gave me a resigned heart. At a suitable opportunity I went to the public-house; and seeing the man amongst much company, I called him aside, and in the fear and dread of the Almighty expressed to him what rested on my mind. He took it kindly, and afterwards showed more regard to me than before. In a few years afterwards he died, middle-aged; and I often thought that, had I neglected my duty in that case, it would have given me great trouble; and I was humbly thankful to my gracious Father, who had supported me herein.[10]

It was a watershed moment in Woolman's life—the first time he recognized that silence can weigh upon the conscience as heavily as speech and that there are times when we know beyond a shadow of a doubt that we are required to bear witness. The outcome of his first trembling attempt cemented his conviction that, like the prophet Ezekiel, all Christians are watchmen. The timid young man who had found it so difficult to speak against the small evils in his own circle would soon find himself called upon to

---

10   Ibid. 32-33.

speak against a great evil overshadowing much of the world and would need every ounce of his growing courage.

A New Ministry, a New Family, and a New Career

Woolman's regional Monthly Meeting, which, somewhat like a diocese or presbytery, held authority over several local Quaker congregations, officially recognized John Woolman as a minister and leader at the age of twenty-three, assigning him to various leadership roles among members of the area's Society of Friends, and endorsing what would become a major focus of his life: a traveling ministry of visiting Quakers along much of the Eastern seaboard, accompanied by one or more other men, to supervise, unite, teach, and encourage Quaker individuals, families, and congregations.[11] As biographer Geoffrey Plank notes, this project—in which Woolman was only one participant—

> was an early manifestation of a widening movement that Jack D. Marietta has described as the "Reformation of American Quakerism." The reformers' ultimate purpose was to strengthen the Quakers as a religious community, remind them of their core principles, and promote the work of salvation.

On such visits, traveling Quaker leaders such as Woolman would stay in families' homes, gather them for family worship, and get to know them. They would also attend local Quaker meetings.[12] Much like the Methodist circuit-riders of the same era, Woolman and other traveling leaders made possible connection and communication among groups of Friends scattered throughout the cities, villages, and wilderness areas of colonial North America. While making his living first as a merchant and later as a tailor and farmer, Woolman would devote much of his time to this ministry in the future, and it would be through these journeys that he would ultimately come to have the decisive impact he did on the issue of slaveholding among Friends. Safeguarding the time, energy, and spiritual preparation demanded by this ministry would also be a formative priority for Woolman during the rest of his life, shaping many of his decisions about work and family.

In his later twenties, then, Woolman's thoughts about the future increasingly focused on two goals: marriage and a line of work that would support a family without requiring the sacrifice of his ministry, and without leading ever deeper into what he increasingly found the morally cloudy world of business and consumerism. As he continued his work in the shop, Woolman found himself "thoughtful about some other way of business."

---

11   Slaughter, Thomas. *Beautiful Soul of John Woolman, Apostle of Abolition.* NY: Hill and Wang, 2008. Page 120.
12   Plank, Geoffrey. *John Woolman's Path to the Peaceable Kingdom: A Quaker in the British Empire.* Philadelphia: UP Press. 2012. Page 63.

My mind, through the power of truth, was in a good degree weaned from the desire of outward greatness, and I was learning to be content with real conveniences, that were not costly, so that a way of life free from much entanglement appeared best for me, though the income might be small. I had several offers of business that appeared profitable, but I did not see my way clear to accept of them, believing they would be attended with more outward care and cumber than was required of me to engage in. I saw that an humble man, with the blessing of the Lord, might live on a little, and that, where the heart was set on greatness, success in business did not satisfy the craving; but that commonly, with an increase of wealth, the desire of wealth increased. There was a care on my mind so to pass my time, that nothing might hinder me from the most steady attention to the voice of the true Shepherd.[13]

Woolman's employer had been a tailor before he opened his shop, and Woolman spoke with him about the possibility of training as a tailor himself. His employer was able to help him, and Woolman had at last found the line of work he would pursue for the rest of his life—one that would enable him to support a family, though in a modest way, and leave him time and freedom for the many journeys he was beginning to take to visit other Quakers all along the east coast. He was not without occasional regrets, but he never doubted that he had made the right choice:

I believed the hand of Providence pointed out this business for me, and I was taught to be content with it, though I felt at times a disposition that would have sought for something greater; but through the revelation of Jesus Christ I had seen the happiness of humility, and there was an earnest desire in me to enter deeply into it . . . [14]

For some years, Woolman continued to work both as a tailor and a shopkeeper, supplementing his income as a tailor by retailing goods to his neighbors. Gradually, he would step away from the retail business and focus on tailoring and tending a small farm and apple orchard. However limited his income, it enabled him to support a wife, Sarah, whom Woolman married in 1749. The couple was to have only one child survive to adulthood, a daughter named Mary. Very little information about Woolman's family life survives, but the Woolmans seem to have been a close and happy family, and in Sarah he seems to have found the perfect wife to understand and support his lifestyle of simplicity and sacrifice. She not only tolerated but also shared Woolman's desire to live a life as free and simple as possible, and as best we can tell, it seems she was supportive

---

13   Woolman 34.
14   Ibid. 35.

and understanding of Woolman's inevitable long absences, during which he wrote her affectionate letters about his travels.

Sarah also seems to have supported Woolman's decision, seven years into their marriage, to give up his retail business entirely, thriving though it was despite his cautious attitude toward expansion. Biographers note that this decision seems to have been influenced by the tragic death of Woolman's infant son some time earlier, and to coincide with a period of reflection and stock-taking in Woolman's life during which he moved his family to a new home, began writing the famous *Journal*, and grappled more than ever before with the moral complexities of trading in goods that often derived from slavery. In the harsh but clarifying light his son's death seems to have shed on Woolman's life and priorities, the very developments many would have interpreted as signs of God's blessing on his work were troubling to Woolman. His business was growing by the year, his customers and their wants were increasing, and he enjoyed and felt drawn to his work as a successful shopkeeper more than he enjoyed tailoring. To Woolman, however, there were some red flags. Wasn't he gradually devoting more and more time and attention to selling things that people didn't really need? "I grew uneasy on account of my business growing too cumbersome," Woolman would write.

> I had begun with selling trimmings for garments, and from thence proceeded to sell cloths and linens; and at length, having got a considerable shop of goods, my trade increased every year, and the way to large business appeared open, but I felt a stop in my mind.

> Through the mercies of the Almighty, I had, in a good degree, learned to be content with a plain way of living. I had but a small family; and, on serious consideration, believed truth did not require me to engage much in cumbering affairs. It had been my general practice to buy and sell things really useful. Things that served chiefly to please the vain mind in people, I was not easy to trade in; seldom did it; and whenever I did I found it weaken me as a Christian.

> The increase of business became my burden; for though my natural inclination was toward merchandise, yet I believed truth required me to live more free from outward cumbers; and there was now a strife in my mind between the two. In this exercise my prayers were put up to the Lord, who graciously heard me, and gave me a heart resigned to His holy will.

Then I lessened my outward business, and, as I had opportunity, told my customers of my intentions, that they might consider what shop to turn to; and in a while I wholly laid down merchandise, and followed my trade as a tailor . . . [15]

Typically, Woolman's decision to give up his shop reflected not only his own priorities but also his concern for others, especially those who might lose more than they gained in the growing economy:

In merchandise it is the custom where I lived to sell chiefly on credit, and poor people often get in debt; when payment is expected, not having wherewith to pay, their creditors often sue for it at law. Having frequently observed occurrences of this kind, I found it good for me to advise poor people to take such goods as were most useful, and not costly.[16]

The boy who had realized so keenly how his recklessness and selfishness had destroyed a family of birds for no good reason was now a man alert to the unintended consequences of the many thoughtless choices made in a consumer economy. Woolman was even concerned by the link he discerned between the pressures of a hectic life in the new economy of trade, and the abuse of alcohol as a comfort and stress-reliever, especially by the poor. Throughout his life, Woolman grew more and more convinced that the expenditure of more time and labor than was necessary, in order to obtain things that were more luxuries than necessities, lay at the root of many social evils. Christians, Woolman believed, should have a very different set of values and should keep themselves free of the entangling complications of the emerging consumer society:

Every degree of luxury hath some connection with evil; and if those who profess to be disciples of Christ, and are looked upon as leaders of the people, have that mind in them which was also in Christ, and so stand separate from every wrong way, it is a means of help to the weaker. As I have sometimes been much spent in the heat and have taken spirits to revive me, I have found by experience that in such circumstances the mind is not so calm, nor so fitly disposed for divine meditation, as when all such extremes are avoided. I have felt an increasing care to attend to that Holy Spirit which sets right bounds to our desires, and leads those who faithfully follow it, to apply all the gifts of divine Providence to the purposes for which they were intended. Did those who have the care of great estates attend with singleness of heart to this heavenly Instructor, which so opens and enlarges the mind as to cause men to love their neighbours as themselves, they would have wisdom given them to manage their concerns,

---

15 Ibid. 46.
16 Ibid. 46.

without employing some people in providing luxuries of life, or others in labouring too hard; but for want of steadily regarding this principle of divine love, a selfish spirit takes place in the minds of people, which is attended with darkness and manifold confusions in the world.[17]

As Geoffrey Plank points out, Woolman's meticulous business records demonstrate that he gradually withdrew from more and more types of trade over a period of approximately two years—first from coffee, molasses, tobacco, and snuff, and then from indigo, rum, cordial, powder, and shot.[18] As Plank summarizes, "By refocusing [and then abandoning altogether] his retail operations, Woolman disengaged himself from several practices that had seemed to compromise his moral principles," from promoting the use of alcohol and tobacco to trafficking in goods derived from the slave trade.[19] Through the remainder of Woolman's life, he would slowly but surely take more and more steps to distance himself from the empire of trade and commerce that he increasingly saw as destructive and perverse. As Woolman's leadership ministry in the Society of Friends focused more and more on speaking against selling and owning slaves, his own steady withdrawal from the many products and branches of trade contaminated by dependence on the slave trade became more important as a proof of his urgency and sincerity.

The Fight Against Slavery

As we shall see, "the darkness and manifold confusions in the world" that troubled Woolman took many forms, but the great evil with which his name would be forever linked was that of slavery. Despite many earlier Quaker voices raised against slavery, and despite the fact that Quakerism would become all but synonymous with abolitionism during the century separating Woolman's lifetime from the American Civil War, at this time "the views of most Quakers on the issue [of owning slaves] were no different from those of other American colonists," writes biographer Thomas Slaughter—meaning that some Quakers condemned slavery entirely, others defended it and felt no shame or hesitation in owning, buying, and selling slaves, and still others were uneasy about slavery and professed concern about it, but continued to rationalize it as a necessary evil, whether for society as a whole or for their own families' livelihoods.[20]

Woolman made a point of emphasizing in his *Journal* that his own response to the issue of slavery began with ambivalence, hesitation, rationalization, and ultimate moral failure.

17 Ibid. 46.
18 Plank 79.
19 Ibid. 80.
20 Slaughter 105.

It happened during the early days of his employment as a clerk and bookkeeper in the shop. One day, offhandedly and quite unexpectedly, Woolman's employer instructed him to draw up a bill of sale for an enslaved woman he owned and wanted to sell. Woolman was distressed and deeply troubled, but he was taken by surprise, and, as he would later write:

> I remembered that I was hired by the year, that it was my master who directed me to do it, and that it was an elderly man, a member of our Society, who bought her; so through weakness I gave way, and wrote it; but at the executing of it I was so afflicted in my mind, that I said before my master and the Friend that I believed slave-keeping to be a practice inconsistent with the Christian religion. This in some degree abated my uneasiness; yet, as often as I reflected seriously upon it, I thought I should have been clearer if I had desired to be excused from it, as a thing against my conscience; for such it was.[21]

The incident troubled Woolman enough that he would never be caught off guard again. When, as we have seen, Woolman was asked sometime later by a friend and fellow Quaker to draw up a receipt for a slave woman that had been presented to the man's wife as a present, Woolman was better prepared. He refused to do it, explaining his reasons. Never again would he knowingly participate in any paperwork relating to slavery, except for releasing and compensating the enslaved.

Once Woolman became a traveling minister, his firsthand experience of slavery in the South, where it was more foundational to the economy and culture than in the northern colonies (although it was legal and widespread there as well), crystallized his conviction that it had no place among Christians in general, and Friends in particular. Woolman saw "this trade and way of life" as what he described as "a dark gloominess hanging over the land; and though now many willingly run into it, yet in future the consequences will be grievous to posterity!"[22] As Slaughter emphasizes, Woolman's discomfort when staying or dining with families who were visibly kept in lives of luxury by the service of slaves prompted him to trace the cause and effect further back, and to begin considering the connections between bloody wars or violent kidnappings on the coast of West Africa and the cloth or sugar he sold in the shop, or the fine schools to which prosperous Quaker merchants could afford to send their children.

Woolman increasingly recognized that his Christianity had radical implications for his life, and specifically for his participation in a society whose wealth was growing because of slavery and imperialism. Woolman knew better than most how deeply

---

21   Woolman 80.
22   Quoted in Slaughter 131.

rooted slavery was in the fledgling society of America, and he was not driven primarily by the determination to eradicate it entirely, although he passionately urged this step in his writings. Rather, Woolman's primary preoccupation was always to preserve the distinction between the world and the church and to protect the credibility of the gospel. Woolman's voice never gained a very wide audience in the world, but within his own Quaker community, he was about to set in motion an irreversible transformation.

Woolman's pamphlet *Some Considerations on the Keeping of Negroes*, begun in 1746 and published eight years later,[23] made fully public the consistent and vocal opposition to the holding of slaves by Quakers that would characterize Woolman during the remainder of his life. It also struck Woolman's distinctive note of appeal and deference. As Slaughter writes:

> [It was] composed in gentle, humble terms and avoids an accusatory tone. He instructs rather than denounces; he pleads rather than threatens. He aims for a genuine expression of empathy that would make the message palatable to Quaker slave-owners and slave traffickers.[24]

The pamphlet made Woolman the first of several Quakers to take a strong public stand against slavery and served as an early signal of what Geoffrey Plank calls "a rising groundswell of opposition to slavery among Quakers."[25] New Quaker voices raised in favor of abolition and new leadership in the North American Society of Friends prepared the way for a pivotal showdown at the Philadelphia Yearly Meeting.

The Yearly Meeting of the Society of Friends in 1758, held in Philadelphia, was a watershed moment for Quakers across the British colonies of the New World. There were several important matters on the agenda, but the issue of slavery was expected to be the most urgent and the most divisive. Would the problem of slavery, with all its economic entanglements, split the Quakers as it would later split the infant United States?

When the time came to discuss the problem of slavery, many delegates spoke. No one defended the institution of slavery directly. Instead, there was reluctance to face head-on a topic that was liable to be so controversial and distressing, and there were some suggestions that the matter should not be rushed. As Whittier reports:

> No one openly justified slavery as a system, although some expressed a concern lest the meeting should go into measures calculated to cause uneasiness to many members of the Society. It was also urged that Friends should wait patiently

---

23   Ibid. 132.
24   Ibid. 138-139.
25   Plank 108.

until the Lord in His own time should open a way for the deliverance of the slave. This was replied to by John Woolman.[26]

Silence fell as Woolman rose to his feet. This moment would not be Woolman's first attempt to address one of the Quakers' governing assemblies on the subject of slavery, and none of his previous efforts had gone very well. Despite his leadership role and his growing ministry of speaking and writing, Woolman's dread of confrontation was still very much part of his personality, and he seems to have been intimidated as well as saddened by the strength of the opposition he had encountered, and the atmosphere of tension and controversy he had created after some earlier attempts to raise the issue of slavery at meetings of the Friends' leadership. At an Annual Meeting four years earlier, one observer recorded, Woolman had risen to speak and was "publicly opposed," whereupon he took his seat again, visibly weeping, and "without attempting any justification."[27] Two years later at the Annual Meeting of a different region, on Long Island, Woolman's urging to consider the "inconsistency of [owning slaves] with the purity of the Christian religion" provoked so much hostility that he compared himself to the prophet Jeremiah, whose warnings to the Old Testament Israelites made him a persecuted outcast accused of everything from lack of patriotism to being a false prophet.[28]

But in the years leading up to this moment, at the 1758 Philadelphia Annual Meeting, Woolman had made yet another visit to the Quaker homes and gatherings of the South. Here slavery confronted the travelers everywhere, even in Quaker homes and communities. Woolman had grown bolder and more articulate as he saw more of what he considered the destructive effects of slavery, not only on the enslaved Africans but also on the white Quakers who owned slaves, and who, Woolman believed, were morally and spiritually weakened and damaged by living in luxury on the labor of the oppressed, while professing to be Christians. Woolman now both wrote and spoke with greater confidence and clarity about the evils of slavery, and he also began to refuse the free hospitality of Quakers who owned slaves, insisting, instead, on paying for his board and lodging so that he was not profiting from slave labor. These experiences, with his continued reflection upon and discussion of the issue, had prepared Woolman for this moment at the Annual Meeting. When many voices proposed caution and delay, Woolman rose to his feet. This time, the moment was ripe, and this time, he did not back down. Instead, he challenged the assembled crowd in these words:

26   Quoted in Woolman 11.
27   Quoted in Plank 108.
28   Ibid. 111.

My mind is led to consider the purity of the divine Being, and the justice of His judgments; and herein my soul is covered with awfulness. I cannot forbear to hint of some cases where people have not been treated with the purity of justice, and the event has been most lamentable. Many slaves on this continent are oppressed, and their cries have entered into the ears of the Most High. Such are the purity and certainty of His judgments, that He cannot be partial in our favour. In infinite love and goodness He hath opened our understandings from one time to another, concerning our duty towards this people; and it is not a time for delay. Should we now be sensible of what He requires of us, and, through a respect to the private interests of some persons, or through a regard to some friendships which do not stand upon an immutable foundation, neglect to do our duty in firmness and constancy, still waiting for some extraordinary means to bring about their deliverance, God may by terrible things in righteousness answer us in this matter."[29]

Woolman's appeal made a great impact. Soon, the whole assembly, including slave-holding members, was ready to agree that all future buying and selling of slaves should be banned. But there were now, at last, many voices to argue this was not enough and that the root of the issue would not be dealt with until owning slaves was forbidden to Friends. In the end, a resolution was adopted, virtually unanimously, agreeing that Christ's command to do unto others as we would have them do unto us meant that all Quakers who owned slaves should be urged to set them at liberty, and "make a Christian provision for them."

It might have felt, for a moment, like the triumphant end of a hard journey, but of course it was really only the beginning. It often happens that those who speak up to argue that something be done find themselves saddled with the job of doing it; thus, John Woolman was one of several Quaker men appointed by the assembly to visit slave-owning Quakers, urging them to release and provide for their slaves and helping them to make the required arrangements.

It was an astronomical task. Another of the four men doing the visitation reported visiting the owners of more than eleven hundred slaves, according to Whittier's account. And it was not the numbers but the predictably endless exceptions and excuses they were offered that were most daunting. One man wanted to free his slaves, but his wife couldn't bear the idea. One pointed out that he had brought up, cared for, and educated his slaves since they were children, and now he needed and expected them to care for him in his old age. Another man said he wanted to free his slaves, but just didn't see how he could possibly manage it financially. Others admitted bluntly that they knew what they were

---

29 Quoted in Woolman 11.

doing was wrong, but simply weren't willing to make the financial and lifestyle sacrifices it would require to change their whole way of life. Many, however, were eager to free their slaves, and to free themselves from the moral burden of living off the exploitation of other human beings.

Woolman seems to have had a very realistic attitude toward the task he was undertaking and expected it to be long, slow, difficult, and frustrating. His journal records how he continually steadied his own mind and emotions as he prayed for understanding, humility, and compassion towards slaveholders, as well as toward the enslaved:

> In the beginning of the 12th month I joined in company with my friends, John Sykes and Daniel Stanton, in visiting such as had slaves. Some, whose hearts were rightly exercised about them, appeared to be glad of our visit, but in some places our way was more difficult. I often saw the necessity of keeping down to that root from whence our concern proceeded, and have cause in reverent thankfulness humbly to bow down before the Lord who was near to me, and preserved my mind in calmness under some sharp conflicts, and begat a spirit of sympathy and tenderness in me towards some who were grievously entangled by the spirit of this world.[30]

Much of the unique and lasting power of Woolman's quiet crusade can be attributed to this most rare and precious combination of human characteristics—unyielding conviction and patient compassion in the same person. Many who raise their voices against injustice, recognizing the urgency of great wrongs and refusing to accept them as others do, alienate those whose help and support they need. They often experience frustration and disillusionment, even rage and contempt, when so many others are unwilling to sacrifice and take the bold steps the situation demands. On the other hand, many who recognize the need to take action fail to do so because of the sympathy they feel with those who would encounter hardship, or they simply quail before the overwhelming investment of time and energy it would require to walk beside the unwilling and unprepared. Woolman had a very rare gift, captured in his remarkable journal, for committing both to the bold first step, and to the long, tedious, unromantic journey. He also combined humility and compassion for those on the wrong side of an issue with a refusal to compromise.

Woolman knew the task he had begun would need to be carried on not only through the rest of his own life but also by others after his time. The real tragedy and the true

---

30   Ibid.13.

magnitude of the evils of slavery can be seen in the fact, which was recognized from the beginning and has continued to haunt all the countries affected by the African slave trade, that once the first great wrong was committed, there was no easy or just way to undo it. It was obvious, of course, that those who had lived all their lives in slavery, often prevented from accumulating either skills or capital of any kind, could not be given back the lost years of their lives. So many of the sins of slavery, from the destruction of childhood to the separation of families to the exploitation of labor, simply could not be undone. Should slaves be sent back to Africa? Some thought so—but by Woolman's time it was already the case that generations of slaves had been born in the New World, and did not even know from which African locations and cultures their ancestors had come. Furthermore, many of the people groups decimated by the slave trade were vanishing from Africa. Their villages were destroyed, their culture and language were all but obliterated, their political structures were irreparably disrupted. There was nothing to go back to.

Meanwhile, it was clearly adding another wrong to the first to simply turn slaves out of their homes to make their own way in such a hostile world—a world they had been prevented from fitting into in any way other than as slaves. They must have homes, some way to make a living, some way of educating their children, some way of navigating a world of ingrained racism where they would not be fully accepted, and where they would often spend the rest of their lives on the outside looking in.

In 1779, just over twenty years after the momentous meeting at which Woolman had been able to sway the consensus toward the freeing of all Quakers' slaves, the Society of Friends passed a resolution that former slaveholders should recompense or compensate their former slaves in some way. While the release of all the slaves was still incomplete, the Society's letter on reparations shows how far the Quakers had come in two decades:

> We are united in judgment that the state of the oppressed people who have been held by any of us, or our predecessors, in captivity and slavery, calls for a deep inquiry and close examination how far we are clear of withholding from them what under such an exercise may open to view as their just right; and therefore we earnestly and affectionately entreat our brethren in religious profession to bring this matter home, and that all who have let the oppressed go free may attend to the further openings of duty.

> A tender Christian sympathy appears to be awakened in the minds of many who are not in religious profession with us, who have seriously considered the oppressions and disadvantages under which those people have long laboured;

and whether a pious care extended to their offspring is not justly due from us to them is a consideration worthy our serious and deep attention.[31]

The Society formed committees for the aid and support of former slaves and their children, and many Quakers who had previously owned slaves voluntarily submitted to the judgment of appointed arbiters who determined what payment was due to the freed men and women for their past services. The money collected was then distributed by the committees.

After describing the holdout Virginia society of Quakers acting in 1784 to disown members who continued to own slaves, Whittier sums up:

> So ended slavery in the Society of Friends. For three-quarters of a century the advice put forth in the meetings of the Society at stated intervals, that Friends should be "careful to maintain their testimony against slavery," has been adhered to so far as owning, or even hiring, a slave is concerned. Apart from its first-fruits of emancipation, there is a perennial value in the example exhibited of the power of truth, urged patiently and in earnest love, to overcome the difficulties in the way of the eradication of an evil system, strengthened by long habit, entangled with all the complex relations of society, and closely allied with the love of power, the pride of family, and the lust of gain.[32]

In the decades separating this decision from the Civil War and Reconstruction, the Quakers would lack the political voice to influence America's views on slavery, and they would also fail to sway much of the church. But they would produce powerful advocates for Abolition who spoke against slavery, keeping the open wound before the public eye and conscience. John Woolman's words and work opened a trail, however rugged and narrow, in which other opponents of slavery could walk.

The Problem of War

Woolman saw his work against slavery not as an isolated crusade, but as one outgrowth of a consistent Christian testimony—nor was it the only issue on which he challenged his fellow Quakers to a more thoughtful, more authentic life. Even as his antislavery work and his traveling ministry continued, Woolman confronted new and disturbing challenges to his convictions as the colonial government was at war with local Native American tribes, and began levying taxes to support the war effort. These demands did not seem at all unreasonable to colonists who were terrified of Indian

---

31   Ibid. 14.
32   Ibid. 17.

attacks, and who knew the taxes were paying directly for the protection of their own homes, farms, and families.

But Quakers are by definition—and had been since they first emerged as a deeply unpopular sect in England—pacifists and conscientious objectors. They believe that all wars, even those in self-defense, are wrong for Christians to participate in, since followers of Christ are not at liberty to repay violence with violence, however great the provocation. This was one of the articles of faith that most sharply divided Quakers from their fellow Christians, as well as being, not surprisingly, one of those which most frequently landed them in trouble with secular governments.

By Woolman's time, however, changes both inside and outside the Society of Friends, as they called themselves, had made it possible for Quakers to coexist peacefully with other colonial Americans most of the time. Perhaps they coexisted *too* peacefully. Woolman had long been distressed, for example, that many Quakers were perfectly happy to own slaves; thus it was certainly not surprising that the vast majority of Quakers had no qualms at all in paying the required tax to support what was almost universally viewed (though quite inaccurately) as a defensive war against the terrifying Indians, who were known to capture women and children and scalp the wounded. The fact that European settlers were already beginning to employ even more violent and less humane methods in their warfare on the Native Americans did nothing to assuage the terrible fear communities experienced when confronted with the specter of armies of "savages," scalping and burning their way through defenseless settlements.

Perhaps it was Woolman's natural timidity that enabled him to recognize so clearly that it is fear, even more than greed or arrogance or racism or self-indulgence, that is often the face of human selfishness. For Christians, it is often fear that reveals or attempts to justify a failure to trust God when the stakes seem higher. Thus, Woolman found himself virtually alone in being unable to reconcile the payment of taxes to support the Indian wars with his Christian convictions. In a familiar pattern, he no sooner began to grow uneasy about the issue than he felt deep apprehension at realizing that he was the only one, even among his own Society, friends, and mentors, who had any problem with it:

> I had conversation with several noted Friends on the subject, who all favoured the payment of such taxes; some of them I preferred before myself, and this made me easier for a time; yet there was in the depth of my mind a scruple which I never could get over; and at certain times I was greatly distressed on that account.

I believed that there were some upright-hearted men who paid such taxes, yet could not see that their example was a sufficient reason for me to do so, while I believe that the Spirit of truth required of me, as an individual, to suffer patiently the distress of goods, rather than pay actively . . . .

To refuse the active payment of a tax which our Society generally paid was exceedingly disagreeable; but to do a thing contrary to my conscience appeared yet more dreadful. When this exercise came upon me, I knew of none under the like difficulty; and in my distress I besought the Lord to enable me to give up all, that so I might follow Him wheresoever He was pleased to lead me.[33]

This part of Woolman's story is important because it demonstrates his approach to matters which he considered less clear and certain than the issue of slavery. Woolman felt it his duty to demand that all Christians release their slaves; he felt that no authentically Christian defense of owning other human beings and living off their labor was possible. In the case of the war taxes, by contrast, Woolman realized others might be morally justified in taking a different position from his own—he even respected their judgment so much that at times he considered them more likely than he to be correct in their response to a difficult question. Yet ultimately, he believed all Christians must respond to "what the Spirit of truth required of me, as an individual."

As many have noted, Woolman's words and example have inspired subsequent generations of war protestors, like the more famous words and example of Henry David Thoreau. But unlike Thoreau, who refused to support an obviously aggressive war distant from his home, and unlike many protesters who have been in no personal danger from armed attack, Woolman raised his objections to what was widely seen as a defensive war, and one in which he knew that the property, family, and personal safety of both himself and his audience were threatened. Woolman was fully aware of the difficulty of what he felt called to do, and of the risk he was suggesting Christians should run:

It requires great self-denial and resignation of ourselves to God, to attain that state wherein we can freely cease from fighting when wrongfully invaded, if, by our fighting, there were a probability of overcoming the invaders. Whoever rightly attains to it does in some degree feel that spirit in which our Redeemer gave His life for us . . . [34]

---

33 Ibid. 62.
34 Ibid. 63.

Woolman's convictions were soon put to a hard test, for the war was very real, and it was coming closer. Woolman knew that in refusing to pay the tax he faced a double danger—that of being considered a traitor by a government confronting a state of emergency and a community increasingly full of fear, and that of seeing his own home, livelihood, family, and safety threatened by Indian attacks that seemed to grow closer and closer, more and more frequent:

> The calamities of war were now increasing; the frontier inhabitants of Pennsylvania were frequently surprised, some were slain, and many taken captive by the Indians; and while these committees sat, the corpse of one so slain was brought in a wagon, and taken through the streets of the city in his bloody garments, to alarm the people and rouse them to war.

> Friends thus met were not all of one mind concerning the tax, which, to those who scrupled it, made the way more difficult. To refuse an active payment at such a time might be construed into an act of disloyalty, and appeared likely to displease the rulers not only here but in England . . . [35]

Woolman's exceptionally sensitive conscience seems often to have made him a kind of "forerunner"—a leader in confronting approaching challenges who, by the time others became aware of them, was ready to offer advice, encouragement, a listening ear, and a calm head. In this case, his own lonely struggle with his conscience in the earlier days of the war equipped him to offer remarkable compassion, understanding, wisdom, and support to younger Quaker men who soon found themselves facing the still more immediate problem of how to respond to being drafted into the militia. Woolman seems to have felt great empathy both for the officers charged with raising the required number of recruits, and for the young men whose principles forbade them to participate in the fighting:

> When officers who are anxiously endeavouring to get troops to answer the demands of their superiors see men who are insincere pretend scruples of conscience in hopes of being excused from a dangerous employment, it is likely they will be roughly handled. In this time of commotion some of our young men left these parts and tarried abroad till it was over; some came, and proposed to go as soldiers; others appeared to have a real tender scruple in their minds against joining in wars, and were much humbled under the apprehension of a trial so near. I had conversation with several of them to my satisfaction. When the captain came to town, some of the last-mentioned went and told him in

---

35   Ibid. 64.

substance as follows:—That they could not bear arms for conscience' sake; nor could they hire any to go in their places, being resigned as to the event. At length the captain acquainted them all that they might return home for the present, but he required them to provide themselves as soldiers, and be in readiness to march when called upon. This was such a time as I had not seen before; and yet I may say, with thankfulness to the Lord, that I believed the trial was intended for our good; and I was favoured with resignation to Him.[36]

Visiting the Native Americans

It was not only Woolman's view of war in general that set him apart from many of his fellow colonists on the colonial frontier but also his more general respect and compassion for Native Americans. He was deeply concerned about the exploitation and injustice that already characterized so much of the interaction between European settlers and Native Americans, and he respected Native Americans as individuals and as cultures in a way that was highly unusual for his time. Despite the danger of these interactions in a tense and hostile atmosphere, he made a long and difficult journey to befriend, listen to, speak with, and preach to the neighboring Native Americans. Perhaps his ability to be critical toward his own culture increased his ability to appreciate others, and to see things from another point of view. "[A]t this place," Woolman would write,

> we met with an Indian trader lately come from Wyoming. In conversation with him, I perceived that many white people often sell rum to the Indians, which I believe is a great evil. In the first place, they are thereby deprived of the use of reason, and, their spirits being violently agitated, quarrels often arise which end in mischief, and the bitterness and resentment occasioned hereby are frequently of long continuance. Again, their skins and furs, gotten through much fatigue and hard travels in hunting, with which they intended to buy clothing, they often sell at a low rate for more rum, when they become intoxicated; and afterward, when they suffer for want of the necessaries of life, are angry with those who, for the sake of gain, took advantage of their weakness. Their chiefs have often complained of this in their treaties with the English. Where cunning people pass counterfeits and impose on others that which is good for nothing, it is considered as wickedness; but for the sake of gain to sell that which we know does people harm, and which often works their ruin, manifests a hardened and corrupt heart, and is an evil which demands the care of all true lovers of virtue to suppress. While my mind this evening was thus employed, I also remembered that the people on the frontiers, among whom this evil is too common, are

---

36   Ibid. 64-65.

often poor; and that they venture to the outside of the colony in order to live more independently of the wealthy, who often set high rents on their land. I was renewedly confirmed in a belief, that, if all our inhabitants lived according to sound wisdom, labouring to promote universal love and righteousness, and ceased from every inordinate desire after wealth, and from all customs which are tinctured with luxury, the way would be easy for our inhabitants, though they might be much more numerous than at present, to live comfortably on honest employments, without the temptation they are so often under of being drawn into schemes to make settlements on lands which have not been purchased of the Indians, or of applying to that wicked practice of selling rum to them.[37]

Woolman's early recognition of the damage being done to Native American cultures and lands by the European settlers was exceptionally insightful and prescient in a time when many Europeans assumed it didn't matter if their own "superior" culture displaced an "inferior" one, and when many European Christians assumed it could only, automatically, be for the benefit of the American Indians if European settlements spread among them. Woolman, because he took dangerous journeys to see for himself, recognized a different picture:

The sun appearing, we set forward, and as I rode over the barren hills my meditations were on the alterations in the circumstances of the natives of this land since the coming in of the English. The lands near the sea are conveniently situated for fishing; the lands near the rivers, where the tides flow, and some above, are in many places fertile and not mountainous, while the changing of the tides makes passing up and down easy with any kind of traffic. The natives have in some places, for trifling considerations, sold their inheritance so favourably situated, and in other places have been driven back by superior force; their way of clothing themselves is also altered from what it was, and they being far removed from us have to pass over mountains, swamps, and barren deserts, so that travelling is very troublesome in bringing their skins and furs to trade with us. By the extension of English settlements, and partly by the increase of English hunters, the wild beasts on which the natives chiefly depend for subsistence are not so plentiful as they were, and people too often, for the sake of gain, induce them to waste their skins and furs in purchasing liquor which tends to the ruin of them and their families.

My own will and desires were now very much broken, and my heart was with much earnestness turned to the Lord, to whom alone I looked for help in the

---

dangers before me. I had a prospect of the English along the coast for upwards of nine hundred miles where I travelled, and their favourable situation and the difficulties attending the natives as well as the negroes in many places were open before me. A weighty and heavenly care came over my mind, and love filled my heart towards all mankind, in which I felt a strong engagement that we might be obedient to the Lord while in tender mercy He is yet calling to us, and that we might so attend to pure universal righteousness as to give no just cause of offence to the Gentiles, who do not profess Christianity, whether they be the blacks from Africa, or the native inhabitants of this continent. Here I was led into a close and labourious inquiry whether I, as an individual, kept clear from all things which tended to stir up or were connected with wars, either in this land or in Africa, my heart was deeply concerned that in future I might in all things keep steadily to the pure truth, and live and walk in the plainness and simplicity of a sincere follower of Christ. In this lonely journey I did greatly bewail the spreading of a wrong spirit, believing that the prosperous, convenient situation of the English would require a constant attention in us to divine love and wisdom, in order to their being guided and supported in a way answerable to the will of that good, gracious, and Almighty Being, who hath an equal regard to all mankind. And here luxury and covetousness, with the numerous oppressions and other evils attending them, appeared very afflicting to me, and I felt in that which is immutable that the seeds of great calamity and desolation are sown and growing fast on this continent.

Nor have I words sufficient to set forth the longing I then felt, that we who are placed along the coast, and have tasted the love and goodness of God, might arise in the strength thereof, and like faithful messengers labour to check the growth of these seeds, that they may not ripen to the ruin of our posterity.[38]

Woolman's recognition of the need to listen to and learn from the Native Americans about their lives and cultures was especially unusual in a man of his time:

Twelfth of Sixth Month being the first of the week and rainy day, we continued in our tent, and I was led to think on the nature of the exercise which hath attended me. Love was the first motion, and thence a concern arose to spend some time with the Indians, that I might feel and understand their life and the spirit they live in, if haply I might receive some instruction from them, or they might be in any degree helped forward by my following the leadings of truth among them; and as it pleased the Lord to make way for my going at a time when the troubles of war were increasing, and when, by reason of much wet weather,

---

38   Ibid. 94-95.

travelling was more difficult than usual at that season, I looked upon it as a more favourable opportunity to season my mind, and to bring me into a nearer sympathy with them. As mine eye was to the great Father of Mercies, humbly desiring to learn His will concerning me, I was made quiet and content.[39]

Woolman's sense of urgency and indebtedness about the Native Americans was very far from academic. His journeys to visit them, taken during the mid-eighteenth century in what was then, quite literally the "frontier" of the American colonies, were full of hardships and dangers that have become so remote for us that they are hard to imagine— including the very real risks of everything from starvation in the woods, to drowning, to catching incurable diseases, to being killed or captured, to freezing to death, to financial hardship caused by unforeseeable delays. All of these dangers had long been realities for the settlers of the American colonies—a reality that contributed to the extreme rarity of Woolman's respect, understanding, and compassion toward people that were simply too far away and too much work for many others to seek out. Woolman's understated journals capture a harrowing journey through an unfamiliar and threatening landscape:

> Between the English settlements and Wehaloosing we had only a narrow path, which in many places is much grown up with bushes, and interrupted by abundance of trees lying across it. These, together with the mountain swamps and rough stones, make it a difficult road to travel, and the more so because rattlesnakes abound here, of which we killed four. People who have never been in such places have but an imperfect idea of them and I was not only taught patience, but also made thankful to God, who thus led about and instructed me, that I might have a quick and lively feeling of the afflictions of my fellow-creatures, whose situation in life is difficult.[40]

The escalating "Indian Wars" of the period meant that visiting the Indian villages often meant traveling, unprotected, into hostile territory. Woolman's journals make clear that there were immediate physical dangers on his trip that he had not foreseen when setting out, and that he confronted decisions about what would happen to him and his family if he were killed by hostile or suspicious Indians:

> On reaching the Indian settlement at Wyoming, we were told that an Indian runner had been at that place a day or two before us, and brought news of the Indians having taken an English fort westward, and destroyed the people, and that they were endeavouring to take another; also, that another Indian runner

---

39   Ibid. 93.
40   Ibid. 100.

came there about the middle of the previous night from a town about ten miles from Wehaloosing, and brought the news that some Indian warriors from distant parts came to that town with two English scalps, and told the people that it was war with the English.

Our guides took us to the house of a very ancient man. Soon after we put in our baggage, there came a man from another Indian house some distance off. Perceiving there was a man near the door I went out; the man had a tomahawk wrapped under his matchcoat out of sight. As I approached him he took it in his hand; I went forward, and, speaking to him in a friendly way, perceived he understood some English. My companion joining me, we had some talk with him concerning the nature of our visit in these parts; he then went into the house with us, and, talking with our guides, soon appeared friendly, sat down and smoked his pipe. Though taking his hatchet in his hand at the instant I drew near to him had a disagreeable appearance, I believe he had no other intent than to be in readiness in case any violence were offered to him.

On hearing the news brought by these Indian runners, and being told by the Indians where we lodged that the Indians about Wyoming expected in a few days to move to some larger towns, I thought, to all outward appearance, it would be dangerous travelling at this time . . . .Then I was again strengthened to commit my life, and all things relating thereto, into His heavenly hands, and got a little sleep towards day.[41]

Woolman's health failed as the journey continued through difficult country and dangerous weather, and he admits with his characteristic engaging frankness that he did not find it easy to shake off his fear:

Before our first meeting this morning, I was led to meditate on the manifold difficulties of these Indians who, by the permission of the Six Nations, dwell in these parts. A near sympathy with them was raised in me, and, my heart being enlarged in the love of Christ, I thought that the affectionate care of a good man for his only brother in affliction does not exceed what I then felt for that people. I came to this place through much trouble; and though through the mercies of God I believed that if I died in the journey it would be well with me, yet the thoughts of falling into the hands of Indian warriors were, in times of weakness, afflicting to me; and being of a tender constitution of body, the thoughts of captivity among them were also grievous; supposing that as they were strong and hardy they might demand service of me beyond what I

---

41   Ibid. 95.

could well bear. But the Lord alone was my keeper, and I believed that if I went into captivity it would be for some good end. Thus, from time to time, my mind was centred in resignation, in which I always found quietness. And this day, though I had the same dangerous wilderness between me and home, I was inwardly joyful that the Lord had strengthened me to come on this visit, and had manifested a fatherly care over me in my poor lowly condition, when in mine own eyes I appeared inferior to many among the Indians.[42]

Voyage to England

Woolman's concern for individuals and cultures outside his own, and especially for those who had been oppressed and defrauded by his own people, seems to have gradually expanded in concentric circles that spread wider and wider throughout his life. Years after he had stopped selling the rum, sugar, and other products imported from the West Indies, Woolman grew increasingly distressed by the effect of the West Indian trade on those enslaved there and began to think seriously of visiting the West Indies—as he had visited the Native American tribes—to see for himself what their lives were like and to show them kindness and share the gospel with them. A severe attack of pleurisy, then a highly life-threatening illness, intervened, not only bringing Woolman to the brink of death but also putting a stop to all thoughts of visiting the West Indies in person. But after his recovery, thoughts of an even more dangerous journey and even more distant land began to stir in his mind. A long-cherished impulse to visit Quaker congregations in the north of England (a country which had been the birthplace of the Society of Friends) grew into a definite goal, and, after conferring with his wife and several friends and mentors, Woolman began planning his trip.

Typically, Woolman insisted on traveling in the cheapest accommodations, where the very poorest passengers were housed, and he spent much of his time on the long and difficult voyage not only being seasick but also learning about the life of the sailors he met—especially those very young boys who were preparing for a seafaring life:

> As my lodging in the steerage, now near a week, hath afforded me sundry opportunities of seeing, hearing, and feeling with respect to the life and spirit of many poor sailors, an exercise of soul hath attended me in regard to placing our children and youth where they may be likely to be exampled and instructed in the pure fear of the Lord . . . .Oh that all may take heed and beware of covetousness! Oh that all may learn of Christ, who was meek and lowly of

---

42 Ibid. 98.

heart. Then, in faithfully following Him, He will teach us to be content with food and raiment without respect to the customs or honours of this world. Men thus redeemed will feel a tender concern for their fellow-creatures, and a desire that those in the lowest stations may be assisted and encouraged, and where owners of ships attain to the perfect law of liberty and are doers of the Word, these will be blessed in their deeds.

A ship at sea commonly sails all night, and the seamen take their watches four hours at a time. Rising to work in the night, it is not commonly pleasant in any case, but in dark rainy nights it is very disagreeable, even though each man were furnished with all conveniences. If, after having been on deck several hours in the night, they come down into the steerage soaking wet, and are so closely stowed that proper convenience for change of garments is not easily come at, but for want of proper room their wet garments are thrown in heaps, and sometimes, through much crowding, are trodden under foot in going to their lodgings and getting out of them, and it is difficult at times for each to find his own. Here are trials for the poor sailors.

Now, as I have been with them in my lodge, my heart hath often yearned for them, and tender desires have been raised in me that all owners and masters of vessels may dwell in the love of God and therein act uprightly, and by seeking less for gain and looking carefully to their ways they may earnestly labour to remove all cause of provocation from the poor seamen, so that they may neither fret nor use excess of strong drink; for, indeed, the poor creatures, in the wet and cold, seem to apply at times to strong drink to supply the want of other convenience. Great reformation is wanting in the world, and the necessity of it among those who do business on great waters hath at this time been abundantly opened before me.[43]

Woolman had insisted on traveling by steerage—despite admitting to some anxiety about the hardships and dangers of the voyage—because he believed it would be wrong to waste money on the comforts of a cabin. Thus, during a very stormy voyage in which bad weather and seasickness plagued many on board, Woolman found himself observing the life of the poorer passengers and the crew at very close quarters indeed—an opportunity he grew glad of, and one which prompted further thoughts on the familiar theme of how the desire for profit could claim many victims not even thought of by those who bought and sold commodities from around the world:

43   Ibid. 115-118.

As I continue to lodge in the steerage I feel an openness this morning to express something further of the state of my mind in respect to poor lads bound apprentice to learn the art of sailing . . . .To silence every motion proceeding from the love of money, and humbly to wait upon God to know His will concerning us have appeared necessary. He alone is able to strengthen us to dig deep, to remove all which lies between us and the safe foundation, and so to direct us in our outward employment that pure universal love may shine forth in our proceedings . . . I was now desirous to embrace every opportunity of being inwardly acquainted with the hardships and difficulties of my fellow-creatures, and to labour in His love for the spreading of pure righteousness on the earth.[44]

Woolman thus expressed gratitude for the opportunity this voyage gave him to experience firsthand the hardships of others—just as he had been glad to see what life was like for the Native American tribes he had visited. His sincere gratitude for an opportunity few would have coveted is even more significant because his journals record steadily worsening health on the voyage—in fact, it probably shortened his life considerably. His visit to England was to be his last, and he would not live to return to his home and family.

Final Months in England

Woolman spent several months in England first, and, characteristically, he made full use of the time to learn all he could about life in England. He soon recognized that, even in a land where the oppression of the Africans and American Indians seemed very far away, there was much suffering and injustice. The gap between the lives of rich and poor distressed Woolman intensely, as always, and with his old bookkeeper's precision, he recorded what he learned about the wages, cost of living, and price of various commodities in different areas of England as he traveled. "Great numbers of poor people live chiefly on bread and water in the southern parts of England," he wrote, "as well as in the northern parts; and there are many poor children not even taught to read. May those who have abundance lay these things to heart!"[45]

The meticulous detail and wide-ranging "research" Woolman recorded are endearingly characteristic of a man who took great pains in forming his opinions and in learning about other people's lives and problems. He was particularly concerned about the stagecoaches that carried the mail with such superb efficiency through the British Isles and refused to use them himself:

---

44 Ibid. 118-120.
45 Ibid. 127.

Stage-coaches frequently go upwards of one hundred miles in twenty-four hours; and I have heard Friends say in several places that it is common for horses to be killed with hard driving, and that many others are driven till they grow blind. Post-boys pursue their business, each one to his stage, all night through the winter. Some boys who ride long stages suffer greatly in winter nights, and at several places I have heard of their being frozen to death. So great is the hurry in the spirit of this world, that in aiming to do business quickly and to gain wealth, the creation at this day doth loudly groan.

As my journey hath been without a horse, I have had several offers of being assisted on my way in these stage-coaches, but have not been in them; nor have I had freedom to send letters by these posts in the present way of riding, the stages being so fixed, and one boy dependent on another as to time, and going at great speed, that in long cold winter nights the poor boys suffer much. I heard in America of the way of these posts, and cautioned Friends in the General Meeting of ministers and elders at Philadelphia, and in the Yearly Meeting of ministers and elders in London, not to send letters to me on any common occasion by post. And though on this account I may be likely not to hear so often from my family left behind, yet for righteousness' sake I am, through divine favour, made content.[46]

Woolman longed for other Friends to learn contentment with him:

Of late years a deep exercise hath attended my mind, that Friends may dig deep, may carefully cast forth the loose matter and get down to the rock, the sure foundation, and there hearken to that divine voice which gives a clear and certain sound; and I have felt in that which doth not receive, that, if Friends who have known the truth, keep in that tenderness of heart where all views of outward gain are given up, and their trust is only in the Lord, he will graciously lead some to be patterns of deep self-denial in things relating to trade and handicraft labour; and others who have plenty of the treasures of this world will be examples of a plain frugal life, and pay wages to such as they hire, more liberally than is now customary in some places.[47]

Despite his compassion for them, it was not so much the distress of the poor that Woolman found hard to bear as the hypocrisy of those who represented the name of Christ. Woolman even had a dream, during a serious illness in England, in which he was tormented by the inconsistencies he saw in the lives of those who proclaimed the gospel:

---

46   Ibid. 127.
47   Ibid. 128.

I was then carried in spirit to the mines where poor oppressed people were digging rich treasures for those called Christians, and heard them blaspheme the name of Christ, at which I was grieved, for His name to me was precious. I was then informed that these heathens were told that those who oppressed them were the followers of Christ, and they said among themselves, "If Christ directed them to use us in this sort, then Christ is a cruel tyrant" . . . .My natural understanding now returned as before, and I saw that people setting off their tables with silver vessels at entertainments was often stained with worldly glory, and that in the present state of things I should take heed how I fed myself out of such vessels. Going to our Monthly Meeting soon after my recovery, I dined at a Friend's house where drink was brought in silver vessels, and not in any other. Wanting something to drink, I told him my case with weeping, and he ordered some drink for me in another vessel. I afterwards went through the same exercise in several Friends' houses in America, as well as in England, and I have cause to acknowledge with humble reverence the loving-kindness of my Heavenly Father, who hath preserved me in such a tender frame of mind, that none, I believe, have ever been offended at what I have said on that subject.[48]

Woolman's words suggest that he knew he risked offending his English hosts, Quakers or not, with many of his concerns—and indeed, Woolman's reception in England, the birthplace of Quakerism, was at first a rather hesitant, even chilly one. The Quakers of England, perhaps unsurprisingly, did not immediately know what to make of the intense, serious, rustic man from the wilderness, who was troubled by so many things they took for granted, and whose accent, clothes, and manners must have seemed very strange to them. Thomas Slaughter explains that by this time Woolman's clothing was extremely unusual, since he refused not only dyes (usually produced by slaves) but also things he deemed wasteful such as cuffs and collars that consumed extra cloth (often, in his view, at the expense of poorly paid workers or of other needs crying out for money). A British Quaker who met Woolman described this exotic American visitor in fascinated detail, and commented that "John Woolman . . . was remarkable for the singularity of his dress."[49]

As if his American accent and bizarre appearance were not enough to make Woolman stand out, he refused to eat or drink sugar, tea, and imported liquor of any kind, and he wouldn't use silver utensils. Instead of drinking from a silver cup, he would politely request a different one. He also insisted on walking whenever he could instead of riding in carriages. It would not have been surprising if he had found few English homes to welcome him.

48   Ibid. 128-129.
49   Slaughter 353-354.

But during his brief stay in England, Woolman won them over. The man who was so intrigued by Woolman's costume also described him as "mild and benevolent," and remarked upon the respect felt for Woolman by all who knew him. Woolman made an impression, not so much of eccentricity, as of "a striking pattern of temperance and humility."[50] As we have seen, Woolman often prayed for protection from an arrogant and judgmental attitude, asking God for humility, compassion, and understanding toward all others, and most especially those he believed to be in the wrong in some important matter. It seems that, increasingly toward the end of his life, his prayer was answered.

Woolman lived only a few months after he arrived in England, but by the time he died of smallpox (probably exacerbated by a weakened condition caused by his rough journey in steerage), so far from home and from the family and friends he had known and loved all his life, he was surrounded by attentive friends who could not do enough for him. The eccentric, inconvenient frontiersman had proved his genuine care and concern for his hosts, and won his place in their hearts and community.

Woolman's Legacy

According to the *Norton Anthology of American Literature*, "In a catalog of American writers, John Woolman stands almost alone as a model of unqualified integrity, decency, and forthrightness."[51] This summation perhaps explains why Woolman is both unforgettable, and obscure; why he becomes a hero to many who read his book, but never became a hero of our nation; why his *Journal* has never been out of print, yet is far less popular than the writings of men whose lives are shadowed by much inconsistency and selfishness. We cannot help admiring Woolman, but at the same time, we may find it much harder to relate to this simple Quaker than to many towering figures in our nation's history, whose talents and achievements become less intimidating to us when offset by the little hypocrisies and false notes in their lives. Perhaps character of Woolman's stamp makes us uncomfortable. Reading *The Journal of John Woolman* can be too poignant a reminder, especially to other Christians, that a life like Woolman's is not impossible. It is just difficult.

---

50   Ibid. 356.
51   *The Norton Anthology of American Literature*. 6th ed. Ed Baym, et al. NY: Norton, 2003. Page 610.

CHAPTER 4
Richard Allen
GOD'S FREEMAN

It was partly the quiet—the eerie stillness of the streets where children did not play, where tradesmen did not make deliveries, where visitors did not stroll. It was partly the look of the watchful houses—the way they seemed to be closed off and sealed up despite the stifling summer heat. It was partly the smell—the smell that seemed to cling to your skin and clothes, the smell that would awaken haunting memories for the survivors as long as they lived. But mostly it was the fear. More than the heat, humidity, or stillness, you could feel the fear, seeping out of the houses and filling the streets and weighing down the people who glanced at one another with such a strange mixture of relief and suspicion. Relief that a friend or neighbor was still alive and well. Suspicion that he or she might be carrying the horror without even knowing it.

The fear was enough to send all who could afford to flee the city as far away as they could get. It was enough to make those still well enough to care for the sick shrink in terror from the houses visited by the dreaded disease. But one man with the courage to look death in the face walked boldly up to door after door, on street after street, and went in, again and again and again. He brought with him others of courage and compassion. He tended the sick, sat with the dying, buried the dead. In places abandoned by others to disease and despair, he brought hope.

It was, in part, two mistakes that had set him apart, marking him for this mission. One mistake was that of the country's leading physician, Dr. Benjamin Rush, who had believed in the early days of the epidemic that black people were immune to the dreaded fever. The man knew now that this had been a mistake because he had survived his own life-threatening brush with the disease. The second mistake was his own. He hoped—he even believed—that this was a moment of opportunity for him and other black Philadelphians. While the fever raged, white people feared it more than they feared

75

his black skin. And surely, he hoped, if he and others proved themselves courageous, compassionate, reliable citizens during this crisis, it would change things. White Philadelphians would remember. They would recognize the injustice and the irrationality of the racism that caused them to view their black neighbors as people who could never be fully their fellow citizens.

Like the doctor's unfounded conviction that dark-skinned people could not get yellow fever, this belief in the outcome of his courageous service would turn out to be a mistake. But even if he had known his error, the Reverend Richard Allen would have continued to visit the sick and would have continued to serve the community that would never fully accept him. He would have continued to lead the members of his black congregation to risk their own lives for the help and comfort of the frightened and the dying. He would have continued to urge them to be the free citizens, the courageous leaders, and the compassionate Christians they were, rather than the timid, intellectually stunted, naturally inferior human beings Philadelphia, and the infant nation, believed they were. Richard Allen would have just kept showing up. He always did.

Childhood and Youth

Richard Allen was born to an enslaved married couple owned by Benjamin Chew, a white Philadelphian, in or around the year 1750.[1] Allen's parents and their four children were then at some later date—also poorly documented but probably about 1768—sold to another owner in Delaware: Stokely Sturgis. Decades in the future northern states would be proud of their slave-free status, but the importation, sale, and ownership of slaves flourished throughout the colonies for generations before they were outlawed even in Quaker Pennsylvania. At the time of Allen's childhood there, Delaware contained an estimated 11,000 black slaves, most of whom worked on comparatively small farms rather than on vast plantations like those in the South. There was also a much larger free black population in Delaware than in the southern colonies, and there was a robust tradition of owners voluntarily freeing slaves or allowing them to earn freedom.

Many slaves, Allen would recall, worked hard for their masters all day long and then worked for themselves in the evening, perhaps earning money to buy their freedom or simply supplementing the comforts of their family. "The slaves would toil in their little patches many a night until midnight," Allen would recall.[2] Thus, Allen's childhood

---

1   Newman, Richard S. *Freedom's Prophet: Bishop Richard Allen, the AME Church, and the Black Founding Fathers*. NYUP. 2008. Page 30.
2   Ibid. 36.

and youth as an enslaved African American in the colony of Delaware was a genuine experience of what he would remember all his life as the bitterness of bondage, but also one that offered tantalizing glimpses of a possible hope of future freedom. This hope must sometimes have sustained and encouraged Allen and his siblings as they grew up, and at other times only increased the harshness and frustration of their captivity. For the possibility of future freedom was not the only outcome on the horizon. The very real possibility of being sold into a far more hopeless situation was also always on Allen's mind as he grew up. Sturgis's finances were insecure; Allen had already been separated from his parents and three of his four siblings, and the knowledge that Sturgis or his heirs might well sell slaves to pay Sturgis's debts haunting the teenaged Allen. "When we would think that our day's work was never done," Allen would remember, "we often thought that after our master's death we were liable to be sold to the highest bidder . . . and thus my troubles were increased and I was often brought to weep between the porch and the altar."[3] Allen always spoke with respect of Sturgis as a kind man, but this experience only deepened his realization that slavery was itself a cruel, unjust, and corrupting system, not simply one that was abused by a few cruel individuals. Later, when he had gained a voice, Allen would always identify with and defend his enslaved countrymen across the soon-to-be United States, even as he recognized with gratitude the unique opportunities he had been granted.

Freedom—and Freedom Again

The first kind of freedom Richard Allen found was spiritual freedom, and the first hope he found was one that laid hold of a future beyond the power of any human greed and injustice. In 1777, when he was around seventeen years old, Allen heard the gospel from an itinerant Methodist preacher, and became a Christian. "The memory of his conversion experience stayed with him until the day he died," writes a biographer. "Indeed, Allen's autobiography trumpeted two birthdays; the one that put him on earth . . . and his rebirth . . . as a teenager."[4]

Even as he chafed more and more against the oppression of slavery, Allen recognized as a seventeen-year-old, attending Methodist meetings in the evenings after his grinding day's work, that the freedom he needed most urgently was from his own sin. "My sins were a heavy burden," Allen would write in his autobiography, until

3   Ibid. 37.
4   Ibid. 40.

I cried unto Him who delighteth to hear the prayers of a poor sinner, and all of a sudden my dungeon shook, my chains flew off, and glory to God I cried. My soul was filled. I cried, enough for me—the Saviour died. Now my confidence was strengthened that the Lord, for Christ's sake, had heard my prayers, and pardoned all my sins.[5]

Allen would become famous for laboring to bring hope and justice to his fellow black Americans on earth, but he would always believe the eternal life beginning at death is the most important issue for every human being, whether white or black, slave or free. Throughout his life, Allen would consider judgment by God after death the greatest danger facing oppressors, and the justice and deliverance granted by God the greatest hope of the oppressed. "What though my body be crumbled into dust, and that dust blown over the face of the earth," Allen would later write,

yet I undoubtedly know my Redeemer lives, and shall raise me up at that last day; whether I am comforted or left desolate; whether I enjoy peace or am afflicted with temptations, whether I am healthy or sickly, succoured or abandoned by the good things of this life, I will always hope in thee, O my chiefest, infinite good.[6]

Thus, the young Richard Allen realized after his conversion that, in an ironic twist, he now had a freedom and status the man who owned him did not. All his life, Allen would warn white Americans against slavery for their own sake, as well as for that of the black men and women who suffered under it. Allen knew firsthand the weight of the knowledge that one day he would stand before a just and righteous God, and he argued that slavery and other kinds of injustice and oppression would ultimately prove more dangerous to those who committed and profited from them than to those who suffered under them. A righteous and merciful God could and would one day restore to the unjustly oppressed all that had been taken from them. But what would it be like for those who might refuse to cast themselves on His mercy and might face Him with innocent blood on their hands?

5   The Life, Experience, and Gospel Labours of the Rt. Rev. Richard Allen. To Which is Annexed the Rise and Progress of the African Methodist Episcopal Church in the United States of America. Containing a Narrative of the Yellow Fever in the Year of Our Lord 1793: With an Address to the People of Colour in the United States: Philadelphia Martin & Boden, Printers 1833 This electronic edition has been transcribed from a photocopy supplied by the Library Company of Philadelphia. Text scanned (OCR) by Chris Hill Text encoded by Lee Ann Morawski and Natalia Smith First edition, 2000 ca. 135K Academic Affairs Library, UNC-CH University of North Carolina at Chapel Hill, 2000. https://docsouth.unc.edu/neh/allen/allen.html. Page 5.

6   Wideman, John Edgar, ed. *My Soul Has Grown Deep: Classics of African-American Literature.* Philadelphia: Running Press. 2001.

Thus, Allen's immediate concern for the salvation of Sturgis, his master, was undoubtedly genuine. At the same time, however, it is impossible not to think that Allen must have also realized how his own chances of gaining freedom would be increased should Sturgis hear the same Biblical teaching Allen and his brother had been listening to. In these early days of the Methodist movement, it was especially well-known for its antislavery stance. While this stance would later be eroded in the United States, during Allen's youth it was widely understood that a man who became a Methodist could be expected to renounce slaveholding just as he would drunkenness, swearing, or theft.

In fact, some of his neighbors had already warned Sturgis, seemingly an easygoing character whose laidback approach to running his property may well have gotten him into the heavy debts he carried, that allowing "his Negroes" to attend so many church meetings would ruin them. They would waste on church attendance and Bible reading the time they should be spending on their work, such neighbors believed, as well as getting dangerous ideas about equality and freedom and literacy. Sturgis dismissed these fears, often telling Allen and his brother, "Boys, I would rather you would go to your meeting: if I am not good myself, I like to see you striving yourselves to be good."[7]

Allen and his brother were determined that Sturgis should never have cause to regret having permitted their attendance at the Methodist meetings, or their becoming Christians. They "held a council," Allen reported in his autobiography, and made their first real plan as young adults, as new Christians, and as men who hoped they might soon be free. They would prove to Sturgis and everyone else that Christianity was authentic and powerful, and they would not give anyone reason to speak against it. They threw themselves into their work on Sturgis's farm with renewed commitment, often refusing to attend meetings if their work was not done, even when he urged them to go. "So we always continued to keep our crops more forward than our neighbours," Allen would recall, "and we would attend public preaching once in two weeks, and class meeting once a week. At length our master said he was convinced that religion made slaves better and not worse, and often boasted of his slaves for their honesty and industry."[8]

Having established his own credibility and that of his new faith, Allen was ready to make his next move. He asked Sturgis if he would be willing to listen to a Methodist preacher himself if one came to speak at the farm. Sturgis consented at once, and preachers began to visit and preach regularly over the next several months. One day when the visiting speaker

---

7   Allen 6.
8   Ibid. 6.

preached on the text "thou art weighed in the balance and found wanting," Sturgis saw himself in need of salvation, and professed Christianity. He also immediately announced that he no longer felt it was right to own slaves and that he would make it possible for Allen and his brother to earn their freedom, or, in Allen's phrase, "to buy our time." Sturgis does not seem to have considered simply drawing up a document that would declare the young men free, as some owners did; perhaps he felt that his debts made this impossible. Instead, he followed another common practice of the time and made an arrangement whereby the two could earn the price of their freedom by working for money of their own after their regular work for their master was completed. Allen reports that he agreed with Sturgis in the year 1780 on "sixty pounds gold and silver, or two thousand dollars continental money." Based on the fact that Allen was able to earn fifty dollars a month at a brickyard and somewhat less sawing wood, the arrangement was that Allen would be free in five years if he spent almost nothing and worked hard at grueling manual labor every day after his master's crops and farm chores were taken care of.

Allen managed to secure his freedom in just three and a half years. He was highly motivated, and he worked incredibly hard—"feverishly," in a biographer's apt phrase.[9] On the very first day of his deal with Sturgis, Allen cut so much wood that at the end of the day he found he could barely open or close his hands; they were so stiff and sore and covered with throbbing blisters. "I kneeled down upon my knees and prayed that the Lord would open some way for me to get my living," Allen would recall. His prayers were answered in a way that would become very characteristic of Richard Allen—not through the miraculous removal of difficulties, but through a fresh infusion of strength and endurance to face them. "In a few days my hands recovered and became accustomed to cutting of wood and other hardships; so I soon became able to cut my cord and a half and two cords a day," Allen wrote.[10] The term "cord" has always been used differently in different regions and different contexts, but probably the "cord and a half" of wood Allen cut in a day in eighteenth-century Delaware would have made a stack of logs roughly around four feet high, four feet tall, and twelve feet long.[11]

Later Allen would work in a brickyard each morning before returning to his work on Sturgis' farm, even as he began to find more and more time for the ministry to which he hoped to devote himself as a free man:

---

9   Newman 43.

10   Allen 7–8.

11   Stevenson, Chris. "How Much Firewood Did Colonial Americans Use?." Wordpress. https://chrissteven-sonauthor.com/2016/01/24/how-much-firewood-did-colonial-americans-use.

> After I was done with the brick-yard I went to days' work, but did not forget to serve my dear Lord. I used oftimes to pray sitting, standing, or lying; and while my hands were employed to earn my bread, my heart was devoted to my dear Redeemer. Sometimes I would awake from my sleep preaching and praying.[12]

As this recollection shows, Allen was not only working his way toward becoming a free man but was also working his way toward becoming a preacher. His own life transformed by the gospel brought to him through traveling Methodist preachers, Allen became one of many colonial Americans who embraced this ministry, so uniquely suited to reaching the remote rural communities of scattered farmers that dotted the woods and fields of the American colonies. As he had the opportunity, Allen himself became a beloved and widely recognized preacher at such meetings—especially because Allen's own bid for freedom overlapped with that of the colonies. During the Revolutionary War, Allen was employed to drive a salt wagon and had regular stops along his route for preaching and prayer meetings.

Thanks to his relentless hard work, Allen was able to pay Stokely off early, and in 1783, at the age of twenty-three, he obtained his freedom. It was the same year in which the United States gained its independence from Great Britain through the Treaty of Paris. As a newly free man in a newly free country, Richard Allen would play a unique role in the swirling controversies that would shape the Constitution of the emerging country. It was a moment of tremendous historical hope and opportunity for black Americans, both slave and free. Although their hopes were ultimately not to be realized and the moment of opportunity was to slip away, during these heady decades many voices, of both white and black men and women, heralded the creation of a new country based on the principles of liberty, justice, and equality enshrined in the Declaration of Independence. It was a time when black Americans hoped for a chance to participate in the process of shaping the new country and felt the weight of history on their shoulders.

The Travelling Preacher

When he and his country first became free in 1783, Richard Allen was still young and inexperienced and had not yet earned the voice he would one day have both inside and beyond the black community. His first goals upon achieving freedom—and with it the sole responsibility for earning his own home and bread and building his own future—were to make an honest living and to preach the gospel wherever and whenever he could.

---

12   Allen 8.

Taking full advantage of his years of singleness and rootlessness, Allen became himself a beloved and successful itinerant minister, like the ones who had changed his own life by bringing him the gospel of Christ, and by being the first white men to treat him as an equal. Allen became the lifelong friend of the famous Francis Asbury, the Methodist leader who most famously shaped the establishment of Methodism beyond the shores of its native England and up and down the coast of the United States. Asbury and Allen often traveled, preached, and led prayer meetings together. Allen also grew to know and love other early American Methodists, some whose names have gone down in history and others now forgotten.

Allen spoke to black, white, and mixed congregations. In later years, when racial segregation began to permeate churches, even his beloved Methodist ones, Allen must have had especially bittersweet memories of these days when he saw the power of the gospel to change hearts, lives, and communities—days when he was, occasionally, listened to with respect and pleasure by white audiences who received the Word of God from him without hesitation. One of the memories Allen describes with the most evocative detail and the most emotion in his autobiography, written many decades later, is that of a white couple who invited him to tea in their home. Allen's feet, which were sometimes in almost crippling pain from his life of walking, would not allow him to come to the table, and his hostess had the table moved to his seat, and also bathed and bandaged his damaged feet.

Yet Allen always understood that he was not safe in the way white traveling ministers were safe. He was in very real danger not only of being misjudged or treated with rudeness but also of being captured or arrested on suspicion of being a runaway slave—in fact, Allen was once arrested and not released from the local jail until white friends arrived to attest to his legal status. He very prudently asked his former master for a legal certificate validating that he was not a runaway, and he was, increasingly, known to many prominent white citizens, but even so he was never entirely safe from slavery. He fully experienced the bitter reality encountered by so many free black men and women in the northern states: the reality that they could always be suspected of being runaway slaves and called upon to produce proof or white witnesses, and that they could be kidnapped and sold into slavery by unscrupulous slave hunters and traders. Allen restricted his own travel to the northern states in which slavery was gradually being abolished and becoming less profitable and therefore less common. Here the authorities were at least accustomed to a large population of free blacks and did not have good grounds to suspect unknown blacks arriving in a community of being runaways—although of course they sometimes did. In the southern states where a far larger percentage of the black population lived in slavery and where antislavery sentiment was fighting a losing battle with the tremendous financial incentives of the plantation economy, Allen knew he might simply disappear one day without anyone being able to find him, or willing to believe him.

These years of travel were taxing in other ways too, even for someone who had accustomed himself over the past several years to hard labor and physical hardship. Allen had several serious or even life-threatening illnesses during his travels, in addition to the pain in his feet. He was scrupulously careful to avoid relying too heavily on the support of his companions or the congregations he visited. Instead, like the apostle Paul, he earned his own living. "My usual method was, when I would get bare of clothes, to stop travelling and go to work, so that no man could say I was chargeable to the connexion. My hands administered to my necessities," Allen wrote, quoting the apostle.[13] The years of ruthless discipline, self-denial, and hard work that had earned Allen his freedom had also prepared him for the demands of his ministry.

Allen was also becoming a self-taught scholar, a gifted speaker, and a compelling writer. It is not clear exactly when or how Allen learned to read—whether he perhaps had been taught the rudiments of literacy as a boy or simply taught himself to read the Bible with the help of the Methodist ministers he knew during his days in slavery. It is one of the most endearing things about Allen that he never even mentions this. He seems not to consider it an achievement of any significance that a man with no formal education whatsoever became a rhetorician who could cross swords in print with the highly educated leaders of the early American "republic of letters." He became a scholar not only of the Bible but also, to judge by his personal library, of classical authors including the historian Josephus and of the same Bible commentators with which his white counterparts were intimate. Allen was aware of the need for black men and women to counteract the racist arguments and assumptions, prevalent everywhere, that African people were intellectually inferior to whites, impossible to educate, and not capable of engaging language and ideas on the same level as whites.

Allen would later write an extended and influential argument urging the social experiment of educating black children in the same way as white children. But he omits many personal details from his writings—which, as biographer Richard Newman wrote, reflect the "public" character of Enlightenment autobiographies rather than

---

13   Ibid. 11–12.

the confessional nature of nineteenth-century ones—and one of the most tantalizing omissions is any explanation of when, where, and how he learned to read and write. Allen seems almost to have assumed that the best way to demonstrate the intellectual equality of blacks and whites was for black people who had been denied an education to simply teach themselves from books as if there were nothing remarkable about it. In the early American republic where the writings of Franklin, Jefferson, and others shaped the national ideal of the thoughtful, literate, well-instructed citizen, and of a nation in which not a privileged elite but all citizens would have access to the learning of the ages and would participate in well-informed and closely reasoned debate, Allen and other black leaders recognized the importance of participating in the national conversation. Perhaps Allen felt that simply taking it for granted that all black men and women could read, write, think and speak well if they had the opportunity of an education was the most powerful way to demonstrate that they deserved to be taken seriously.

In any case, if Allen's years of earning his freedom had given him character, self-discipline, confidence, and relentless determination, his years as a traveling minister gave him the leadership and communication skills that would shape the rest of his life. It is a testament to his character and faith that when he at last earned his freedom, he worked just as hard and lived with just as much self-denial as he had while laboring to buy it. He had wanted his freedom to spend not on himself, but on others, and on the One Whose blood he believed had bought the ultimate freedom and dignity that no one could ever take away from him.

A New Home, a New Life, and a New Church in a New Capital

Richard Allen's move to Philadelphia, then the capital of the infant republic and the city with which he would become closely identified, was less a momentous decision and more the organic and gradual outgrowth of his traveling ministry. When he was first invited to speak at Philadelphia, Allen later remembered, "I thought I would stop in Philadelphia a week or two." He spoke in many different locations and was overwhelmed by the response, especially among black Philadelphians who were often neglected and excluded by the existing churches. Allen would record:

> I preached at different places in the city. My labour was much blessed. I soon saw a large field open in seeking and instructing my African brethren, who had been a long forgotten people and few of them attended public worship. I preached in the commons, in Southwark, Northern Liberties, and wherever

I could find an opening. I frequently preached twice a day, at 5 o'clock in the morning and in the evening, and it was not uncommon for me to preach from four to five times a day. I established prayer meetings; I raised a society in 1786 of forty-two members.[14]

In this understated, matter-of-fact paragraph Allen, soon to be recognized as a leader of the thriving black community in Philadelphia, recounts his work in Philadelphia during his first year of residence there, as a young man of twenty-six. It was an important transition in Allen's life and ministry. After spending his first years of freedom and adulthood on the road and having, as Richard Newman writes, "traveled to a half-dozen states in the new American nation and worked at well over half a dozen different jobs,"[15] Allen was now putting down roots. In his private life, he would rapidly become, a homeowner, an employer, a husband, and a father over the next few years. He purchased a piece of property, started a chimney sweeping business, and married his beloved first wife, Flora. Sadly, Flora would die in 1801 after eleven years of marriage, but during those eleven years, she was vital to Allen's establishment of a home, ministry, vital network of friends and allies, and ultimately a church.

Meanwhile, in his ministry Allen had a completely new focus on building a permanent congregation. No longer the itinerant guest speaker, Allen was becoming the pastor in charge of a growing, permanent, local congregation. At first, Allen's forty-two black congregants were members of St. George's Church, a Methodist congregation which had included only five black members when Allen arrived in the city. As focused and enthusiastic as Allen was about the neglected black community of Philadelphia and their potential to establish vibrant churches, he also seems to have remained committed to the Christian, and more specifically the Methodist, vision of a church in which white and black Christians worshipped, served, and led together. In Philadelphia, the capital of a new nation founded on promises of freedom and home to an expanding free black population and a large and vocal abolitionist community, and in the Methodist church, known around the world for its strong stand on abolition and racial equality, it still seemed to Allen and other optimists as if anything was possible. It would be hard work, but he had worked hard before. There would be prejudice, false accusations, and racial hostility to face, but he had faced them all before. With a few decades of commitment, sacrifice, and persistence from black Methodists and their white allies, a community of

14   Ibid. 12.
15   Newman 53.

Christians who embraced the Bible with its principles of equality in Christ and humility toward others should be able to build something extraordinary—something that showed the gospel of Christ could defeat racism even if the young nation's lofty words about freedom and equality could not.

Allen also formed with seven others, in 1787, the Free African Society, a rare organization with all-black leadership and a specific focus on helping the black community. At a time when even the few organizations most specifically dedicated to the abolition of slavery or the socio-economic advancement of free blacks were run by whites, the Free African Society "epitomized black independence in the Post-Revolutionary period."[16] Members of the society would contribute one shilling a month to the society, and in return the society would provide financial help to those in the vulnerable black community who were widowed, orphaned, in need of temporary help, or facing other needs. In addition, the society, greeted warmly by white Philadelphians at least in principle, would become an official voice for the city's black community, organizing political initiatives such as petitioning to establish the first "African Burial Ground."[17]

Ironically, however, even as opportunities opened to establish and promote the black community of Philadelphia culturally, politically, and economically, the one thing Allen considered most important—the spreading of the Christian gospel and the building of the church among blacks as well as whites—began to seem vulnerable. As Allen continued to see the huge and unique needs of the black community, and sought to respond to them by developing black leaders and cultivating a sense of unity, the confines of St. George's began, ever so slowly, to narrow around and against Allen and its other black members. White elders were suspicious of the louder, more emotional style of Allen's preaching, and especially of the prayer meetings and preaching he conducted outside the church. They instructed him to preach in a style that mirrored their own, and while he complied, his feeling grew that the expanding black membership of St. George's was considered "a nuisance"—even as it fueled the overall numerical growth and increasing prosperity of the congregation and helped necessitate and fund an expansion of the building.[18] Allen began to dream, to pray, and even to discuss with other St. George's members the idea of a black congregation with its own leadership and its own building—still firmly and loyally connected to St. George's and within the Methodist fold, but able to grow without being cramped and overshadowed by the suspicion and condescension of an all-white

16 Ibid. 60.
17 Ibid. 61–62.
18 Ibid. 59–60.

leadership that, it was increasingly clear, neither fully trusted nor fully respected its black brothers and sisters.

The exact timing of the creation of what Allen would call "the first African church in America" is complicated and elusive; it is impossible to be entirely certain how much of the planning, fundraising, and organizing went on before the famous and climactic confrontation at St. George's and how much began after. The founding of the church was not an impulse, but a project that had engaged several people in planning, at the very least, over a period of years. Not only could the black members of St. George's see at least as well as their white counterparts which way the wind was blowing in a city where both race and class were becoming ever more important, but they also had their own big dreams for the city's black community, and their own plans for the future of the black church there. Thus, they certainly cannot have been caught off guard in any way by the notorious incident at St. George's—they must have been waiting for and may even have been planning the confrontation at which pretenses could be laid aside and issues simmering below the surface could be brought into the open.[19]

"The First African Church in America"

None of this background reduces the dramatic impact or the painful ugliness of the morning on which the black members of St. George's were informed that they would now be required for the first time to sit in new segregated seating. Americans are familiar with the iconic photographs of black men and women kneeling outside the doors of segregated churches during the Civil Rights era, white congregants standing with grim faces and folded arms to bar their way. But there is something even more jarring and even more sad in the image of people who had been faithful members of a church for years showing up for prayer and worship one Sunday morning, then being directed without explanation to segregated seating in the church's newly completed balcony. Whether through misunderstanding, incredulity, or resistance—or perhaps a combination of all three—Allen and the other black congregants went, instead, to their usual seats, the service already in progress. As they reached their seats, the elder leading the service announced a time of prayer, and just as they had done, week after week, for years, the black members knelt on the floor alongside white members and bowed their heads for prayer. Instead, however, of a reverent hush dominated by the voice of a man praying for God's blessing on the preaching of His Word, Allen reported that he heard

---

19   Ibid. 64–66.

whispering and shuffling all around him. At last, raising his head and opening his eyes, he saw white trustees of the church trying to physically raise the Reverend Absalom Jones, Allen's friend and mentor and an important leader among black Methodists, from his knees. "Get up; you cannot kneel here," Allen heard them say. Shocked, Jones urged the trustees to wait until the prayer was over, but the leader, never letting go of Jones's shoulders, refused. "You must get up now, or I will call for aid and force you away," he said. Jones continued to insist that they be allowed to finish the prayer, and in response the trustees summoned a body of white officials to force all black members to their new seats, even as the service continued. Waiting only until the prayer was finished, the black members of St. George's rose together and walked out of the church, never to return.[20]

It was the beginning of Bethel Church. The black Methodists first met for a while in a storefront, during fundraising, building, and doomed "negotiations" with St. George's. Many white church members were grieved and ashamed by what had happened, but a critical mass of the church's leadership reacted with outrage and demands for submission to the news that the black congregants planned to start their own church without white supervision or consent. Allen, Jones, and the other black Methodists were blamed for creating division and seeking to keep to themselves financial resources that should have been funneled back into the general funds of the church—this despite the fact that black members had helped in raising the funds used in building the balconies to which they were to be exiled. Ultimately, the treatment of its black members by St. George's could only legitimate their actions; they could not possibly be viewed as aggressors or as anything but the injured parties in a very nasty business. Some black members who had remained reluctant to give up their efforts to make a place for themselves within St. George's were now convinced that they had no choice.

Both Allen and his friend and ally Jones started churches, seemingly in large part because Jones allied himself with the Episcopal denomination, and Allen, despite what had occurred, still wanted and would want for years to come to remain connected to the Methodist denomination. Since both Episcopalianism and Methodism had originated in the Anglican Church they were not at this time very different, but Methodism retained a flavor of moral rigor and an emphasis on reaching the poor and uneducated that Allen treasured. Though Jones and Allen remained friends and allies and would become co-leaders of and co-spokesmen for Philadelphia's black churches and black people, the exodus from St. George's, therefore, led to the founding of two all-black churches, not just

---

20   Ibid. 64–65.

one. In July of 1794, the building of Allen's Bethel Church opened for services, and in 1796 the church was officially recognized by the state under its own "Articles of Association." The original congregation of forty swelled to over a hundred within a year, sparking years of remarkable numerical growth. Thus began not merely one local Philadelphia congregation but the African Methodist Episcopal Church, although it would take time for the new denomination to gradually and painfully cut its ties to Methodism and to fully emerge as a separate entity.

Epidemic

The famous walkout of St. George's and the birth of Bethel nearly coincided with the terrifying Philadelphia yellow fever epidemic of 1793—a fact which makes still more remarkable the achievements of both Jones and Allen during these months. Yellow fever is a virus carried by mosquitoes, but this would not be discovered for decades. In 1793 medical and scientific controversy and misinformation swirled around both the causes and the suggested treatments of the disease, only adding to the fear its name evoked around the world with its rapid progression, its obvious contagion, and its horrifying symptoms. As Jim Murphy writes, "Yellow fever was one of the most vicious diseases in the world and could create panic anywhere . . . .While mortality rates for yellow fever varied widely, it was not unusual for it to kill 50 percent of those who contracted it."[21] The death rate of the Philadelphia epidemic was probably closer to twenty percent of those infected, but about 4,000 people, or ten percent of the city's population, were to die in the epidemic of 1793 between August and November.[22]

Not only the speedy transmission and high death toll of the disease but also the course and symptoms of the illness itself were frightening. In the first stage, the patient would develop chills, headache, body aches, and a high fever, and would feel terribly ill for about three days. Then the fever would break and for just a few hours the patient might feel much better and seem to be recovering. In the dreaded second stage, however, the fever returned and the skin and eyeballs took on the yellow tinge that gave the disease its name. Soon the patient would begin to bleed from the nose, mouth, and intestines, and would vomit black blood every few minutes, often complaining of terrible abdominal pain. As death approached the patient often became delirious or even deranged.[23]

---

21   Murphy, Jim. *Yellow Fever*. Pages 15–16.
22   Gehlbach, Stephen H. *American Plagues: Lessons from Our Battles with Disease.* Updated Edition. Lanham, MD: Rowman and Littlefield. 2016. Page 6.
23   Murphy 13–14; Gehlbach 5–6.

The terror surrounding the disease did as much as the virus itself to add to the misery of Philadelphia in the summer and autumn of 1793, because as citizens poured out of the city or sealed themselves in their houses to escape contagion, many refused to deliver food and other vital supplies to the city. A haunted silence settled over the city's usually bustling waterfront, and schools and businesses were closed. The smells of camphor and tobacco believed to ward off contagion were everywhere. As gravediggers, undertakers, garbage men, and public officials stopped showing up for work, bodies appeared in the streets, and the feeling of a city coming apart at the seams was everywhere.[24] In the eerie stillness, the relentless tolling of the church bells to announce yet another death was impossible to escape. Instead of the typical three to five burials per day in the city, there were seventeen on August 24, twenty-two on August 28, twenty-four on August 29—and the epidemic, which would last into November, was just getting started.[25]

Against this backdrop, the Free African Society held a special meeting on September 5, to consider how they could help. Benjamin Rush, a famous Philadelphian who was a noted abolitionist and a medical doctor in addition to being a signer of the Declaration of Independence, was a personal friend of Richard Allen's and an early supporter of Bethel Church. Now he appealed to the Free African Society for help. Black people, Rush wrote, were evidently immune to yellow fever. Because of this, might they not have a unique opportunity to serve their desperate white neighbors?

Rush was, of course, mistaken about black immunity to yellow fever—just as he and all other doctors of the era were mistaken about its cause, its transmission, and its treatment. A very small percentage of black Philadelphians who had come from Africa or the West Indies would have had exposure to the disease as children and therefore would have been immune to it, but the course of the epidemic would quickly prove that most black Philadelphians were every bit as susceptible to the fever as their white neighbors.[26] At this moment, however, just as true severity of the epidemic was being recognized, Rush's error may have lent weight to an appeal that Allen and other members of the Free African Society were already inclined to consider seriously. The Society had been founded, six years earlier, to focus on the needs of the black population Philadelphia and its churches had so neglected. But now that white Philadelphia was in crisis, Allen and his fellow leaders considered seriously how they should respond, first as Christians and

---

24 Murphy 37–42.
25 Miller, Richard G. "The Federal City, 1783–1800." *Philadelphia: a 300-Year History*. NY: W.W. Norton. 1982. Page 182.
26 Murphy 18.

second as citizens who—whether white Philadelphians recognized it or not—deserved and desired to participate fully in the life of the infant republic in general, and its capital city in particular.

Many considerations might have justified the Free African Society in at least hesitating to answer Rush's appeal. Among the Society's leaders and members were many former slaves and many who had suffered injustice, prejudice, and poverty in a city that still held 200 black slaves and in which more than half of the black population served as domestic labor for whites.[27] There was a certain irony in the city's turning, in its hour of need, to an organization founded by and for the very blacks who were so often accused of being incapable of managing their own lives and communities—and just as the morale and public services of white Philadelphia, the proud capital of the New United States, were collapsing under the pressure of the epidemic.

Yet it is clear that Allen, Jones, and the rest of the Society did not hesitate, because they set out in pairs the day of the meeting to visit the homes of fever victims and assess the situation, and the day after the meeting Jones and Allen called upon the mayor to offer help. As Murphy writes:

> To say that [Mayor] Clarkson was grateful for their aid is an understatement; everyone else the mayor had counted on to help battle the spreading fever— leaders in the business community, church groups, elected representatives, and civil servants had fled in terror. The Free African Society was the one and only group to step forward and offer its services.[28]

The work of the Free African Society during the yellow fever epidemic is one of the great untold stories of heroism and sacrifice in the early years of the United States. Allen, Jones, and other black men and women who had been bought, sold, mistreated, oppressed, and excluded by white Americans all their lives stepped forward to do for their white neighbors the things that no one else was doing—burying the dead, finding homes for newly orphaned children, nursing the dying, providing the most intimate and the most menial services in the homes of the sick despite the stomach-turning sights and smells of rooms and furniture soaked with blood and vomit. We do not even know the names of most of the men and women who served their neighbors in this way. As Murphy writes:

> Exactly how many blacks were involved in the relief effort is not known. They stepped forward to save lives and relieve suffering, and did so without any

27 Ibid. 48.
28 Ibid. 51.

thought of receiving individual acclaim. We know that Jones and Allen were in direct contact with approximately three hundred blacks, and that there were far more black nurses (both male and female) than white nurses. The names of most of these nurses have been lost to history . . . "[29]

Exhausted, sleepless, neglecting their own families, the army of black volunteers answered every call for help as soon as they could. Many would stay with one patient until he or she died then hurry off to the next one. Allen himself was tireless in the work; he and Jones both visited about twenty families a day during much of the epidemic.[30] As the epidemic burned through the city, Murphy records, the Society

> took more and more of the burden of caring for the city's ill. When the men hauling victims to Bush Hill [the city's makeshift emergency hospital] reported the appalling conditions there, the Free African Society sent nurses. With most carpenters gone from the city, the supply of coffins soon ran out. The society set about purchasing boards and constructing coffins.[31]

Inevitably, black volunteers began to catch the fever. Allen himself was hospitalized with it but continued his relief work when he recovered. Ultimately black Philadelphians would die in roughly the same numbers as whites.[32] The fact that Allen and others continued to serve the sick once it became clear that they were risking their lives by doing so underscores the courage and generosity of the Free African Society.

Sadly, the outcome of this heroic story was to be a very sad one, and even more, perhaps, than the treatment of black congregants at St. George's, it would permanently scar Allen's previously invincible optimism about the future of black people in the infant United States. As the epidemic began to wane, ugly stereotypes and accusations about black Philadelphians began to circulate. Black nurses became scapegoats for the inevitable incidents of looting and price-gouging that had occurred during the epidemic, and vague fears of the black population taking over the ravaged city appeared in newspapers. With white citizens more likely to afford to flee the city or retreat to their homes, the larger percentage of black residents visible on streets and in other public places struck residents and visitors alike. The Free African Society had donated labor and resources and had served many poor fever victims at no cost, but some black laborers and nurses were paid or reimbursed by the city for their services. Even though many whites had refused to go

29 Ibid. 53.
30 Newman 90–91.
31 Murphy 55.
32 Newman 88.

anywhere near the tasks black aid workers undertook, there was grumbling about the black workers being paid as much as the few white workers available.[33] Ugly suspicions about a black population that had seized its opportunity to profit from the distress of its white neighbors appeared more and more frequently in discussions of the epidemic as racial fears and hostilities provided a focus for white Philadelphians' panic.

Publication

The last straw came with the publication in November—on the very heels of the epidemic—of a bestselling pamphlet account of the epidemic by Matthew Carey. Carey made a point of praising "the elders of the black church," but he portrayed unidentified masses of "the vilest blacks" wandering the empty streets of the ravaged city, looting, stirring up trouble, and financially exploiting their suffering white neighbors.[34] A heroic sacrifice that Allen had hoped and believed might not only vindicate the gospel of Christ but also prove that black Philadelphians were worthy—and trustworthy—fellow citizens had turned, with cruel irony, into the opposite: a backlash against the black population that reinforced all the stereotypes and prejudices Allen had been battling and associated black Philadelphians with disease and disorder instead of with courage and compassion toward neighbors in need.

With racial hostility already in the air in the wake of the fever, Allen feared that Carey's pamphlet would have both widespread and lasting impact and might do irreparable damage to black citizens seeking full acceptance into the public life of their fledgling country. In just two months, it was estimated, Carey's pamphlet went through four editions and sold around ten thousand copies, and a year later new editions were still being advertised. For curious and concerned readers throughout Philadelphia and far beyond, Carey's account of the epidemic was a definitive source of information.[35] If no one set the record straight, Allen feared, Carey's radically inaccurate characterization of the black response to the fever would be accepted without question.

And so Allen and Jones embarked on another first: becoming the first copyrighted black authors in the United States. In their own pamphlet, they explicitly replied to Carey's as was typical of the robust, debate-oriented print culture of the early republic. Allen and Jones countered Carey's vague, ill-defined, and unsupported accusations and innuendos with specific details, names, and stories. There was a poor black man named

---

33   Ibid. 93.
34   Ibid. 95.
35   Ibid. 94.

Lampton who "went constantly from house to house . . . and gave assistance without fee or reward." There was Sarah Bass, a black woman who lost her husband but "gave all the assistance she could . . . for which she did not receive anything." There was Caesar Cranchal, a black man who "offered his services to attend the sick and said, I will not take your money, I will not sell my life for money" and who himself died of the fever.[36] Of course, there were black nurses and laborers who accepted payment for their services as did many of their white counterparts, but Carey's very "partial account," as Allen and Jones called it, fell far short of doing justice to the overall black response to the epidemic. Allen and Jones themselves, they reported, so far from making money off the city's misfortune as Carey implied, had ended up paying out of their own pockets for many needs such as laborers coffins, and carriages.[37] The picture Carey painted of a black population enriched at the expense of vulnerable whites failed entirely to reflect either the sacrifices made or the losses sustained by black Philadelphians who had also suffered heavily under the epidemic and who were least able to absorb the loss.

Carey's response to the pamphlet was both dismissive and injured—he had made a point of publicly thanking the leaders of the black church, Carey pointed out, and it was not in very good taste for Allen and Jones to repay his courtesy and gratitude with accusations.[38] Indeed, nothing could undo the damage that had been done, and nothing could recapture the moment Allen had once dreamed of creating in which black Philadelphians might be trusted, accepted, and respected as equals after their heroic response to the epidemic. But the pamphlet was important in other ways and was the beginning of an important new role for Allen.

"With his coauthorship of the yellow-fever pamphlet," writes Newman, "Richard Allen entered national and international reform circles."[39] Allen and Jones were now the first copyrighted black authors in the United States, and their pamphlet was printed and distributed in both the U.S. and Britain. Allen was rapidly becoming the voice of black America in the way that Frederick Douglass would one day be.

Characteristically, Jones and Allen seized the moment to maximize the impact of their book by appending to it another, separate document: a direct appeal to slaveholders. It was a bold move. Rather than simply rebutting the false accusations made about black Philadelphians during the fever, Allen and Jones made their attack on racism complete

---

36   Ibid. 95–97.
37   Ibid. 98.
38   Ibid. 105.
39   Ibid. 105.

by tackling the issue of slavery head on. Their timing was perfect; five years after the ratification of the United States Constitution, slavery was becoming a more divisive and controversial issue, especially in Philadelphia, where the abolitionist movement was gathering strength. The Constitution had been ratified in some degree because the states managed to force the issue of slavery to a back burner; as the new country expanded and built its economy, the issue of adding slave states to the Union was beginning to erode the hopes of some founders that slavery would inevitably, if gradually disappear, either through the action of states or perhaps simply through the voluntary manumission of their slaves by individual owners. Founders such as Patrick Henry and Thomas Jefferson recognized and agonized in print over the irony and hypocrisy of their own slave-holding and attacked slavery not only for its cruelty and injustice but also for its bad moral effect on white Americans. Jefferson, in his *Notes on the State of Virginia*, was reduced to hoping that slavery was naturally on its way out, along with other bad habits American still retained after centuries of European despotism, and might with luck vanish before the judgment of God descended on the new nation:

> [W]ith what execration should the statesman be loaded, who permitting one half the citizens thus to trample on the rights of the other, transforms those into despots, and these into enemies, destroys the morals of the one part, and the amor patriæ of the other. For if a slave can have a country in this world, it must be any other in preference to that in which he is born to live and labour for another: in which he must lock up the faculties of his nature, contribute as far as depends on his individual endeavours to the evanishment of the human race, or entail his own miserable condition on the endless generations proceeding from him. With the morals of the people, their industry also is destroyed. For in a warm climate, no man will labour for himself who can make another labour for him. This is so true, that of the proprietors of slaves a very small proportion indeed are even seen to labour. And can the liberties of a nation be thought secure when we have removed their only firm basis, a conviction in the minds of the people that these liberties are of the gift of God? That they are not to be violated but with his wrath? Indeed I tremble for my country when I reflect that God is just: that his justice cannot sleep for ever: that considering numbers, nature and natural means only, a revolution of the wheel of fortune, an exchange of situation, is among possible events: that it may become probable by supernatural interference! The Almighty has no attribute which can take side with us in such a contest.—But it is impossible to be temperate and to pursue this subject through the various considerations of policy, of morals, of history natural and civil. We must be contented to

hope they will force their way into every one's mind. I think a change already perceptible, since the origin of the present revolution. The spirit of the master is abating, that of the slave rising from the dust, his condition mollifying, the way I hope preparing, under the auspices of heaven, for a total emancipation, and that this is disposed, in the order of events, to be with the consent of the masters, rather than by their extirpation.[40]

With the importation of slaves already scheduled to end in 1808, many shared Jefferson's hope that slavery might naturally wither away. Nor was Jefferson's hope, however cowardly or self-serving, entirely groundless. Historians agree that at the time of the Constitution's ratification, "slavery was actually a dying institution,"[41] to some degree because of growing abolitionist sentiment, but to a far greater degree for economic reasons. Much of the agriculture and industry developing in the new United States did not require the use of slaves; in fact, in many cases it was more economical to employ indentured servants or other paid labor.

Though no one realized it at the time, everything changed in the same year Allen and Jones published their appeal. In 1794, Eli Whitney patented the cotton gin, and already by 1800, slavery had become an entrenched, thriving, and growing institution as cotton became the cash crop fueling American growth, development, and expansion. During these six years, slavery would go from being something no one actually defended—something all Americans were more or less embarrassed by and wanted to go away—to something that was vigorously defended as natural or beneficial to black people, or something that was inevitably the way of the world.

At the very same time, the Haitian revolution against France was underway. Many Haitian refugees, both white slaveholders escaping the island's violence and newly freed slaves seeking a new life, came to Philadelphia, and their presence breathed new life into both the controversy over slavery and the deeply held fears of whites who dreaded the violence and revenge of a slave revolt.

Thus, Allen's and Jones' published appeal echoes from a crossroads of history—a moment of missed opportunity that has haunted the nation. But while writers such as Jefferson focused their arguments on black and white Americans as large groups, Allen appealed to individuals who would one day stand before God, as well as to those who

---

40 Jefferson, Thomas. *Notes on the State of Virginia.* Text transcribed by Apex Data Services, Inc. Images scanned by Brian Dietz Text encoded by Apex Data Services, Inc., Amanda Page, and Sarah Ficke First edition, 2006 ca. 556K University Library, UNC-Chapel Hill University of North Carolina at Chapel Hill, 2006. https://docsouth.unc.edu/southlit/jefferson/jefferson.html Pages 173–174.

41 "Pre-Civil War African American Slavery." Library of Congress. www.loc.gov/teachers/classroommaterials/presentationsandactivities/presentations/timeline/expref/slavery.

were shaping the new nation. To those who, like Jefferson, felt oppressed by the guilt of slavery and feared its effects on the developing country, Allen spoke directly: "If you love your children, if you love your country, if you love the god of love, clear your hands from slaves, burthen not your children, nor your country with them."[42] He and Jones also offered specific responses to two major ideas that surfaced again and again in discussion of slavery: that black people were in a "debased" or barbarous condition and could not be given freedom until they were carefully prepared for it by whites, and that abolition might unleash hordes of angry former slaves seeking revenge on their oppressors. To the first, he replied simply that no one could determine if black people could become literate, competent, well-educated citizens if no one ever tried:

> We believe if you would try the experiment of taking a few black children, and cultivate their minds with the same care, and let them have the same prospect in view as to living in the world, as you would wish for your own children, you would find upon the trial, they were not inferior in mental endowments.[43]

Allen's claim strikes us as commonplace but was revolutionary in a time when many scientists and philosophers argued that, through some accident or mischance, black Africans had failed to develop the same capacity for learning and civilization as white people had. His language is also, however, exactly suited to his audience—an audience of highly literary post-Enlightenment readers and thinkers trained in the arts of argument and rhetoric, valuing both the experimental science he refers to and the logical argumentation he employs.

In response to fears of bloody reprisals from former slaves, Allen urges the transforming power of Christianity. "That God who knows the hearts of all men, and the propensity of a slave to hate his oppressor, hath strictly forbidden it to his chosen people," Allen writes. "The meek and humble Jesus, the great pattern of humanity . . . hath commanded us to love our enemies, to do good to them that hate and despitefully use us." He speaks both for and to currently and formerly enslaved Christians:

> I feel the obligations [to forgiveness and repaying evil with good], I wish to impress them on the minds of our colored brethren, and that we may all forgive you, as we wish to be forgiven, we think it a great mercy to have all anger and bitterness removed from our minds . . . [44]

---

42   Wideman 57.
43   Ibid. 57.
44   Ibid. 57.

He concludes the passage with a characteristic twist of irony—black Christians rejoice in being free from anger and bitterness because "I appeal to your own feelings, if it is not very disquieting to feel yourselves under dominion of wrathful disposition."[45] In one masterful rhetorical flourish, Allen and Jones manage to suggest that white and black people have the same natures and the same need of God's salvation, that those who believe Christianity is true should be able to trust the power of forgiveness, and that the worst kind of slavery is one that white slaveholders may experience even when their oppressed slaves do not: slavery to the worst passions of fallen human nature.

Allen's writing showed white leaders that he was capable not only of the stereotypically black Methodist preaching of which the white leaders at St. George's had been so skeptical but also of the kind of highly literate, closely reasoned argumentation that was the lifeblood of the eighteenth century and in particular of the early American dream of the "republic of letters." Allen would go on to write several other important works, including his own autobiography and a powerful and moving eulogy to George Washington upon his death. Allen embodied in his writing, as in his life, the belief that black people, black Christians, and black Americans were both qualified and responsible to enter the national conversation. The works of this self-educated man—still remarkably compelling to read—are a testament to his belief that black and white people are equal and ratify each other's humanity before God when they engage in communication and even debate—even if they do so unwillingly, as many of Allen's readers undoubtedly did. They also reflect his ongoing commitment to building his life and ministry on the knowledge of the gospel and of the Bible—the only hope, he believed, for lost humanity, and carrying the power to transform others as they had transformed him.

Buying Back The Church

But even as he was expanding his impact on those outside, Allen found himself embroiled in a frustrating and exhausting struggle with the white leadership of his own beloved Methodist church. Just as the white leadership of St. George's had gradually restricted Jones, Allen, and other black leaders more and more from full participation and influence in the life of the church, so now they began gradually seeking to restrict and confine the activities of Bethel church, still under the authority of the larger Methodist denomination. In the years following the War of 1812, an event which hardened racial attitudes in Philadelphia and across the nation, and during a period of explosive numerical

---

45   Ibid. 57.

growth at Bethel, the white Methodist leadership began to treat Bethel more and more differently from other congregations, seemingly seeking out ways of forcing the black leaders to submit to white ones, however contrary to the traditions of Methodism. "As far as white elders were concerned," Newman summarizes, "black congregants must always defer to white clerics."[46]

Allen, in turn, believed it was essential to defend Bethel's equal status within Methodism. Black church members and leaders must be involved in all decisions affecting the individual congregation, just as white members and leaders would in the case of any other Methodist congregation. Bethel should be no more subject to unilateral decisions announced from outside than any other congregation should be, whether those were sending a visiting minister to speak without prior arrangements with Bethel leaders, to announcing Bethel's expulsion from the Methodist communion or assuming control of Bethel's property. Records of the recurring conflicts which lasted for years are surprisingly sparse, and as usual the intricacies and legalities of any conflict related to quasi-legal church documents are dauntingly complex. But ultimately the tension reached a climax when Methodist leadership announced that they were both morally and legally in control of Bethel and that they would be selling the property and building.

As far as can be ascertained, the first Richard Allen knew of this may well have been when he saw public notices of a sheriff's auction posted around town. The church he and his members had built on land he owned had been "seized and taken" by the city and would be sold to the highest bidder.[47] Allen and his congregation had almost no notice. His response, which he barely discusses in his autobiography, was typical of Allen's faith, resilience, and determination: "On that June day Allen awoke early, prayed to the Lord for strength and wisdom, and then travelled roughly four blocks to bid on his church."[48]

During his time in Philadelphia, Allen had achieved a remarkable degree of financial security, despite his generosity, and he owned several properties. Everything he had achieved was now on the line to enable him to buy back the church he had founded. And at the astounding cost of $9,600, Allen did just that—to the palpable shock of white Methodist leadership who had assumed they would win the auction. In 1815 the annual salary of a United States congressional member was only $1,500, and the average wage of an artisan in Philadelphia in the same year was $1.91, or very roughly around $500 a year. No wonder the Methodist leadership was blindsided by the ability of a black congregation

---

46   Newman 162.
47   Ibid. 164.
48   Ibid. 165.

to raise this sum. Just as he had during the yellow fever epidemic, Richard Allen had put his own hard-earned social and financial security on the line and made bold sacrifices to serve others.[49]

Undeterred, the white Methodist leadership continued to insist that as a Methodist congregation, Bethel must submit to their demands, and ultimately they took Bethel to the state supreme court to insist on their right to send speakers to Bethel any time they chose, with or without the consent of the congregation's own leadership. Challenging Bethel in court was a big mistake for Methodist leadership and a triumph for Allen and his fellow members because the court ruled that Bethel was an independent congregation and might invite or disinvite any speaker it chose, just like every other Methodist congregation. White officials who did not even belong to the congregation, the court ruled, had "held too high a hand over the colored people . . . and had no right to the church."[50]

At last, Allen felt he and his black congregation had been forced out of the larger Methodist denomination in which he had first found salvation, and which he had loved and served all his adult life. Promptly, Allen joined with other black congregations in the region to form the African Methodist Episcopal Church, a denomination that would become "the single most important black-led group in North America," and one that would ultimately choose Allen himself as the first ordained black bishop in the Western world.[51]

As he became an ever more prominent public figure, Allen's private life reflected the values of strict morality, generosity, unity, and compassion he preached. After the death of his beloved first wife, Flora, Allen married Sarah Bass, the same widowed nurse who had served so heroically during the fever epidemic and been mentioned in Jones and Allen's book. The couple had six children, but records show there were nearly always other people living in the family's home, whether guests, family members, apprentices, employees, friends, or people in need of help.[52]

Allen's life reflected, in many ways, the tragic trajectory of black people in America between the revolutionary and civil wars. He began his free adult life amid the heady optimism of the decades in which many believed the principles enshrined

49 Historical Statistics of the United States. https://babel.hathitrust.org/cgi/pt?id=uiug.30112104053548&view=1up&seq=181."Salaries of Members of Congress" by Fraser St. Louis Federal Reserve. https://fraser.stlouisfed.org/title/salaries-members-congress-5996?start_page=19.
50 Newman 169.
51 Ibid. 173.
52 Ibid. 172.

in the Declaration of Independence would be promptly extended to the abolition of slavery and the granting of full citizenship to blacks. He lived to see slavery both entrenched and expanded, to see America's stance harden on both race and slavery, to see Philadelphia increasingly segregated and increasingly hostile to blacks, and to lose the sense of belonging to his beloved Methodist church, where he had first heard the gospel and had preached to mixed black and white audiences who took it for granted that Christianity would abolish slavery. So differently did Allen view the American situation in his later years that he, who had worked so hard and made so many sacrifices to establish blacks as participating citizens of the United States and to contribute to the shaping and growth of the new nation, supported three different "colonization" schemes for sending black Americans overseas to build their own futures in new countries free of white domination. One of these plans focused on Africa, one on Haiti, and one on Canada. None was ultimately to prove successful, any more than Allen's younger hopes of a newborn republic keeping its lofty promises of freedom and equality, or his youthful belief that black Americans who worked hard, served others, and contributed to the society around them would become fully accepted as citizens of the new United States. In his later years, Allen feared that it was becoming far less possible, rather than more, for other young black men like himself to rise out of slavery and poverty and achieve respect and financial security either in Philadelphia, or in the United States as a whole.

Allen also faced divisions and disputes within his own church, including accusations of mismanagement from some, and a splinter group that left Bethel to form another church. Allen's determination and rigid code of conduct did not always make him a popular leader, and could undoubtedly make him demanding and dictatorial at times, even as he strove to establish a church where the power would rest with the congregation. He consistently urged very high standards of personal morality and devotion on his fellow Christians in general and his fellow black Christians in particular, and the same tenacity that had enabled him to endure so many hardships and make so many sacrifices could make him difficult to reason or negotiate with.

Yet Allen continued throughout his life to embody in his preaching, his writing, his ministry, his friendships, his citizenship, and his home life the same ideals and values he had taught as a young pastor—ideals and values that, for him, flowed out of Biblical truths and the reality of the gospel. He was hospitable, generous, and compassionate, always looking for ways to offer opportunity and hope to those most in need. He was courageous, operating a station for many years on the Underground Railroad and welcoming into his home a minister from Charleston, South Carolina, whose life was in danger in the wake of Denmark Vessey's slave uprising. He was fair and thoughtful, always seeking to tell the whole truth and never to sacrifice truth to partisanship—for example, when two young black men murdered a white woman and robbed her shop, Allen's response was thoughtful, balanced, and deeply personal. He condemned the actions of the two men, using their tragic story to warn his own black congregation about the urgency of the gospel and the danger of sin, and to warn white readers that the human capacity for evil transcends race and that white people should fear God's justice and black people hope in His mercy to exactly the same degree. He disputed the stereotypes that black people were more prone to violent crime. He condemned the injustice, poverty, and inequity that left directionless young black men vulnerable to temptation and desperation because they were debarred from the education, the jobs, the opportunities, and the respect young white men enjoyed. And he himself spent hours speaking and praying with the two men, hearing their stories and writing the confessions of the two illiterate prisoners. He believed both had put their faith in Christ before they died. It was typical of Allen that he saw even the most tragic situation as an opportunity to both speak truth and show kindness to all concerned, and that he involved himself in intimate and sacrificial ways with the needs and struggles of those around him.[53]

When Allen died in 1831 at the age of seventy-one, as Newman writes, "black Philadelphia stopped in its tracks."[54] Despite Allen's own clear wishes not to have a grandiose funeral, so many were determined to honor him that a vast procession followed his corpse to its simple interment. Characteristically, Allen had paid for his own burial in advance so that no one needed to spend a penny on it that could be used for other purposes.

Richard Allen, who had lived to see so many of his earthly hopes for his country and his people tarnished, died just a few days before Easter. He would have appreciated the reminder that an undying heavenly hope is the only final security for the justice and kindness so many seek in vain on earth. "I believe," Allen had written in a prayer to God years before, "that thou hast prepared for those that love thee, everlasting mansions of glory . . . O blessed eternity! When shalt thou be my portion forever?"[55] And in another

---

53   Ibid. 199–202.
54   Ibid. 288.
55   Wideman 41.

passage: "Let my last breath, when my soul shall leave my body, breathe forth love to thee, my God; I entered into life without acknowledging thee, let me therefore finish it in loving thee; O let the last act of life be love, remembering that God is love."[56]

56   Ibid. 42.

CHAPTER 5

Hannah More

BOTH WORD AND DEED

She stood at the back of the church, smoothing the folds of her wedding dress with a damp palm. She inhaled the familiar smells—flowers, beeswax, old wood, slightly damp stone. She heard the chiming bells and the restless stirring of the waiting congregation in the pews. But most of all she heard the pounding of her own heart, the throb of blood in her temples.

She could see forward along the aisle to the front of the church—the minister waiting, family and friends gathered, glimpses of her four sisters' excited faces. But it seemed she could see beyond them to her future home—down the lane that wound toward the elegant house and the bright flourishing gardens she had been helping to design and decorate over the past years. The very whiff of the flowers in her hands—the two of them had always shared such a love of flowers!—brought echoes of the endless conversations they had shared as they wandered the house and grounds arm in arm, envisioning their future together. As she saw those rooms and flower beds and paths, she could picture the life she would have there—the "lady of the manor" she would be, opening her home to artists and writers, supporting education in the community, helping the poor, drawing her family and friends to her new home, an oasis of warmth and kindness and beauty. She could see it all. But as she looked down again, at the stone floor of the dim church, she could see her own feet in her wedding shoes, standing, waiting—waiting again.

And there was one important thing she could not see anywhere: the groom.

And with that, the vision dissipated. How many times had she imagined it over the past six years? How many times had it vanished like a bubble brushing a blade of grass? But this time was different because now, at last, she knew. It was only a dream, and it would never be more. Her mind was made up. This was the third time in six years, and it would be the last. Today was the third time Hannah More's wedding day had been postponed by the same man—her fiancé of six years, a man who had first asked her to marry him when she was twenty-two. Today was the day Hannah More began to imagine the rest of her life in a completely different way—not for the first time, and not for the last.

Childhood and Early Life

Hannah Moore was the fourth of five daughters born to a country schoolmaster in a four-room cottage. She and her sisters grew up in economically precarious circumstances but surrounded by books and devouring knowledge. Their parents, unlike many contemporaries, believed in providing girls as well as boys with an excellent and challenging education—or rather, Hannah's mother believed in it wholeheartedly and her father, who in theory did not, shared with his wife a desire to equip their five daughters to support themselves by running a school, and shared with the whole family a tendency to dote on Hannah, who was always sickly and fragile. He was in fact alarmed by her skill and confidence with mathematics, Latin, and other masculine subjects, and curtailed her progress in them, but he seems to have found her sweetness, precocious intelligence, and eagerness as hard to resist as her fragility (which probably led to the very real fear of losing her to death as the Mores had lost their only son).[1] In any case, the house full of chattering little girls was a house full of curiosity, intelligence, and determination. Hannah, in particular, was a gifted student, with a striking talent for reading and writing and an unusual imagination and memory. When Hannah was three or four, her mother decided it was time to teach the bright child to read, and discovered, upon beginning the first lesson, that Hannah had already learned to read from listening to her older sisters' lessons. So real to her were the stories she read that the first time she read Shakespeare she was too deeply moved to sleep afterward, and during one of the doctor's all-too-frequent visits to the sickly child, Hannah was so eager to tell him a story she had been reading that they both forgot the purpose for his visit entirely until he was on his way out the door.[2] Her favorite present as a little girl was paper—a relatively rare and expensive commodity—on which to write her stories and poems, and stories and poems poured from the little girl.[3]

Hannah's older sisters dutifully—and, as best we can tell, eagerly—fulfilled their parents' plan for their future economic security by opening a school in the booming

---

1   Prior, Karen Swallow. *Fierce Convictions: The Extraordinary Life of Hannah More.* Nashville: Nelson, 2014. Pages 3-4.
2   Ibid. 39.
3   Metaxas, Eric. *7 Women and the Secret of their Greatness.* Nashville: Nelson, 2015. Page 61.

port city of Bristol, and Hannah joined them as a pupil at age thirteen, and as a fellow teacher when her education was complete at sixteen. Bristol had become the second-most populous city in England thanks to the British empire's ever-expanding network of trade, and thanks to an influx of people just like the Mores who found in England's new industrial cities economic opportunity and social mobility they could never have found in rural communities.[4] In Bristol, a school for young ladies run by sisters of excellent education and unquestionable reputation—and offering, according to their advertisement, "French, Reading, Writing, Arithmetic, and Needlework," as well as dancing lessons—would be a magnet for families struggling upward into the middle class.[5] In such an environment, and thanks to their parents' preparation for just such an undertaking and their own lifelong practicality and teamwork, the More sisters' school was immediately and increasingly successful.

Hannah More, Spinster Schoolteacher

Hannah More now seemed destined for life as a "spinster schoolteacher"—a fate that threatened many unmarried young women who were well educated but not born to wealth. Not only were their opportunities for meeting eligible men often sharply limited, but even if they met and fell in love with a young man of the appropriate background and class—say a young minister or schoolmaster—it would not be uncommon for his income to be far too small to afford a house or support a wife. Becoming a teacher or governess was often an alternative to a family of one's own, not a path toward it. (Indeed, all five of the More girls remained unmarried their whole lives and were always recognized as a kind of unit even though they did not always all live together.)

For Hannah and her sisters, however, running a school together was the fulfillment of a plan the family had long—and enthusiastically—shared. Hannah, in particular, found very real and exciting challenges in sharing her love of books, words, and knowledge with her students. What might have struck others as a dreary situation was, to Hannah, an opportunity to offer an engaging and substantial education to young women—the mothers of a future generation—who might otherwise have no chance of receiving one. While the school offered the fashionable accomplishments her students' parents would be looking for—including music, dancing, and needlework—Hannah More rejected the superficiality of much education offered to girls in her time. She believed girls should

---

4   Prior 14-16.
5   Ibid. 16.

learn foreign languages not just to drop the occasional clever phrase, but so they could converse intelligently and read important books in their original languages. Girls, like boys, should read good books so they could learn, understand, think deeply, and develop their minds. In fact, More would later write specifically against the cultivation of a taste for instant gratification in study and reading—a taste that would immediately spit out anything that wasn't a "delicious morsel."[6] Female students, just like male ones, should be expected to "maintain the most critical accuracy in facts, in dates, in numbering, in describing, in short, in whatever pertains, either directly or indirectly, closely or remotely, to the great fundamental principle, truth."[7] The widespread tendency for girls to gain a surface veneer of accomplishment by skimming through anthologies of only the most sensational, accessible, or immediately pleasing passages of books they did not bother to actually read struck More as a dangerous one that greatly undervalued the minds, souls, and lives of women. What she called the superficial nature of much women's education stemmed, she argued, from a "false and low standard of intellectual excellence," and she blamed women who merely dabbled in the lighter and showier pursuits for much of the suspicion and contempt with which educated women were viewed by society. The last thing the world needed, More believed, was more "accomplished" but intellectually lazy women prepared only to show off in society and have a good time. "One would be led to imagine, by the common mode of female education, that life consisted of one universal holiday," More would complain in a 1777 essay. An education focused on "ornamental accomplishments" would, she wrote, "but indifferently qualify a woman to perform the duties of life . . ."[8]

Unlike some pioneers of women's education, More did not want to reduce the moral, cultural, or social distinction between men and women, or to undermine the importance of women's roles in the family. Rather, she reflected a tradition that believed all human beings, regardless of their different places in the family and the world, could and should develop their minds and imaginations. During the preceding two centuries, the Puritan influence in England had particularly stressed the importance of education for women, who needed to be able to read, understand, and reflect upon the Bible for themselves, to be genuine spiritual and intellectual companions to their husbands, and to be responsible for instructing their children. In More's time many outside this tradition believed that education was harmful for women, making them unattractive

6   Ibid. 23.
7   Ibid. 22.
8   Ibid. 21.

or even destroying their health, but the More sisters exemplified the persistence of a different belief—a belief that both men and women could be best equipped to fulfill their purposes and to serve others by developing their minds and building on a solid foundation of knowledge and reflection. As Prior writes, More "sought to advance female education in order to fulfill women as women, not to make them like men." She asked rhetorically in *Essays on Various Subjects, Principally Designed for Young Ladies,* "Is it not better . . . to be good originals, rather than bad imitators?"[9] For More, women had a unique and crucial role to play in both the family and the world that it was high time to value more highly and take more seriously.

More may also have stressed the importance of application, discipline, and precision in part because she was naturally prone to the same quick, impatient, eager habits of work and study she warned against. It was a lifelong uphill battle for her to counteract her own tendency to emphasize the imagination to the neglect of the more analytical approach, to work quickly with more inspiration than discipline, and to rely more heavily on her natural abilities than on good work habits. All her life she struggled to live up to her own high standards of discipline and practicality, much like her friend William Wilberforce who recognized in himself a bad habit of relying on natural talent and avoiding sustained mental effort and discipline—and indeed, much like many naturally talented students who can succeed without effort during their early years.

In any case, the work of bringing together Hannah More's high ideals of intellectual discipline and her inborn imaginative spark could have been begun in no better place than her Bristol classroom. It was the perfect laboratory in which More could test her commitment to the idea that deep truths and big ideas could be learned with discipline and hard work—but also with fun and creativity. In fact, as Karen Prior notes, More's own struggles to curb her imagination and apply her mind may have made her a much better teacher, as they would undoubtedly make her a better writer. She instinctively knew that the pill of education goes down much easier with a little sweetener and that many people will refuse even to try to swallow it without that. "Do not fancy that a thing is good merely because it is dull," More would write later in advice directed to teachers, "enliven the less engaging parts of your discourse with some incidental imagery which will captivate the fancy; with some affecting story, with which it shall be associated in the memory."[10]

---

9   Ibid. 24.
10   Ibid. 27.

Hannah More sparked infectious excitement in the classroom with her enthusiasm, playful wit, and sense of fun. She was decades ahead of her time in thinking that school could and should offer more than dull, uninspired, and repetitive drill and memorization. More delighted in finding ways to engage her students in their lessons through fun and imagination, and especially through incorporating stories that might captivate the students' attention, whether from the Bible, history, mythology, nursery rhymes—anywhere. She brought these stories to life in such a way that one witness remembered her hearers "fancied [More] must have lived among them herself."[11]

She loved her students, she loved working with her sisters, and she loved teaching. What would have seemed a hard fate to many would probably have contented Hannah More for the rest of her life—especially since the school increasingly gave her opportunities to write, and to have her work read, published, and performed. Not only did More write a play for her own students to perform but she also found that doors opened for her through the school's proximity to the Royal Theatre of Bristol, and through visits to the city by important British writers, thinkers, and statesmen. More, who frequently attended plays at the theatre with her sisters and pupils, wrote a prologue to accompany a performance of *Hamlet* by a distinguished London actor,[12] she wrote a poem in response to a series of lectures delivered by Thomas Sheridan, father of the famous playwright, and she was hailed as the unofficial local poet of the parliamentary campaign of Edmond Burke, who would become one of the leading statesmen and political theorists of the age, as well as a friend of Hannah More's.[13] Much as she loved teaching, More increasingly thought of herself as a writer, too, and as she developed her abilities, she attracted the support and encouragement of highly qualified readers and thinkers such as Burke and Sheridan, who recognized in her a rare talent.

Engagement: Hannah More, Lady of the Manor

But then, at the age of twenty-two, she became engaged to a local landowner, and her future seemed to shift in a bright new direction. William Turner was twenty years older than Hannah, but this age difference was not uncommon in her time, when many women died young in childbirth, and when men often had to wait a decade or two for sufficient financial security to marry. Neither of these factors seems to have been relevant to William Turner's case, but they explain why there was nothing remarkable

---

11   Ibid. 26.
12   Ibid. 26.
13   Ibid. 45-46.

in the age disparity between him and the precocious and responsible Hannah More. In any case, it seems certain that the engagement was a love match on both sides. Hannah was bright, articulate, and accustomed to friendships with those—both men and women—older than herself, and the two had many interests in common. Both found instant enjoyment in discussing books and pictures and ideas; both loved art and gardens; both enjoyed the company of clever and creative people, and if the rather shy Turner had the inviting environment to make such gatherings possible, More was gifted in putting people at their ease and drawing them out. Turner was captivated by the cheerful, witty young schoolteacher, and proposed marriage; Hannah's acceptance was eager and joyful. Judging from what we now know of their doomed relationship and its effect on both of them, both parties, and especially Hannah More, were very genuinely in love and found great happiness in each other's company. Both could envision a future of shared interests and friendships and of leading and nurturing the community they both loved in countless ways. For Turner was a wealthy man. As Eric Metaxas points out, the future for which Hannah now begin to plan and compare was in sharp contrast to her first twenty-two years of life, and she took seriously the responsibility to plan and prepare for the life she now expected to live and the role she planned to fill:

> The new and glamorous life that now lay ahead would be dramatically different from what she had known as a teacher or as a child growing up in her parents' humble cottage. She immediately began preparations for her future as the Lady of Belmont: she gave up her share in her sisters' school and began spending much time and money buying clothes suited to the life she would soon be leading. The engagement lasted six years, during which time Hannah visited Turner often and appropriately played the role of wife-to-be, consulting with her future husband on everything, including the landscaping and design of the gardens . . . Turner had some of More's poems engraved and posted on plaques around the estate and even gave her a cottage to use as a place to write, naming it after her.[14]

It is difficult for modern readers to fully grasp the real importance of the many roles played by the wife of a landowner like William Turner. For scores, perhaps even hundreds of people, she would be—or could be if she chose—a leader, an organizer, a friend, a philanthropist, a coordinator. She could be a catalyst for the life of a whole community and of each family within it. Such a woman might play a leading role in providing

---

14 Metaxas 63.

medical care and emergency relief of all kinds to the most financially vulnerable in a community—the elderly, the disabled, the widowed mother of several young children, the family of a working man temporarily laid up by an accident, the young adult children of a family who desperately needed them to find work and contribute to the family's income. Everything from extra firewood sneaked onto the right woodpiles to the tactful gift of "unwanted" extra fruit or meat to a proud but needy family to the finding of work, through an extensive network of potential employers, to those who needed it most—such activities are only a small sampling of the ways in which a landlord's wife might be expected to nurture and oversee the families who lived on her husband's estate. She might take a leading role in organizing the work of the local church and the local school. She might be the hostess to educational, seasonal, and social events of all kinds. She might provide opportunities for talented but impoverished young artists, scholars, or musicians who would otherwise never have a chance to pursue their interests. She could know who was barely making ends meet, who was looking for work, who wanted to get married but couldn't afford a house, who needed an introduction to someone who needed a piano teacher or a lady's maid, who had an idea for a church fundraiser. Of course, a woman of this class might also choose to spend all her time, money, and energy on dancing, card-playing, and gossip, ignoring the suffering of those whose labor made such a lifestyle possible—and many did just that. But from what we know of both Turner and More, it seems likely that they shared an eagerness to develop the opportunities they would have to improve the life of the community they both loved in ways neither could achieve alone.

As we have seen, Hannah More's engagement with Turner lasted for six years—a length of time highly unusual at the time and still unexplained today. It must have provided time not only for anticipation and preparation but also for at least some moments of doubt. Turner refused again and again to set a date for the wedding, and on three different occasions, he got cold feet and asked to postpone the wedding. He never wanted to break the engagement, and when, after his third postponement, Hannah severed the connection herself, Turner begged her repeatedly to set any date she chose, promising to go through with it this time. Indeed, Turner seems to have regretted for the rest of his life letting his opportunity to marry Hannah More slip away. Both families treated the matter discreetly with such success that no biographer has been able to learn much more about what happened, and we will probably never understand what Turner was thinking or what divided the couple who had seemed so well-matched.

Heartbreak and Opportunity

What is certain is that Hannah, despite her determined refusal of Turner's pleas for a fourth opportunity, was distraught, and her health was devastated. As we have seen, she was sickly and fragile as a child, and all her life she would suffer occasional bouts of illness often brought about or worsened by times of severe stress. This time, after finding, at her sisters' and friends' united urging, the strength to refuse Turner's pleas once and for all, More collapsed and was ordered by doctors to the seaside to rebuild her shattered health.

Here, as luck would have it, she became friends with a young doctor who, after weeks of conversation and horseback riding together, suddenly proposed marriage to her. But More, perhaps still in love with Turner, perhaps beginning to savor her newfound independence, or perhaps still too bruised from her recent heartbreak, refused him—just as she refused Turner again when he met her upon her return with a last desperate appeal for one more chance. Hannah More may or may not have known it, but she would remain unmarried for the rest of her life. She would earn the admiration and friendship of many men throughout her life, and may have received other proposals of which we have no record, but she had rejected the two men who had begged during the same year for her hand in marriage. There is no reason to think she ever regretted either decision, but the woman who had spent six years looking forward to marriage and family life had now to reimagine her future as a woman who would never marry. She would give herself now to her writing.

Yet it was thanks to William Turner that Hannah More, the author, ever existed. Although he had lost her through his own inexplicable and hurtful behavior, Turner was determined that the woman he loved should not lose the opportunity their marriage would have given her to develop her exceptional talents and pursue her most cherished dreams. Turner insisted on providing More with the annual payment, or annuity, that he would have been expected to offer after such a long engagement failed to end in marriage—and, with a kindness verging on tenderness, he explicitly insisted on making the payment large enough that More would not have to teach, but could devote herself fulltime to writing.

This payment strikes modern readers as odd, but was normal for the time. More's plight was no laughing matter for a young woman of the eighteenth century. She had spent what were quite literally, given the life expectancies and average marriage ages of the time, the best years of her life waiting for the man who had said he loved her and had promised to make her his wife and give her a home. She had entirely missed the most marriageable age, and her reputation could have been dented by the suspicion, ridicule, or pity of the neighborhood. She had spent her twenties planning for the marriage that kept receding into the distance. Now here she was, at twenty-eight, her attractiveness as an ideal marriage partner gone forever, and all her ideas about what the rest of her life would look like having to be rebuilt from scratch. Turner's behavior to her would have been considered indefensible by many at the time, and it would certainly have been considered his obligation—perhaps by himself, and certainly by others—to compensate her for the years she had spent trusting his promise of marriage, rather than feeling free to marry someone else.

At first, More adamantly refused the annuity. Presumably, she planned to support herself as a schoolteacher again, rejoining her sisters and giving up the dreams she had allowed herself to dream of devoting more time to writing. But both Turner and her sisters were insistent, the hurt and exhausted More was in no state to resist the united certainty of everyone whose opinion she trusted, and the siren call of being free to devote herself to writing must have been alluring at some level. In any case, she ultimately accepted, and Hannah More the author was born—in a very real sense, William Turner's gift to the world.

So Hannah More embarked on a new chapter of her life: becoming a fulltime author and playwright. For the second time, she reinvented herself—no longer the schoolteacher, no longer the soon-to-be lady of a country manor and wife of a doting husband, she was now a poet and playwright whose work soon began to bring her the notice and the friendship of some of the greatest minds of her time. Devastated as she had been by the end of her engagement with Turner, as she recovered her health, she put the disappointment resolutely behind her and embraced the excitement of fulfilling another dream: developing to the full her talent for writing and finding an audience for it.

The next decade of More's life was pivotal for four important reasons: it introduced her to an extraordinarily diverse and influential network of lifelong friends which would not only enrich her life but also give her remarkable widespread influence; it made her a writer renowned both nationally and internationally; it brought a gradual but ultimately a very deep transformation in her mind and heart; and it turned her life, her energies, and her writing in a completely new direction.

As we have seen, Hannah More had already begun to be noticed for her writing—in fact, the play she had written for her students to perform became her first published work, and sold well.[15] But thanks to William Turner's annuity and the encouragement and guidance of an important mentor, she was about to look beyond Bristol to a much larger audience: the London stage. Sir James Stonhouse, a doctor and clergyman who had befriended the younger More and guided some of her reading, was so convinced of her talent that he was not only instrumental in arranging her annuity from Turner, but also himself sent the manuscript of her play *The Inflexible Captive* to the famous London actor and theatre manager—and one of More's personal idols—David Garrick. The response was immediately favorable; indeed, Garrick's enthusiastic reception of this manuscript marked what Prior calls the opening of the door to England's literary capital.[16] *The Inflexible Captive* was performed in Bristol to great acclaim, but it was toward London that its author was now looking. And thanks to Stonhouse's introduction, both literary and personal, to David Garrick, she would be welcomed with open arms.

Hannah More, Bestselling Author

The London of Hannah More's time was not simply a big city. It was *the* big city—the beating heart of an empire that stretched around the globe, and in some ways the one major metropolis of the English-speaking world. London was probably home to more than ten percent of England's population, and an estimated one in six residents of England would visit this center of power, commerce, trade, and high society at least once in their lives, whether as privileged young women attending balls in search of a wealthy husband, rising politicians in search of advancement, or desperately poor teenagers looking for work to keep them from starving. There had been no census of London's population, but the evidence we do have makes it clear that London had surpassed in population density not only its European rivals such as Paris and Naples, but also other major world centers including Constantinople, Cairo, and Peking.[17] This was the London of which Hannah More's friend Dr. Samuel Johnson famously said, "When a man is tired of London he is tired of life," because it was so rapidly transforming itself into one of the first modern cities—a place of astonishing diversity where men, women, and children from the opposite extremes of wealth and poverty and from places all over the world could be encountered, and where the news, the currency, the power, and the knowledge of the world was drawn like iron filings to a magnet.

---

15   Prior 48.
16   Ibid. 49.
17   Picard, Liza. *Dr. Johnson's London*. NY: St. Martin's, 2000. Page 3.

Certain times and places in history seem to bring together an astonishing community of talented thinkers who challenge and bring out the best in one another, creating something greater than the sum of its parts—a sudden explosion of achievement that causes the clustering of many famous names of scientists or artists or thinkers around one place on the timeline. The group of writers and artists Hannah More was hoping to enter in eighteenth-century London was such a group. For while London was several orders of magnitude larger than any other city in England at the time, it was still small by modern standards—probably around 650,000.[18] In a city this size, those who had the time, talent, and taste to devote themselves to writing, publishing, and performing composed a small world, and they all knew each other as friends, rivals, biographers, and critics. Dr. Samuel Johnson, the leading literary figure of his age, the editor and writer of two influential journals and the author of the first English dictionary, James Boswell, his protégé and writer of what is often considered the first modern biography, Fanny Burney, one of the first important female British novelists—the list goes on, comprising actors and actresses, playwrights and directors, editors and poets, speakers and pamphleteers, scholars, and statesmen. They were men and women whose words were read and performed all over the English-speaking world, men and women who were in the process of creating the most influential and enduring literary works of their time in Britain. To venture into these exalted circles was a big, brave step for a Bristol school teacher recovering from a broken heart. Turner had given Hannah More the money she needed to try her wings. But did she really have the talent to work on this level? And did she have the confidence to find her feet in London society?

The answer to both those questions quickly proved to be yes, thanks in part to More's courage, talent, and natural gift for networking, but thanks also to the support at crucial moments of others who, like Turner, Stonhouse, and her sisters, valued her ability and wanted her to have a chance. The most important of these were certainly the Garricks, David and his wife Eva. This couple became More's closest friends, her frequent hosts, her mentors, almost her family—something between surrogate parents and adopted siblings. David Garrick was the manager of London's Theatre Royal and perhaps the most famous actor of the time. When he and his wife met Hannah More on her second visit to London, as Eric Metaxas writes "that one meeting commenced the strongest friendship of all their lives."[19] Thanks to the Garricks' connections and

---

18   Ibid. 3.
19   Metaxas 64.

support, all the right doors in London society and in the literary world would be thrown open for Hannah More, but there is no question that she valued her close friendship with both Garricks for its own sake, and far beyond any of the ways they helped her. Their affection for her seems to have been equally strong; indeed, they soon invited More to live with them like a daughter or younger sister whenever she was in London, for as long as she liked.

Through the Garricks and through her own natural readiness to make friends with all kinds of people, More quickly established other important lifelong friendships in London, including playwright Richard Sheridan, artist Sir Joshua Reynolds, historian of the Roman Empire Edward Gibbon, and influential author, orator, and politician Edmund Burke.[20] The former schoolteacher's name was soon recognized by the greatest men and women of her era, and she was welcomed and sought out by the leading lights of London. She was rapidly becoming what Jonathan Aitken calls her: "one of the most influential women of her generation in London."[21]

More was welcomed especially into two of the most remarkable circles of the age. One was the distinguished and diverse intellectual circle collected around the great Samuel Johnson, who prized her charm, wit, vivacity, and engaging conversation. Another was the so-called "Bluestockings," a group that included some of the best-known writers of the day, and was famously (or notoriously) led by a group of well-educated women. More sometimes felt that she did not really belong in these exalted circles—a certain insecurity about her own abilities and humble background always seems to hover in the background. But as Eric Metaxas notes, "Her talent at winning the trust and friendship of notable people followed her through life," and would be no small part of what she was able to achieve.[22]

Especially remarkable is the degree to which, throughout her long life, Hannah More had the power to cultivate and maintain a startlingly diverse circle of friendships that included men and women, rich and poor, those who shared her own beliefs and those with whom she strongly disagreed, fellow writers and those of entirely different backgrounds. Despite her conservative background and what would later become her famously Evangelical convictions, More's lifelong friendships included the Roman Catholic Eva Garrick as well as the flamboyant and notorious unbeliever Hugh Walpole. Biographer Karen Swallow Prior refers to "More's love and embrace of those of different

20   Ibid. 64.
21   Aitken, Jonathan. *John Newton: From Disgrace to Amazing Grace*. Wheaton IL; Crossway, 2007. Page 283.
22   Metaxas 62.

religious and political convictions, a quality not always found in years marked by wars over those very differences."[23] And not only did More's friendships cross ideological lines but they also bridged the widest gaps of background, class, and education. As Prior writes, "More was establishing herself as one uniquely able to bridge the worlds of the great and the low. Her ability to connect the likes of [an uneducated poor woman] with supporters such as Elizabeth Montagu [a wealthy and influential society woman] depended on relationships that were more than superficial . . . More considered both women—otherwise worlds apart—genuine friends."[24] As Prior emphasizes, and as we have already seen in her relationship with the Garricks, it is important to note that More's gift for networking was also a genuine gift for friendship. She did not establish connections to abandon them when they were no longer useful; rather, she made lifelong friends that she continued to care about and correspond with however different their lives and opinions became. This ability to connect and communicate across boundaries would increasingly become characteristic of More's writing as well.

Because her writing is so rooted in and responsive to the tastes and perspectives of her own time, More's literary reputation has all but vanished between her time and ours—a fact that leaves modern readers with no idea of the astounding impact she made on her own time. As Eric Metaxas points out, she was "a best-selling playwright and author whose works at the time outsold Jane Austen's ten to one"[25] and she achieved the extraordinary double success of both pleasing an extraordinarily diverse swathe of the reading public, and impressing the greatest and most exacting writers and critics of her time, including Samuel Johnson, whose expositions and critiques of such great writers as Milton and Shakespeare are still valued by scholars, and who considered More one of the greatest poets in the English language.

More's literary first love was the theatre. She loved everything about the theatre—reading and writing and watching plays, meeting and learning from actors. Upon arriving in London after the end of her engagement, therefore, More's major focus was the writing of plays, though she wrote poetry as well. Indeed, during her early years of friendship with the Garricks and establishing herself in London, More seemed destined to be remembered by history as a playwright. Thanks to Garrick's support and her own talent, More's plays were spectacularly successful—her 1777 tragedy "Percy" was "literally

---

23   Prior, Karen Swallow. *Fierce Convictions: The Extraordinary Life of Hannah More*. Nashville: Nelson, 2014. Page 72.
24   Ibid. 80.
25   Metaxas 59.

the most acclaimed play of that era," selling four thousand copies in two weeks and being staged across the country and on the continent.[26]

Thus, More's time in London society (she never lived there full time but made long and regular visits) brought money, success, fame, friendship, an international audience for her writing, and extraordinary opportunity. Yet as the years passed, More felt less at home in London, not more—and it was she, not London, that was changing. More had a growing sense that she was being pulled in two directions. On the one hand was the "fashionable world," with its competitive striving, its lavish excess, its obsession with image, social climbing, and impressing "the right people," and its lifestyle of endless social engagements and pleasures such as dancing, gambling, parties, and entertainment. On the other hand, More increasingly realized, were her own convictions and her growing desire that her life and her work should reflect those convictions. The more she found her feet in society, overcoming her sense of social inferiority and her feeling of being a fish out of water, the more she realized that in some ways she wanted to belong in the world around her, but in other ways she did not. She grew increasingly uncomfortable with the hypocrisy, excess, and shallowness of the society around her, and she felt torn as she struggled for a balance between functioning in society and making the kinds of connections she needed to survive as a writer and gain an audience for her work, and maintaining her own convictions. She found the over-the-top women's fashions of the day ridiculous (it was the era of Marie Antoinette and the towering hairstyles we associate with her), and felt silly and extravagant trying to fit in. "Nothing," wrote More to her sisters, "can be conceived so absurd, extravagant, and fantastical, as the present mode of dressing the head."[27] She wasn't always free to observe Sunday as she liked to do, and she was troubled by the fear that her own life lacked the integrity and simplicity she celebrated in her writing.

More loved literature, language, stories, and wholesome entertainment of all kinds, and all her life she would resist the idea that there was something unchristian or unbiblical about laughter and entertainment. On the contrary, she believed that all the gifts of intellect and imagination were ideally suited to convey Biblical truths and reach the world with the Christian gospel. But there was only a very limited fashionable market for the kind of moral viewpoint she sought to incorporate into all her literature, and while her plays had been successful so far, she had already been told by one publisher

---

26   Ibid. 66.
27   De Rusha, Michelle. *50 Women Every Christian Should Know*. Grand Rapids, MI: Page 100.

that she was "too good a Christian for an author." Also, it seems that as she grew older, More may have recognized the uniquely dangerous power that theatre had over her own mind and imagination—that, as Prior suggests, she loved it too much, in a way she could not fully master or discipline.

Thus, even as she achieved both success and happiness during her time in the London spotlight, More increasingly felt unsure of her place there and her direction in life. It seems almost certain that she could have established herself as a successful playwright with a lifetime of celebrity ahead of her, and perhaps it would have taken only minor compromises to make it happen. But the feeling was gradually growing on More that she was at a moral and spiritual crossroads, and as she considered it, events overtook her. Two heavy blows coming close upon each other in 1779 drew a line under More's roughly five years of scaling the peaks of social and literary success. The first was the death of her mentor David Garrick. As we have seen, More was close to both Garrick and his wife—perhaps closer than she would ever be to anyone but her sister Patty. Not only had she lived with the couple for extended periods several times but also after Garrick's death she shared a home with his widow for a while. Her friendship with the Garricks had, for years, provided an anchor, a home, and what she called her London conscience—for while the Garricks did not share More's far more conservative theological bent, they respected and were sensitive to it, and if they sometimes urged her to sacrifice her preferences for the sake of appearing in the right places and meeting the right people, they also protected her from pressure or ridicule when she drew the line, and they created openings for her to gracefully absent herself from situations where she would feel uncomfortable or conflicted. Without Garrick, More felt more heavily the burden of navigating the moral complexities of her London life, as well as far less taste—for a time, at least—for its pleasures.

In the same difficult year, More faced a devastating and completely unfamiliar setback as a writer. Her new play, *Fatal Falsehood*, not only failed spectacularly but also, ironically in view of its title, attracted accusations of plagiarism which were soon proved false, but which, in the cutthroat world of the London theatre, had already inflicted ugly wounds on More's reputation. Perhaps in part because she had been such a center of attention in her family—both the precociously talented charmer and the one so often ill—More struggled all her life with the tendency to be excessively sensitive to criticism and verbal attacks, although as we shall see she had no choice but to increasingly overcome this tendency. For now, in any case, she was deeply shaken by the undeserved attacks on her. Between the loss of her friend Garrick—followed shortly by the death of another great friend, Samuel Johnson—and the brutal battering of her literary career and legacy, London increasingly seemed a harsh, lonely, and hostile environment. With the death of Dr. Garrick (and his wife's retreat from society to mourn), the death of the great Samuel Johnson, the plagiarism scandal, the failure of her latest play, and her growing unease in the fashionable world, it seemed like the obvious time for taking stock.

A Time of Reflection and Redirection

During the secluded winter of 1779-1780, during which Hannah More and Mrs. Garrick lived together in a country house, nursing their shared grief and reassessing their lives, More's new direction began gradually to come into focus. The catalyst for this transformation was an encounter with John Newton, the slave-trader turned pastor and hymn writer. Newton's book, *Cardiphonia*, made a profound impact on More, as did several of Newton's sermons she attended during this period. Through the upheaval of these hard years and the influence of Newton and others, Hannah More's faith in the Christian gospel and her relationship with Christ became the focus and driving force of her life and work. Newton's biographer describes the gradual but definite change: "She became less social and more evangelical . . . .It was Newton's influence on Hannah More through his writings and sermons in the early 1780s that changed the course of her life toward Christian service and education."[28] When More reemerged into society after this period of mourning, she would have a different set of priorities—and she would soon find herself gradually turning more and more away from London and toward the countryside. In fact, More soon began to work and save toward the purchase of a cottage at Cowslip Green where she would make her beloved home for most of the rest of her life (and where she could spend hours each day in her beloved flower garden). To some degree she kept a foot in both worlds for the rest of her life, but her real "London era" was rapidly drawing to a close. More would remain one of the best known and most influential authors of her generation. She never wrote for the London stage again, but she wrote poetry, fiction, and nonfiction in an unstoppable torrent, no matter how much her other work demanded of her time and energy. She never faded from the public view, and the huge audience of people who recognized her name and wanted to read what she wrote would be central to the impact she would have during the rest of her life.

During the next several years, however, More increasingly lived and wrote with a new clarity of purpose. Her move to the cottage at Cowslip Green was gradual too—at

---

28   Aitken 283-284.

first, it was her country refuge while her busy London life continued unabated—but somehow it was the visible outward symbol of an inner change that was ultimately to be as profound as it was subtle and gradual. The country air seemed to clear her head, to bring things into focus and hush the confusion of voices she heard during the giddy years of her rise to London fame. More wrote to her mentor John Newton from Cowslip:

> While I am in the great world, I consider myself as in an enemy's country, and am beset with snares, and this puts me upon my guard. I know that many people whom I hear say a thousand brilliant and agreeable things disbelieve, or at least disregard, those truths on which I found my everlasting hopes. This sets me upon a more diligent inquiry into those truths; and upon the arch of Christianity, the more I press, the stronger I find it.[29]

As Prior writes, More "continued to winter in London for many years but not to the same ends as before . . . her heart had turned elsewhere."[30] Her first focus was on challenging the privileged, the leaders of society and fashion, to consider the truths of the gospel and to evaluate how they used the opportunities they had to influence others for good or ill. More's books addressed to the aristocracy, and in one case even the royal family, sold well and gained a wide audience, but still More was not satisfied. Increasingly, she had a more specific cause to advance: the abolition of the slave trade.

Hannah More, Abolitionist

To the degree that Hannah More is remembered today, it is mostly as the woman described by historian Thomas Kidd as "the heart and hands" behind the British abolition movement.[31] Hannah More's influence on the campaign to abolish the slave trade is one of the great untold stories of that epic battle. A large, diverse, and dedicated group of men and women poured their time, money, and energy into the decades-long struggle to outlaw the slave trade, but More's role is one of the most intriguing and most neglected. Perhaps her most important contribution was that she, with several others, recruited the young William Wilberforce to the cause, handpicking him as the best spokesman for the effort and educating him about the horrors of the slave trade. The two would spend the rest of their lives fighting the trade with tireless tenacity. "In Wilberforce, More found a counterpart," writes Prior. "It was as if all she had done and accomplished so far in her life had been merely practice for this historic mission."[32] More herself

---

29 Prior 104.
30 Ibid. 104.
31 Prior iii.
32 Prior 119.

wrote to her sister about an early meeting with Wilberforce, describing how she and Wilberforce "had four or five hours of most confidential and instructive conversation, in which we discussed all the great objects of reform."[33] More became a dear friend, a cheerleader, and a mentor to Wilberforce, a surrogate mother or older sister—although, as we shall see, the influence worked both ways. She was also the best spokesperson he could possibly have had—a talented writer at the height of her fame and popularity, able to communicate compellingly with the rich, powerful, and well read, and with the impoverished and uneducated. Her name on the cover of a pamphlet or the title of a piece in the newspaper instantly guaranteed a wide audience. And the sick little girl who had once held her own doctor so spellbound with the discussion of books and stories that he forgot his examination, the young woman who had captivated a classroom full of girls with her vivid tales from history and mythology, was now an experienced and beloved writer whose imagination, captured in words, had power and impact across the English-speaking world and beyond. She turned her voice and her moral imagination to the task of making it impossible for the British people to ignore, forget, or feel indifferent to the horrors perpetrated in their time. Her writing made the enslaved Africans most English men and women would never see into human beings she hoped they would never be able to stop thinking about.

Nor was she limited to published writing—More wrote poems against slavery that made a tremendous impact across the English-speaking world, but she spoke and wrote endlessly to everyone she knew on the subject. She joined the sugar boycott, refusing, with many others, to use in her tea and in her kitchen the sugar that was produced under horrific conditions on the plantations of the West Indies. The impact of the sugar boycott may have been very small economically and politically, but it was important in solidifying the commitment of the abolitionists to their cause—and in any case, Hannah More was finished with making compromises. She no longer had any need for the approval of the fashionable world; her position in public life was secure, even if it could not protect her from criticism. And she could not go back to a life—or to words—that compartmentalized life and work, or faith and social life. Increasingly for the rest of her life, Hannah More would have an almost impulsive readiness to jump in with both feet to any worthy cause—as Noel Brewer Yeatts writes, the answer to the question "what would Hannah More do?" is always "More would do something."[34]

---

33   Ibid. 119.
34   Ibid. iiii.

More's commitment to every cause she espoused was lifelong. Remarkably in a woman who moved in such diverse circles and whose life passed through several very different phases, More never discarded the friends, connections, or commitments she made, but accumulated and nurtured them throughout her life. As she grew older, she accumulated causes (the education of the poor, the treatment of animals, and others), but she never discarded or neglected one. As the campaign for abolition dragged on for the rest of her life through failure after failure, More used her gift for language and the power of her moral imagination to apply unrelenting pressure to the public opinion of her country, forcing the humanity of African men and women and the inhumanity of their oppressors into the public eye again and again. She would die just before the victory was at last achieved, but there has never been any question that "More was the single most influential woman in the British abolitionist movement," and she never ceased to believe in its eventual triumph.[35] More's "resilient willingness to use her words for good when others were comfortable keeping quiet," writes Yeatts, "allowed her to literally move the world."[36]

A New Mission

But if More was a catalyst for Wilberforce's campaign against the slave trade, the power of influence worked both ways. Just as More had played a key role in drawing William Wilberforce into the battle against the slave trade, so Wilberforce, on a visit to More's cottage, was to draw More into a battle closer to home—one that would become the second major facet of her enduring legacy. More's biographer describes the moment:

> More and her sister Patty urged [Wilberforce] to take a day to travel to the beautiful Cheddar Gorge nearby . . . When he and his sister returned to Cowslip Green later that day . . . Wilberforce was distracted and offered only passing praise of the scenery . . . [After dinner] He asked the servant to leave the room and spoke to the two sisters in earnest.

> "Something must be done for Cheddar," he expostulated. He had spent the day not gazing on the dramatic cliffs as the sisters had urged him to do, but making inquiries about the condition of the poor people he saw there. He shared his distressing findings with the Mores. "There was no resident minister. No manufactory, nor did there appear any dawn of comfort, either temporal or spiritual," he explained.

35　Ibid. iiii.
36　Prior 140-141.

The friends spent the next few hours discussing what might be done to alleviate the suffering of the people in the neighboring village. "If you will be at the trouble," Wilberforce vowed, "I will be at the expense."[37]

Both Hannah and Patty were eager to respond. Many ideas were discussed, but not surprisingly, the beginning they eventually decided on was a school—one of the new "Sunday schools" recently established here and there to provide the only formal education for the children of laborers who, on the other six days of the week, would be in the mines, the fields, or the factories from sunup to sundown.

The two sisters began to travel into the surrounding countryside to assess the needs and possibilities for their school. What they found appalled them. The desperate poverty, the rampant crime, the hopelessness, the lack of education and opportunity—above all, the sheer neglect and indifference of the nation and of much of the church toward its forgotten poor—were beyond anything the sisters had realized. In one village, More reported, "a single cup of broth cannot be obtained; for there is none to give, if it would save life. I am ashamed of my comforts when I think of their wants."[38] At one gathering of local parents, the sisters saw "more ignorance than we supposed existed anywhere in England."[39]

One village was known as "Little Hell," both for the filth of the mines that covered the town and its people, and for the swearing, drunkenness, theft, violence, and hopelessness of the community. In village after village, formal education was almost unknown and illiteracy widespread. Not only the wealthy landowners and mine owners who employed them but also the Church of England that was supposed to shepherd them had largely turned their backs on this population, abandoning multiple generations to their brutal lives of ignorance, hopelessness, and deprivation. Indeed, the church often participated, actively or passively, in the exploitation of this most vulnerable population, since it exacted tithes from the residents and often provided nothing in return. In one village More would indignantly report that the clergyman had collected his tithes for fifty years but hadn't preached a sermon for forty. In another, the minister was notoriously drunk six days out of seven, and when he didn't show up to preach everyone knew it was because he had black eyes and bruises from his latest fistfight. Not only the church but also the state had often deserted these backwaters—like police afraid to venture into a notorious inner-city neighborhood, the constables were often reluctant to risk

37 Ibid. 143.
38 Ibid. 145.
39 Ibid. 144.

visiting these rough areas where it was all too easy for an unwelcome visitor to disappear forever, no questions asked—especially since so many pits dotted the landscape.[40] Any idealized visions of the unspoiled simplicity of country life More might have cherished since her partial withdrawal from London society were shattered in an instant. Right on her own doorstep, in the heart of one of the most heartbreakingly beautiful parts of the English countryside, was a staggering abyss of misery, neglect, and exploitation. As More pointed out, while many English Christians were beginning to send resources to African missionaries, there lived under their noses generations of their own countrymen engulfed in desperation and ensnared by ignorance.

Hannah More: Educational Pioneer and Antipoverty Reformer

It is characteristic of More that she set about this new life with the same fearless, matter-of-fact readiness with which she had once worked to prepare herself for the life of a landed gentlewoman, and which she had brought to the navigation of the giddy heights of London literary and artistic society. In an age when women of her class were sheltered from the spectacularly bad language and the open drunkenness and sexual promiscuity of the Cheddar villages, More and her sister were a striking contrast to the stereotypical hypocrisy of the prosperous ladies who might be glad to parade their generosity at lavish tea parties benefitting worthy causes overseas, even as they wouldn't think of engaging in conversation anyone below their own status. Indeed, the idea of not responding in some way to the needs they had discovered seems not to have even occurred to the More sisters. Two unprotected spinster schoolteachers would now venture boldly into areas feared by both the clergy and the police—no matter how many times they were warned not to, often by those they hoped would support their new undertaking.

For not only did Hannah and Patty More find themselves confronting overwhelming obstacles of every kind but they also soon discovered there was very little support for their undertaking among those who might have been expected to offer resources and encouragement. Indeed, the reaction both inside and outside the church, and from both the rich and the poor, often went beyond indifference to active hostility. Many employers and landowners believed education would make the poor discontented and disruptive, and of course many of the villagers themselves were understandably suspicious of the motives of the two women who appeared in town and started trying to convince them that education would benefit their children.

---

40 Ibid. 145.

Prudently, the sisters began their new project by asking the advice of an expert—a poor man in the neighborhood who made his living catching rabbits. Tears came to his eyes when they shared their idea. "You will have much difficulty," he warned the sisters, "but let not the enemy tempt you to go back, and God bless the work."[41] He told the sisters exactly how they should begin, and whose support, or at least permission, they would need. First came the wealthy landowner who controlled much of the land where they hoped to start. The sisters set out to pay a call at the home of a man they described as an "ignorant, cold, unfeeling rich farmer," and were graciously received—until they mentioned that they hoped to open some schools for the poorest villages. Religion, their host warned, "would be the ruin of agriculture"—it made the poor lazy and useless, and had already done great damage where it had been introduced. He begged them not to give another thought to their reckless plan.[42]

The sisters' good manners and gift for conversation stood them in good stead, as did Hannah More's experience raising awareness and support for the abolition movement. Above all, it took all their persistence to wear down his resistance. As skillfully as if they had been canvassing for political votes, they turned the subject deftly to the excellent refreshments they had been offered, praising the wine of which their host was especially proud. They also, however, found several opportunities to emphasize that they had no thought of asking him for any financial support for their school, and this seemed to allay his greatest concern. They left him unconvinced but also in a much better mood than when the conversation had begun.

It was the first of many visits to those in the area who should, from both courtesy and caution, be advised in advance of the new schools, and whose approval should be gained if possible. Over tea or wine or sherry, day after day, the sisters chatted with their new acquaintances and explained their concerns for the residents of Cheddar Gorge and the schools they hoped to open. As Karen Prior notes, the reactions they received emphasize the widespread attitudes toward both religion and poverty that had created the crisis at Cheddar and other communities in the first place. The French Revolution, which awakened widespread fears of social upheaval and radicalism, only underscored the fears of the wealthy that the divinely appointed order of society might be undermined by any closing of the gap between rich and poor. Many cloaked their motives with religious, political, and philosophical arguments, but the sisters saw the same basic attitude of

41   Ibid. 146.
42   Ibid. 147.

selfishness and possessiveness again and again. Whether it was one woman protesting "If a school were to be set up it would be all over with property and if property is not to rule what will become of us," or another family delighted to hear of the proposed school because fewer of their apples would be stolen by the children of the neighborhood if they were confined in school, the underlying determination to hang onto privilege and property was nearly always the same.[43]

But the naysayers had met their match in Hannah More and her sister. The same intelligence, wit, and charm that had made Hannah More a London success, and the same gift for adapting her approach to her audience that had made her writing beloved by such a diverse audience, now enabled her to conduct a masterful charm offensive among the landowners of Cheddar. Always pleasant and polite, never losing their tempers, never showing frustration or impatience, listening to the same complaints again and again with courteous attention, always interesting and engaging, the two could certainly be considered peculiar and eccentric, and perhaps to be classed as religious fanatics, but they must never be accused of being heavy-handed, self-absorbed, tedious, judgmental, or dull. Every evening after a day of visiting, More confessed to Wilberforce, the two sisters would strategize and actually practice their persuasive techniques. And gradually, it worked. The sisters were able to persuade a critical mass of the local landowners that a school which would keep the local children out of mischief during the few hours they were neither working nor sleeping was in everyone's interest. More even persuaded many of the landowners to actively encourage attendance at the school by rewarding parents who sent their children faithfully, and discouraging those who did not. There were still holdouts who forbade or discouraged attendance, but enough of the community had been won over that the plan to open the first school could go ahead.

More described the sisters' campaign and eventual success to Wilberforce with characteristic humor:

I was told we shou'd meet with great opposition if I did /not/ try to propitiate the chief Despot of the Village, who is very rich and very brutal; so I ventured to the Den of this Monster, in a Country as savage as himself, near Bridgewater. He begged I wou'd not think of bringing any religion into the Country, it was the worst thing in the world for the poor, for it made them lazy and useless; in vain I represented to him that they wou'd be more industrious as they were better principled, and that for my own part, I had no selfish views in what I was

---

43   Ibid. 147.

doing; he gave me to understand that he knew the world too well to believe either the one or the other. Somewhat dismay'd to find that my success bore no proportion to my submissions, I was almost discouraged from more visits; but I found friends must be secured at all events, for if these rich savages set their faces against /us/, and inflamed the poor people I thought nothing but hostilities wou'd answer. So I made Eleven more of these /agreeable/ Visits, but I was by this time improved in the Arts of canvassing and had better success. Miss Wilberforce wou'd have been shocked had She seen the petty Tyrants Whose insolence I stroked and tamed, the ugly children I praised, the Pointers and Spaniels I caressed, the cider I commended, the wine I drank, and the brandy I might have drank; and after these irresistible flatteries I enquired of each if he cou'd recommend me to a house; /said/ that I had a little plan which I hoped wou'd secure their orchards from being robbed, their rabbits from being shot, and their game from being stolen /and *might* lower the Poor Rates./ If *effect* be the best proof of Eloquence then mine was a good Speech; for I met with the hearty concurrence of the whole people, and their promise to discourage or favour the poor in proportion as they were attentive or negligent in sending their Children. Patty, who is with me says she has good hope the hearts of some of these *wealthy* poor wretches may be touched; they are as ignorant as the beasts that perish, drunk every day before dinner and plunged in such vices as make me begin to think London a virtuous place.[44]

Of course, the parents who would be asked to send their children to school must also be persuaded to see the value of the plan. They had no reason to trust the two spinsters; some even feared a scheme to kidnap children and sell them into slavery. And in the world they lived in, the point of sending children to sit at desks when they could be working was hard to see. Some said they should be financially compensated for sending their children to school. The sisters had to emphasize the advantages that education could offer the children in the future and explain the marketable skills they would gain.

But the humility and thoroughness of the Mores' approach to the community, patiently visiting and learning from the residents before taking any action, gradually paid off, and, with Wilberforce's financial support, they chose a building, hired a teacher, and opened the first school. The sisters boldly took a seven-year lease on the building—"that's courage for you!" More wrote to Wilberforce.[45]

Approximately one hundred and forty students began attending on Sundays, learning the Bible, the catechisms and creeds of the Church of England, reading, arithmetic, and

44   The Collected Letters of Hannah More. Copyright 2016. (24 September 1789) Accessed May 30, 2022. The Collected Letters of Hannah More (hannahmoreletters.co.uk).

45   Ibid.

knitting and spinning—the major marketable skills which could, in this time and place, almost ensure that students would be able to make their living. As time went on and her relationships with them improved, More collaborated with local manufacturers to incorporate other marketable skills into her curriculum, preparing a way out of poverty and unemployment for those who attended faithfully. Many were even able to enter domestic service, often a significant upward move for those who could otherwise look forward only to work in the fields, the factories, or the mines—if they were able to find employment at all.

The success of the schools was immediate and explosive. The first grew to an enrollment of three hundred, and the sisters opened a second—the second of many schools they would open in the area over the next decade. By 1796, the schools had approximately 1,600 students throughout ten parishes. And, as Prior puts it, "the transformations spilled out beyond the schoolhouse walls."[46] In these tiny, close-knit villages, changes in one or two families could be enough to reshape the community. Places which had never been able to offer their residents any alternative to the crime, poverty, and dead-end hopelessness of the past suddenly glimpsed an entirely different way of life. The seemingly impassable gap between rich and poor was no longer the only contrast; now there was also the sense that even the poorest and most disenfranchised family could make meaningful choices that would shape their future. There could be fathers who didn't spend their evenings in the pub and beat their wives when they got home; there could be laborers who had some hope that their diligence and honesty might be rewarded; there could be young men and women who knew they could prepare themselves for real opportunities and could earn enough to support themselves. The long-empty churches began to fill again in many villages as stories circulated of astounding transformations in the lives of notoriously profane, cruel, or dishonest local residents who became Christians. One church congregation grew from approximately twenty adults to five hundred, as, Patty More recorded, the people hungered and thirsted for the knowledge of God.[47]

Sunday evening classes for adults were added to the schools' programs, and the More sisters started women's clubs which not only brought together the local women in support of the schools but also functioned almost as insurance, using money from the collected dues to pay members a stipulated amount during times of illness or childbirth

---

46 Prior 150.
47 Ibid. 151.

when they were unable to work. Hannah More's characteristic sense of fun and flair for the dramatic did not desert her in the bleakest environment, and she inaugurated an annual tea party at which the poorest women of the area joined the more supportive of their wealthy neighbors in sitting down to tea and being waited on by the More sisters. Many of these women spent their whole lives in unrelenting, backbreaking labor for others, and had never experienced being waited on, drinking from fine china, or sharing a table with the neighborhood gentry. The annual celebration became such a beloved event that, as More recorded with delight, an additional benefit of it was the incentive it provided for the women to save and scheme all year for a nice dress and hat. The once-common excuse that the women were too ashamed to attend church in their worn and filthy clothes all but disappeared. More also held an annual celebration at which the school children had a chance to march in a grand procession, show off all they had learned at school to a gathering of parents, and enjoy a grand feast of roast beef and cake—certainly the best meal many of them tasted all year. One of these celebrations had as many as 4000 spectators in attendance, and fed more than 500 children.[48] More confessed to Wilberforce that she invested her own money in such celebrations because many conscientious donors did not approve of such indulgences. More's own view was, not surprisingly, very different:

> I know some even very good people think these indulgencies so wrong that for the quiet of my own conscience I always take the expence of all the festivities on myself, and never lay out the Money of my *friends* on any Objects of *questionable* usefulness. I have a *System* about these things, which is however controverted, even sometimes by my dear Mrs. Clarke – I do not think the generality are tender enough in their charity – judging of human Nature partly by myself, I believe a kindness is often valued more than a benefit. Including the Woman's Club-feasts and the children's dinner I contrive in the course of this Month to treat about 1700 in what *they* think a *grand Way* for a little more than thirty Pounds – And why shou'd not these poor depressed creatures have *one* day of harmless pleasure in a Year to look forward to? – To know You do not think my principle a wrong one wou'd encourage me a little under the labour which is not small. I encourage much your visit to Cirencester.[49]

The spectacular success of their Sunday schools not only brought joy to the More sisters but also demanded of them incessant work, travel, and problem-solving. It was

---

48   Ibid. 153.
49   Letters of Hannah More. (8 August 1797).

not unusual for them to travel twenty miles on Sunday, scaling the rugged hills and navigating the muddy tracks to visit their schools on foot or on horseback. Often it was dark on their way back, but the very real prospect of a fall, robbery, illness, or other mishap did not deter the dauntless sisters—and neither did the widespread ridicule directed at the two middle-aged spinster ladies traipsing all over the countryside each weekend. This behavior was considered both foolish and unladylike, as readers of Jane Austen's *Pride and Prejudice* will remember—Elizabeth Bennett attracts much criticism for her solitary walk across the fields to visit a sick sister, even though she could not get any other transportation. How much more severe the public opinion of two ladies who had no better excuse for tramping the hills in muddy clothes and worn shoes than visiting the area's worse neighborhoods. If Hannah More had longed to escape from London and the pressure to observe the strict rules of fashionable society, she had certainly found her freedom—although her health, never very good, sometimes suffered, and her other activities certainly did. She reported to Wilberforce that she was so absorbed by her work in the villages that she had hardly any time to read or pursue her writing (although her voluminous correspondence seems to contradict her):

> I am something like a gouty or intemperate General Officer, I am either in my bed or in the Field; pain and Action pretty equally divide my life between them, with some preponderance, however, I thank God on the latter side, but reading and writing are things almost as much out of the question with me as with the poor savages I live with, for if I am well enough to be *up* I am well enough to be *out*, in a general way.[50]

Controversy and Heartbreak

Yet this time of almost unimaginable success and fulfillment brought with it the seeds of its own destruction, and already the clouds were gathering of the worst storm Hannah More was ever to weather. She had survived the heartbreak and humiliation of her broken engagement to Turner, and she had survived the dark time when two of her dearest London friends died and her play failed so publicly amid false accusations of plagiarism—although, in both cases, her health had collapsed for a time. More seems to have had, ever since her childhood illnesses, the tendency to push herself to the edge of complete exhaustion and then suffer very real and serious physical breakdowns at the most stressful times of her life. The illness which would follow the "Blagdon controversy"

---

50   Ibid. (13 August 1798).

about to erupt over her work in Cheddar was to be the most severe of all, and to leave the deepest, most painful scars in More's memory.

As the More sisters' Cheddar project expanded, it inevitably attracted more and more attention—at first regional, but soon national. Many, of course, were supportive, but many others were increasingly suspicious and disapproving. Hannah and Patty More had established their schools at the height of the controversy over the Wesleyan revival—a controversy which divided the church even more deeply than it did the rest of society. Many who were only nominally religious mistrusted Wesleyanism for its identification with the poor and its attacks on poverty and injustice (though of course many among the poor also resented it for its condemnation of alcoholism, profanity, immorality, and other social evils.) This focus on improving the lives of the poor might, it was feared, grow into something much too close to the revolutionary spirit which had destroyed the government of France and brought dreadful rumors of riots and bloodshed from across the Channel. But the condemnation of Wesley's "Methodism" from within the church was even fiercer. No matter how Wesley defended his lifelong loyalty to the Church of England and disclaimed all intention of creating an alternative or challenge to it, many feared that the populism, emotionalism, and anti-authoritarianism of Wesley's movement could destroy the church from within.

Thus, though Hannah and Patty More saw their work in Cheddar as being entirely consistent with the authority and unity of the Church of England, and believed they were simply reaching a population the church had been unable or unwilling to serve as it should in the past, it was all too easy for suspicious eyes to detent hints of "Methodism" in the swelling semi-formal meetings and the women's and children's classes being organized by two women, without official sanction, among precisely the population where Wesleyanism was making its greatest impact elsewhere in the country.

Specifically, the accusation first brought against More was that Sunday evening services held at the Blagdon schoolhouse (though entirely apart from the school itself) included extemporaneous prayers—prayers that people made up and prayed aloud, instead of prayers recited together out of the Book of Common Prayer. It requires great effort of the imagination for modern readers to understand why this was such a contentious issue, but the accusation of encouraging the abandonment of the prayer book, with its sanction of authority and tradition, in favor of prayers that people simply made up out of their own heads was one of the most serious accusations leveled against Methodism. It was seen as irreverent, presumptuous, disrespectful of God as well as of His church, and as an open invitation to heresy. English Christians who felt a responsibility to "hold the line" against the atheism, deism, and populism they saw tearing France apart often felt impelled to defend the liturgy and the authority of the Church of England as well as of the Bible—to take a stand against the dangerous cultural trend toward rejecting all authority and, at least in the case of France, literally inventing new, personalized sects or religions to suit each population's own taste.

Thus, in the fraught climate of More's time, the seemingly minor accusation of extemporaneous prayers at Blagdon school was like the spark to a pile of tinder. The whole country erupted into a ferocious blaze of controversy and accusation that, for a time, all but destroyed the lives of all five More sisters. Signs were posted along the road near their home inviting passersby to see for themselves "the menagerie of five female savages of the most desperate kind." Hannah More was called "The She-Bishop" and accused of everything from being a dangerous revolutionary to "not believing one word of Christianity."[51]

More had already endured one terrible and unjust storm of controversy when she was wrongly accused of plagiarizing her last London play, but, much as she had hated that harsh experience, two painful ironies made the Blagdon controversy even more of a nightmare for her. First, she loved the Church of England and was devoted to it all her life, and she was so far from having revolutionary tendencies that modern historians have tended to criticize her for not being nearly radical enough. She was by political affiliation a Tory, the most conservative major party, and she had made her objections to and rejection of the extremes of "Methodism" very clear. And second, despite her ready wit and facility with language, she detested religious division and controversy above all things. Endlessly tactful, patient, and respectful in even her boldest arguments with those who opposed Christianity, More shrank especially from the many bitter and unnecessary battles that seemed to be tearing the church apart—battles that went so quickly from being doctrinal to being viciously personal. "My soul is sick of religious controversy," she wrote in an 1803 diary entry. "*Bible* Christianity is what I love . . . a Christianity practical and pure, which teaches holiness, humility, repentance, and faith in Christ; and which after summing up all the Evangelical graces, declares that the greatest of these is charity."[52] Years later she would write, "Oh, how I hate faction, division and controversy in religion!"[53]

---

51   Prior 155.
52   Ibid.155.
53   Ibid.156.

Yet there was nothing More could do to stop the toxic flood of accusation and attack that poured over her, her family, and her work for the next three years. Wisely, More appealed to Bishop Richard Beadon, and he, along with other clergymen, spoke in her defense, and in defense of the Cheddar schools. Yet many others continued to attack her, even after the sisters reluctantly closed the Blagdon school, where enrollment had plummeted from two hundred to thirty-five because the families of the students were afraid to find themselves on the wrong side of the clergy who had so much power and influence in their small communities. They hoped by doing this that they might confine the focus of the controversy to the Blagdon school and protect the others.

After raging unabated from 1800 to 1803, the debate resulted in vindication of Hannah More, her sisters, and her work, just as the accusations of plagiarism in London years before had eventually been answered in her favor. But, just as in that case, the damage done to her health and reputation could not be undone. More's health collapsed and for the next two years she endured what she would call her "great illness," perhaps to distinguish it from other severe bouts of illness like the one she had suffered after her final break with Turner. It wasn't until 1805 that More recovered her strength—at least most of it. More was never really quite the same after the Blagdon controversy. She was shamefaced about how devastated she had been, writing in her journal after reading seventeenth-century devotional writer Richard Baxter, who had faced severe criticism in his own highly quarrelsome time, that "through my want of his faith and piety, they [the attacks she herself faced] had nearly destroyed my life." And the resilience she was able to display during the remaining decades of her life could never erase her memory of "a wantonness of cruelty which, in civilized places, few persons, especially of my sex, have been called to suffer."[54] Her confidence was bruised and shaken—she wrote in her journal of a new uncertainty about when to speak of her ideas and beliefs and when to hold her tongue, and she thought for a while she might never write again. She had, she wrote, "hung my harp on the willows, never more to take it down."[55]

Perhaps this was why Hannah More was ultimately prouder of and more pleased by the books and tracts she would go on to write later in her life than any that had gone before. The only remarkable thing she could claim as an author, she once told a friend, was that she had written eleven books after the age of sixty.[56] As the Blagdon controversy

---

54 Ibid.156.
55 Ibid. 239.
56 Ibid. 240.

faded in people's memories, More's reputation and influence as an author were greater than ever during her final two decades.

As always, her influence spilled beyond the printed page and brought remarkably diverse gatherings of friends and visitors around her. She was a kind of matriarch as well as a popular hostess, and visitors of all kinds—rich and poor, famous and unknown, scientists and artists, learned and ignorant, godly and irreligious, flowed through her little home with its bright, beloved flower garden. In a single week, she had eighty visitors, and so many ministers visited that her home was described as "a minor Evangelical centre."[57] Even as she lost sister after sister (Hannah More would be the last of the sisters living) and friend after friend, More found herself surrounded by visitors she could never bear to discourage or turn away.

More's influence continued to spread not only through her books, and not only through those who were shaped and strengthened by their visits and correspondence with her, but also through the causes she continued to support with her writing and her money. These included the fight against animal cruelty, the support of widows, and, always, the long battle for the abolition of slavery. Always she continued to love and support her Sunday schools, which survived the Blagdon controversy and continued to thrive. She raised money with her writing, and through appeals to the wealthy and influential, many of whom continued to number among her friends and visitors. Her financial generosity was such that toward the end of her life, she feared running out of money entirely, but, characteristically, it was not simply money but also time, love, energy, enthusiasm, and a uniquely personal touch that she brought to the needs around her. She defended a local servant girl who had been fired for alleged sexual impropriety, seeking to find her employment. She bought books for impoverished young ministers. She bought ore from miners. She took in the child of a servant and two other orphans.

The harsh criticism she had weathered seems, once she recovered her health and resumed her work, to have made Hannah More gentler and more understanding—one friend complained about More's being treated ungratefully by someone else, and she responded that our response to ingratitude shows us our true motives, and that experiencing ingratitude from others should remind us of our own ingratitude to God. The friend would later comment on the fact that More's words—despite both the strength of her convictions and the readiness of her witty tongue—always reflected "the law of kindness."[58]

---

57 Ibid. 241.
58 Ibid. 242.

Hannah More died in 1833 at the age of eighty-eight. She outlived by roughly a decade nearly everyone she had known for most of her life, and despite the endless flow of visitors who poured into her home she was sometimes lonely, once writing, "I have lost so many of my contemporaries . . . that I am ready to ask with Dr. Johnson, where is the world into which I was born?—they taken, I spared—they of great importance in society, I of little or none; but by thus extending my life, God has been pleased to give me a longer space for repentance and preparation. May it not have been given in vain."[59] Another hard loss came when More was persuaded by her friends that she must leave her beloved cottage, with the flower gardens she had nurtured over the decades, and move to a house in the city where she would be near her doctors and her friends. She compared this move to Eve's being cast out of Eden, but accepted it and enjoyed the visitors she continued to receive on two days a week because of her weakened health. She died after an illness of about ten months. Her last word was "joy."[60]

One of the most remarkable things about Hannah More is that, in unexpected ways, she ended up living all the lives that seemed to have passed her by—and then some. She did not end up as the country schoolteacher she had expected to be as a young woman— yet she opened schools all over her part of England and was responsible, directly or indirectly, for educating thousands of children. She did not end up as Mrs. Turner, the lady of the manor—yet no lady of the manor could have been a more popular or successful hostess, a more influential leader of the community, or the center of a livelier and more impressive group of friends and acquaintances. She did not have children of her own, but her home was always filled with children, and she served as a mother to countless young men and women. She turned away from the peak of her success in London society, yet she remained connected to all the best-known men and women of her time through visits and letters—actresses, royalty, politicians, historians, novelists, and more. She went from being a bestselling playwright who was the toast of Europe to a woman who never wrote for the stage again—yet words poured from her pen and flowed around the world, and the book she published when she was eighty went into eleven editions and was translated into French as soon as it was released.[61]

More was beloved throughout her life but was also the target of recurring criticism and ridicule, not just during the Blagdon upheaval but during her entire adult life. Curiously, the same warm, winning, and courteous persona that attracted such an

59   Ibid. 245.
60   Ibid. 250.
61   Ibid. 240.

astonishingly diverse array of friends and admirers meant that More was attacked from opposite extremes. By some she was ridiculed as prim, preachy, rigid, and moralistic, while at the same time she was accused by others of excessive tolerance and worldliness, especially for her friendship with the scandalous playwright Hugh Walpole. However her convictions and causes were attacked, her whole life and personality contradicted the stereotype of the prim, severe, and joyless Methodist. Once, when she was urged to condemn what some considered the vanity and self-indulgence of wearing flowers, More refused, admitting it "would be ridiculous enough in me who so passionately love them"[62]—and indeed, More's beloved flower gardens were one of the greatest joys of her life.

This contradictory response to More continued after her death, with some early biographers transforming this warm, cheerful, funny, and deeply flawed woman into a repellent plaster saint, only to be followed by modern writers who condemned More, sometimes called "the first Victorian," as the embodiment of all that was dull, joyless, and judgmental. Her writing, once beloved by an audience whose diversity rivaled that of Shakespeare or Dickens, has been rejected by readers whose tastes no longer enjoy the distinctive style of the eighteenth century, of which More's voice was so characteristic. Condemned by many in her own time as a radical for her crusade to educate the poor, she has been criticized by more recent generations as an elitist for her acceptance of the inevitability of class distinctions in society and her belief that the rich and the poor should receive different educations. Tedious to some of her contemporaries for her tireless dedication to an endless array of causes, she has been rebuked by subsequent generations for her failure to recognize the need for legislation to reform the working conditions of factory laborers. Condemned by many of her contemporaries for using fiction, poetry, humor, and imagination to teach Biblical truths, she has been rejected as dull, dry, and pious by readers since her time.

But there could be no better proof of More's real achievement and importance than the very ambiguity swirling around her reputation, in life and in death. She lived in an era of tremendous social, cultural, and ideological upheaval—a polarized period in which fissures divided rich from poor, liberal from conservative, secular from religious, educated from illiterate, optimistic from hopeless. Hannah More was able to bridge all these gaps and more with exactly the blend of qualities her age needed—a sense of fun with a serious purpose; conviction with humility; belief with kindness and generosity;

62   Ibid. 238.

compassion with realism; vulnerability with resilience. Hers was, as biographer Karen Prior calls it in a memorable chapter title, "An Imagination that Moved the World."

Perhaps there is a particular kind of triumph for More in the peace she was eventually able to make with the controversy surrounding her. As we have seen, More's deep sensitivity to criticism was a weakness she struggled with all her life. Even the purest motives, she once confessed, could not always protect a writer from the temptations of pride.[63] She knew she should not be so fragile in the face of false accusation, or criticism, and of rejection, and she worked hard to grow stronger through the battles she faced. Perhaps, then, she might have seen it as her final victory that today, while many of the causes she championed have triumphed and the communities she served have been transformed, her own name, once so famous, has been almost entirely forgotten and the part she played lost to history. Perhaps her best epitaph is found in the words Hannah More wrote, during the Blagdon controversy, when she expressed a fear that her books were probably being "much less read and more condemned." "God can carry on his own work," she wrote, "though all such poor tools as I were broken."[64] God carried on His work through Hannah More, and that would have been enough for her, even if her name were forgotten.

---

63   Ibid. 247.
64   Ibid. 247.

CHAPTER 6

William Wilberforce

CONTAGIOUS COMPASSION

Somewhere in the middle of the Atlantic ocean, a clean, pure wind blew across the deck of a ship. The ship's timbers creaked gently, and the sea whispered against the hull. Sunlight glittered on the waves. A sailor leaned against the rail, closing his eyes to savor the fresh tang of the air and the gentle touch of the sun on his back. Suddenly, from somewhere beneath his feet, a scream splintered the silence—a frantic cry like that of an animal. Its despairing echo floated across the waves and died. The sailor never moved. As he stretched luxuriously, baring his arms to the sun, his deep sigh spoke only of contentment.

Below decks, under the sailor's feet, the endless darkness, the fierce heat, and the suffocating stench pressed down without respite. The sounds of the ship and the waves were drowned by the terrible sounds that never ceased—low moans, muffled sobbing, the inconsolable wailing of little children. Sometimes, too, there was the clinking sound of chains moving as the hundreds of men and women shackled together struggled to find a position that would ease the pain of cramped limbs and chafed flesh, or just to breathe a little new air. Day and night, the horrors of "the middle passage," a name that would cast a shadow over the memory of the whole world for centuries to come, unfolded in the darkness and the stench.

And hundreds of miles away, in green and misty England, a man named William Wilberforce sat struggling to think of a way to galvanize the conscience of his country.

Childhood and Early Life

William Wilberforce was born on August 24, 1759. His parents were privileged and prominent members of the Hull community into which Wilberforce was born, and both had deep roots in local society, including a family history of political involvement. They were cultured and fond of society life, and they were ambitious, both able and eager to provide an excellent education for their only son. Despite suffering already from some of the health problems—especially eye problems and digestive problems—that would plague him all his life, Wilberforce stood out as a precocious student, especially good at reading aloud.

When Wilberforce was only eight, his father died, followed shortly by his older sister. Devastated by this double blow and pregnant with another child, Wilberforce's mother succumbed to a dangerous fever and was, for a time, entirely incapable of caring for herself, let alone her children. Indeed, she was considered unlikely to survive. His eight-year-old world rocked to its foundations, Wilberforce was sent to stay with an uncle and aunt for what would prove a happy and formative four years.

Wilberforce's childless uncle and aunt seem to have welcomed the grieving boy as if he were the child they could not have, and they created such a secure and loving home that they earned Wilberforce's lifelong gratitude and affection. Indeed, by his own account he loved them as parents. The school he attended during these years was strikingly inferior to the one he had attended at his parents' home, but the happiness of his life with William and Hannah more than compensated for this, especially to a lonely boy between eight and twelve. Even after his mother recovered her health, William remained for a time at his aunt and uncle's home.

Two more people the young Wilberforce met during his years in Hull were to prove enduringly significant in his life. One was John Thornton, a relative by marriage, and a wealthy and extraordinarily generous man who financed many philanthropic causes. The other was John Newton, the famous former slave ship captain who had become an Anglican minister and songwriter.

First Encounter with Evangelicalism

What both these men, and his aunt and uncle, had in common was that they all drew the young William into a very different circle within the Anglican church than that to which his parents belonged. The evangelicals, sometimes called "methodists" as a term of contempt and disapproval, were a large, unaffiliated, and diverse body of opinion in England, much as the Puritans had been centuries before. Some were Methodists, Presbyterians, Baptists, Plymouth Brethren, or affiliated with other groups, but many, like Newton, remained within the "low church" Anglican fold. They saw themselves as heirs of the authentic tradition of the Church of England, opposed only by those who valued the church more as a social and cultural institution than as a religious or spiritual entity. Evangelicals emphasized the historicity and reality of supernatural events such as the divine inspiration of the Bible and the resurrection of Christ. They opposed the eighteenth and nineteenth-century movements which valued Christianity primarily as an ethical system, and which sought to remove its supernatural elements in response to developments in science and textual criticism. Evangelicals also emphasized the need for an individual choice to accept or reject the sacrifice of Christ. They stressed the importance of an individual relationship with God, unlike some in the Anglican communion who taught that being baptized and confirmed, as virtually every English child was, was sufficient to ensure salvation, and that participation in the life of the church and submission to its authority were ample guarantors of a healthy Christian life.

Some in the Church of England, such as Wilberforce's mother Elizabeth, viewed evangelicals with a contempt, mistrust, and suspicion difficult to overestimate. "It is impossible for you to have any idea," Wilberforce would tell his son years later, "of the hatred in which methodists were then held."[1] Evangelicals were distrusted and resented on social, cultural, intellectual, and philosophical grounds, by those who associated them with the uneducated and reactionary, or who valued such things as dancing, theatres, cards, and other pastimes the evangelicals sometimes (though not always) opposed. They were mistrusted on theological grounds, not only by modernists anxious to rid the church of many of the supernatural elements evangelicals emphasized but also by other sincere Anglicans who mistrusted the individualism and emotionalism that characterized extreme elements of the evangelical movement.

In any case, Wilberforce's mother, Elizabeth, was one of the prominent and wealthy Anglicans who viewed evangelicalism as a disease from which her son must be protected. As she grew stronger, as William grew older, and as the impact on him of his aunt and uncle's beliefs increased, Elizabeth determined to remove him from their influence. The depth of her contempt for the evangelical circles in which they moved is evident in her refusal to reconsider her decision, despite tearful pleas not only from Hannah but also from William himself, who, at twelve, was once again wrenched from what had become his home and his family. Wilberforce, who by his own later account felt a son's affection for his aunt and uncle and was "almost heart-broken at the separation," wrote his uncle in a poignant letter after his return home, "I can never forget you, as long as I live."[2]

---

1   Belmonte, Kevin. *William Wilberforce: A Hero for Humanity*. Grand Rapids, MI. Zondervan. 2002, 2007. Paperback. Page 29-30.
2   Ibid. 30.

Wilberforce's sense of loss and of permanent separation was not exaggerated, for his mother and other relatives were determined to separate him from his aunt and uncle's influence and to erase as much as possible the impressions made on him during those four years. Though Elizabeth Wilberforce was a committed Anglican who was active in the church, she refused for a time to take her son to any church services at all, for fear of encouraging his alarming tendencies toward "methodism." She was ambitious for her son's future and determined that nothing, least of all religious enthusiasm, should interfere with her bright dreams of his prominent and successful future. She surrounded him, instead, with all the amusements and activities, and all the frivolous and ambitious people, that she possibly could, seeking to distract him from any serious thought except that which focused on his studies and his future career. "[N]o pious parent ever labored more to impress a beloved child with sentiments of religion than [was done] to give me a taste for the world and its diversions," the adult Wilberforce would write.[3]

With a tenacity remarkable in such a young boy, the loyal and deeply affectionate William clung to his memories of his aunt and uncle. For about two years, he also clung to the ideas and desires he had learned from them, and continued writing faithfully to them despite his mother's disapproval. His letters were full not only of his wistful affection for his aunt and uncle but also of precociously sincere and reflective thoughts about the Scriptures, about Christ, and about Christianity. But at last, around the time he was fourteen or fifteen, the gradual transformation of William Wilberforce, the thoughtful, spiritual, and affectionate child into William Wilberforce the witty, ambitious, pleasure-loving young man was complete—or so, at least, it seemed for many years. "I became," Wilberforce would recall, "as thoughtless as any amongst them."[4]

Student Days

During the rest of his student years, Wilberforce adeptly divided his time, his attention, and his energies between two things: his academic preparation for a distinguished career, and his bustling social life. The latter usually took priority, but because of his quick, facile intelligence Wilberforce's success at school didn't suffer even when he neglected his work. At the prestigious grammar school where his mother placed him, Wilberforce soon began to attract attention for his obvious intellectual gifts—especially a quick, agile mind and a talent for written and especially for spoken language. During his years at Cambridge University he continued to excel, with almost no effort, in subjects he happened to enjoy

---

3 Ibid. 30.
4 Ibid. 31.

or find interesting. Thanks to his natural ability, however, Wilberforce's studies left him ample time for boating, dancing, gambling, smoking, parties, attending the theatre, and generally becoming one of the brightest stars in a constellation of popular, privileged young men who were seen at all the best clubs and parties. Wilberforce was in high demand as both a guest and a host, not only for his ability to spend plenty of his mother's money but also for his charm, wit, and gift for conversation—characteristics on which people would remark all his life.

Looking back on this period of his life, Wilberforce would deeply regret the waste of his opportunities and his time. It is important to note, in view of his later reputation as a moralizer, that it was his idleness and vanity he saw as the dominant evils of these years. It wasn't that he came to see card playing or parties as purely evil; rather, he recognized that as a young man with great, perhaps exceptional, potential, he had been only too willing to content himself and impress others with skills and knowledge that came easily to him, while avoiding any real discipline, and without taking any responsibility for developing his potential. The mature Wilberforce recognized the disservice that had been done to a spoiled and lazy young man whose charm and intelligence made it possible for him to excel in school without effort. He felt he had been flattered and actively encouraged to refuse all responsibility for cultivating his intellect or character, and he would repeatedly regret in writing the years he felt he had lost as a result. "I can never review but with humiliation and shame, the course I ran at college, and during the first three or four years of my . . . life which immediately succeeded it."[5] Wilberforce wrote to one of his Cambridge instructors, years after his time at university. He went on to ask directly why this man—indeed, why all his teachers—had not challenged him to consider the choices he was making. Why had they not told him "that I should ere long bitterly lament that I had suffered the years and circumstances . . . for acquiring useful knowledge . . . for cultivating and strengthening the intellectual powers, to pass away wholly unimproved? Ought you not to have reminded me of the great account I had to render of the talents committed to my stewardship, and all the uncommon blessings which had been lavished on me. . . ?"[6]

Wilberforce believed that the natural quickness and elasticity of his intelligence especially needed discipline, and that he should not have been allowed, much less encouraged, to "coast" through his studies without investing effort. "Mathematics, which my mind greatly needed, I almost entirely neglected," he would remember. "Whilst my

---

5   Ibid. 42.
6   Ibid. 43.

companions were reading hard and attending lectures . . . tutors would often say within my hearing that '*they* were mere saps, but that I did all by talent.' This was poison to a mind constituted like mine."[7]

To judge by appearances, however, Wilberforce's university career was triumphantly successful in equipping him for precisely the life and career he had chosen: politics. He was meeting all the right people, he was developing the right reputation, and he was cultivating his gifts of rhetoric. Already he could hold an audience in the palm of his hand, whether in an oral examination at university or around the card table at one of the five clubs he belonged to. And he was already addicted to that headiest of drafts: admiration and acclaim. "Emulation, and a desire of distinction, were my governing motives," Wilberforce would write years later with characteristic honesty, describing himself as "ardent after the applause of my fellow creatures."[8] He summed up, "[m]y own distinction was my darling object."[9]

Entering Political Life

The informal but robust coalition of fellow statesmen Wilberforce would rely on again and again throughout his career was also largely in place. He had forged important alliances with a brilliant group of young men destined to make their mark on history— rising leaders who opposed Britain's opposition to American independence, and who advocated parliamentary reform. Wilberforce had also formed the great lifelong friendship that was to prove the one clear lasting good to come out of this time in his life: his friendship with William Pitt. Wilberforce would share a lasting bond with the future prime minister, based on trust and a mutual respect for each other's political independence and integrity that would survive differences on several important issues. Perhaps his friendship with Pitt helped to safeguard in Wilberforce the capacity for integrity and moral courage, for loyalty to truths larger than himself, which otherwise might have been eroded by the temptations and pressures of political life until there was nothing left but personal ambition and an unscrupulous love of the game for its own sake—surely a common fate for idealistic young politicians.

Wilberforce, then, showed great promise as a politician, making powerful friends and encumbered by few scruples. In the election of 1784, writes Kevin Belmonte in his biography, Wilberforce "freely adopted morally questionable methods of gaining support."

---

7   Ibid. 43.
8   Ibid. 51.
9   Ibid. 67.

And once he was in Parliament, "Wilberforce . . . used one of his most potent oratorical weapons, a gift for devastating sarcasm, to attack [an opponent] with great bitterness." "In short," Belmonte sums up, "he was quite willing to savage his political opponents and bribe voters."[10] Wilberforce was capable of great charm, but also of vicious personal attacks. He used his quick mind and gift for language to slash and publicly humiliate those who stood against him, and he delighted in the rapid growth of his reputation for intelligence, oratory, and influence. He had developed a cringing embarrassment about, and contempt for, the beliefs and lifestyle he had shared with his aunt and uncle as a young boy; he was now, like the majority of well-educated and fashionable men of his day, a rationalist—one who believed that, while there was probably a God of some kind and that morality was important for human society to flourish, ideas such as the fall of man, the need for redemption, the resurrection of Christ, and the inspiration of the Bible were superstitions modern people could not take seriously.

The "Great Change"

Wilberforce was, then, an ambitious young man of average ethical standards and above average gifts, engaged in the universally-approved task of establishing a promising career for himself. And then, as Belmonte records, "Strange reports began to circulate."[11] A gradual but fundamental change occurred in Wilberforce's life—a process he himself referred to as his "Great Change." It is important to note that, despite the suspicions of his mother and others, Wilberforce shared with his evangelical mentor John Newton a conversion experience that was very much a process. He would come to believe that there was a moment at which God gave him new spiritual birth, but he, like Newton, was not certain when this moment was, and did not think it important to identify it. What mattered was where the process ended, and his grateful astonishment at the many seeming coincidences that characterized it—coincidences Wilberforce, like Newton, saw as the merciful interventions of God in his life.

The Great Change began with a holiday abroad. In 1784, Wilberforce planned to travel in continental Europe with his mother and other family members, and he hoped a longtime friend who shared his interest in politics and parliamentary reform would accompany him. However, the man was unable to go. Encountering another old friend, a former tutor nine years his senior, at the races, Wilberforce impulsively invited Isaac Milner to join the trip instead. For the rest of his life, Wilberforce would marvel at the

---

10   Ibid. 68.
11   Ibid. 81.

chance encounter and spontaneous suggestion that made Milner his companion. Milner was to become the first in a quartet of influences—two men and two books—which were to be instrumental in Wilberforce's Great Change.

Isaac Milner was one of the dreaded evangelicals, at least by profession—his lifestyle seemed, at this period, very much like Wilberforce's. He was also warm, charming, funny, intelligent, well and widely read, an endlessly fascinating conversationalist, and a passionate and articulate debater. But he did not see the discussion of serious topics as a game to be won, or a chance to show off, as Wilberforce was beginning to do. Wilberforce would remember years later that more than once Milner replied, "I don't pretend to be a match for you in this sort of running fire, but if you really wish to discuss these topics in a serious and argumentative manner, I shall be most happy to enter on them with you."[12]

Wilberforce was intrigued. Gradually he found himself compelled to take Milner's arguments more seriously, finding that he had a thoughtful, intelligent answer for every objection Wilberforce raised. Wilberforce was curious now, prepared by his conversations with Milner for the next of the four pivotal influences he was to encounter. This was a book, *The Rise and Progress of Religion in the Soul*, by Philip Doddridge. Picking up a copy of the book that belonged to a relative, Wilberforce asked Milner if it was worth reading. Milner said it was an excellent book and suggested that they take it with them and read it together on their journey. As they read and discussed the book, Wilberforce found himself increasingly unable to dismiss arguments and ideas he had not taken seriously since boyhood. Now that he was approaching the whole subject on his own, as an adult, there seemed to be much in evangelical beliefs that was compelling, even inescapable. Wilberforce had to be back in England for an important vote in Parliament, but he and Milner were planning another trip afterward, and they agreed that on this trip, they would tackle a far more challenging reading project together: the Greek New Testament. The daunting task of studying it in the original appealed to the two, and to Wilberforce it seemed the best way of testing Milner's arguments, and the ideas in Doddridge's book, against the original source. No longer either the child, starved for affection, who had embraced his aunt and uncle's teachings, nor the young man preoccupied with climbing the ladder of social and career success, Wilberforce now set himself for the first time to bring all the powers of his mind to bear on the question of whether or not Christianity was credible. He had always retained not only a keen (if sometimes lazy) intelligence but also a certain intellectual integrity—in fact, Wilberforce delayed the official conferring

---

12   Ibid. 73-74.

of his Cambridge degree for several years because he refused to sign a document, regarded by almost everyone as a meaningless formality, assenting to the beliefs of the Anglican church. Now Wilberforce determined he would give Christianity a fair hearing.

The investigation soon became far more troubling and less entertaining than it had seemed at first. Gradually but fairly easily, Wilberforce became intellectually convinced that the tenets of Christianity were true. But then a much longer and harder process began: the process of grappling with the implications of Christianity for his own life. For Wilberforce, deciding whether the claims of Christianity were credible was virtually effortless in comparison with the task of determining his response to them. At first, he was torn between his growing convictions and the lifestyle, the reputation, and the ambition he valued so highly. He knew very well that taking Christianity seriously would probably mean many changes in his life and in his priorities, and that it would certainly mean contempt and ridicule from many who were still as he had been just months before—delighted to poke fun at the "methodists" who were so odd, so ridiculous, and so far outside the mainstream of life and society. But gradually, Wilberforce became even more oppressed by a growing sense of guilt and regret for the waste of time, ability, and energy he now saw in both in his past, and in the future he had planned for himself. How arrogant, how self-indulgent, how careless he had been! And yet, there were times when he was reluctant to give it up. He needed confidence that a new life was possible for him before he could release his hold on the old one.

In fact, Wilberforce—a man who throughout his life suffered from agonizing bouts of ill health and exhaustion, including side effects from the opium he was prescribed for his stomach ailments, and who would encounter repeated crushing disappointments—would recall this period as the most painful and most difficult of his life, even though he also regarded it as the best thing that ever happened to him.[13] It was truly a spiritual and emotional dark night. The previously lighthearted young man now experienced doubt, conflict, and inner struggle such as he had never known. "My anguish of soul for some months was indescribable," Wilberforce would later write.[14] At times he was overcome by guilt and regret; at other times he was appalled by the coldness of his own heart and the fact that he was not moved as he knew he should be when considering the possibility that he was wasting his life and risking his eternal soul. At times he shrank from the thought of giving up everything he had worked for and incurring the scorn of

---

13   Hague, William. *William Wilberforce: The Life of the Great Anti-Slave Trade Campaigner*. Orlando, Harcourt. 2007. Page 84.
14   Belmonte Paperback 78.

his friends and family; at other times he was horrified by the arrogance and hypocrisy that could value reputation above his own eternal destiny. At times he was disgusted by the self-indulgence with which he had squandered his time and energy on pleasure; at other times he could hardly bear the thought of giving those pleasures up. When he was at home with his books and his thoughts he saw everything clearly; on the increasingly rare occasions when he ventured out to spend time among his friends and in his usual haunts, he was distressed to find how easily he slipped back into his old habits of speech and thought. And when he most longed to find peace in trusting Christ's sacrifice for sin, Wilberforce would experience days or weeks of a despairing fear that it was too late for him—that he had so long turned his back on God that it might now be impossible for him to repent or to be redeemed. More and more, as Wilberforce later wrote, "I condemned myself for having wasted my precious time, and opportunities, and talents."[15]

Enter the fourth member of the disruptive quartet that Wilberforce encountered during his Great Change—a name from his past: John Newton. Now elderly and in poor health, Newton graciously received the conflicted young man who asked him for a secret appointment so no one would see the prominent young Parliamentarian calling upon a notorious evangelical minister and writer. The visit brought great hope to both men and cemented a friendship that would be treasured by both for the remaining years of Newton's life. Wilberforce found great encouragement and understanding in the elderly pastor whose gentleness and patience stemmed from the horrific sins and the almost incredible conversion story of his own past, and Newton saw in the young man he had never forgotten a bright hope for the future—a hope that, through his friendship with Wilberforce, he might play a small role in paying his debt to future generations. Newton would later write to Wilberforce, "The joy that I felt, and the hopes I conceived when you called on me . . . I shall never forget."[16]

The strength Wilberforce drew from Newton at this time was increased from an unexpected source: his best friend, William Pitt. Writing to Pitt, like secretly visiting Newton, was one of Wilberforce's very earliest, tentative steps toward emerging from his self-imposed isolation and openly declaring his new convictions. Wilberforce's letter has not survived, but from Pitt's warm and supportive response it is clear that Wilberforce had written with great trepidation, dreading, perhaps all but assuming, that he would probably

15   Metaxas, Eric. *Amazing Grace: William Wilberforce and the Heroic Campaign to End Slavery*. San Francisco. HarperCollins. 2007. Page 52.
16   Belmonte, Kevin. *A Hero for Humanity: A Biography of William Wilberforce*. Nav-Press 2002. Hardback Page 86.

lose Pitt's friendship and certainly his respect, and that their political partnership and Wilberforce's parliamentary career were at an end. Instead, Pitt's unhesitating response of support, affection, and reassurance was one Wilberforce would treasure all his life.

Wilberforce remained preoccupied for months with the inner struggle that preceded his gradual emerging into the confidence and joy he would find at the end of his "great change." "For months I was in a state of the deepest depression," Wilberforce would later write.[17] But during the end of 1785 and the beginning of 1786, the gradual but irrevocable commitment that would transform Wilberforce's life became complete. "By degrees," he would recall, "the offers and promises of the gospel produced in me something of a settled peace of conscience."[18] His transition to confidence in salvation through Christ seemed agonizingly gradual to Wilberforce at the time, but it was so dramatic that he would write years later to a friend that "I seem to myself to have awakened . . . from a dream, to have recovered, as it were, the use of my reason after a delirium."[19]

As he grappled with the implications of his new life and began to explain it to friends and family, Newton and Pitt were yet again an unlikely and unconscious alliance, both agreeing in urging Wilberforce to reconsider a momentous decision he had all but made. One thing that was never in doubt for Wilberforce was that his newfound faith would change almost everything about his life—he canceled his membership to all the clubs he belonged to in one day. Initially he believed, perhaps almost assumed, that he would retire from politics, turning his back on all the motivations and principles which he felt had been such a waste of his time and such an indulgence of all that was worst in his character. But Pitt and Newton both urged Wilberforce not to withdraw from public life. His privileges and achievements had brought him unique opportunities, they argued. He was positioned to make a difference in the country, even in the world. He was prepared as few could be for leadership in the political arena. The fact that he had till now offered all his opportunities and abilities on the altar of his own ambition did not mean that God might not lead him to dedicate them to another purpose.

A New Life, and a Return to Politics

After long and deep consideration of this advice, and after spending countless hours in prayer and Bible study, Wilberforce returned to Parliament—though the sharp-tongued, unscrupulous politician who had begun his career there was never seen again.

---

17   Hague 82.
18   Belmonte Hardback 94.
19   Belmonte Hardback 91.

Two things about Wilberforce had already begun an immediate and irrevocable transformation: his attitude toward his own reputation, and his use of his time and money. Perhaps most noticeable to others was the progress of the formerly ruthless, sharp-tongued young orator, driven by his thirst for public success, toward a man distinguished by rare humility. Over the remainder of his political life, Wilberforce grew into a statesman who had the humility to address opponents and rivals with gentleness and respect, and to live with public ridicule and ferocious criticism that would have been a nightmare for the young man who, just a few years earlier, had been so desperate to fit in and be thought well of. This change in Wilberforce not only attracted notice upon his return to Parliament but also made a striking impression upon his mother, predictably dismayed by his sudden relapse into what she considered an unbalanced religious excitement she had worked so hard to eradicate in him as a boy. Wilberforce's first visit to his mother—which coincided with a visit from friends who had played an active role in helping her to refocus the young Wilberforce on the pleasures of society—brought her at least the consolation of noting that, whatever its disadvantages, Wilberforce's new life had at least greatly reduced his outbursts of irritability and short temper toward her, causing him to treat her and others with far more consistent kindness and courtesy than before. Mrs. Sykes remarked to his mother that, if he was indeed "mad" as some rumors held, she only hoped he would bite them all and spread the contagion of his improved disposition.[20]

His attitude toward his time and money were the other dramatic outward change in Wilberforce at this time. The young man who had found it easy to achieve success and popularity with very little effort or discipline, and who had felt entitled to spend his liberal supplies of time and money as he wished, now felt deep and lasting regret about the sheer waste of time, talent, resources, energy, and opportunities he saw in his own past. Eagerly, yet with remarkable intention and tenacity, he embarked on a project of entirely redirecting his resources. His own fortunate situation as the child of privilege, leisure, and financial security now seemed a very responsible one—a stewardship for which he would owe an account both to God and to the countless millions of his fellow human beings who had so much less.

Wilberforce began to walk instead of paying for a carriage, to eat more simply, and to drastically slash his spending in other areas. For the rest of his life, he would live simply in countless ways and give huge amounts of money away. He also began to spend his time very differently, appalled at what he called the madness of "throwing away" his time as

---

20 Metaxas 66.

he had done in the past. Most important to him was the time he set aside for prayer and Bible study, a discipline he considered essential throughout his life. "How criminal . . . must this voluntary ignorance of Christianity and the Word of God appear in the sight of God," he would later write. "When God of His goodness has granted us such abundant means of instruction, how great must be the guilt . . . of voluntary ignorance! . . . Great indeed are our opportunities. Great also is our responsibility."[21] Wilberforce felt an urgent need for his times of Bible study and prayer to protect the clarity of his focus, writing that without these times "the most pressing claims will carry [my heart], not the strongest," and adding "The shortening of private devotions starves the soul, it grows lean and faint. This must not be."[22]

Wilberforce also embarked immediately on a sustained effort to redress as best he could the waste of his time as a student, especially at Cambridge. For the next twelve summers, until he married, Wilberforce would spend nine or ten hours in a carefully planned and serious course of reading. As Belmonte writes:

> Wilberforce read an astonishing variety of books. He took pains to remain well acquainted with works of classical Greek and Roman literature . . . He read Boswell's *Life of Samuel Johnson* often, as well as works by Gibbon, Adam Smith, Francis Bacon, David Hume, William Blackstone, Locke, Machiavelli, Montesquieu, Rousseau, Voltaire, and Sir Walter Scott . . . He read memories and biographies, biblical and legal commentaries, treatises on economics, essays, histories, collections of letters, linguistic works, novels, philosophical writings, plays, poetry, works on political theory, works of science and theology, and travel books.[23]

Even after family life and other added responsibilities restructured his life, and despite serious problems with his eyes which had begun in boyhood and would progress until he lost the sight of one eye entirely, Wilberforce's passion for and delight in reading remained one of his most striking characteristics all his life. He not only read books but also memorized long passages in both English and Latin and took copious notes. He was famous for stuffing his pockets to bursting with books, notes, pens, and even inkwells, and he carried on a running "conversation" with the authors he read through marginal notes, and loved to share and comment on what he was reading with anyone else in the room. His curiosity and enthusiasm for learning remained strong all his life, and made him interested in everyone he met, and an endlessly fascinating conversationalist.

---

21   Wilberforce, William. *Real Christianity*. Colorado Springs. David C. Cook. 2005. Pages 40-44.
22   Belmonte Hardback 89.
23   Belmonte Paperback 93.

Wilberforce applied the same new discipline to his work in Parliament, immediately becoming a much more diligent member than he had ever been—attending more sessions, however uninteresting, serving tirelessly on dull and unpopular committees, and taking detailed notes on other speakers.

"Two Great Objects"

All of this renewed focus and mental training both prepared Wilberforce for the great task of his life, and led him to it. His reading, his new seriousness about the responsibilities of a life in politics, and the expanded circle of people he now began getting to know converged to focus his mind, his plans for the future, and his political future on the famous 1787 declaration in his diary, "God has placed before me two great objects, the suppression of the slave trade and the reformation of manners."[24]

Wilberforce has become far more famous for the first of these two objects, but it was the second which attracted his attention first, and which he probably thought (mistakenly, if so) would consume more of his time and energy. By the reformation of manners, Wilberforce meant the reformation of morals—a full-scale, sustained attack on the conscience and culture of a society disfigured by cruelty, corruption, and vice. Many of Wilberforce's concerns, such as drunkenness, gambling, prostitution, and the wasting of time in theatres have continued to strike many modern readers, as they struck many of his contemporaries, as excessively severe, petty, or moralistic. But other areas that attracted the attention of Wilberforce and a growing army of fellow reformers are so shocking to readers today that our horror on learning how recently and how widely they were accepted is the ultimate testament to the century of humanitarian reforms ushered in by Wilberforce and his contemporaries. Bear and bull-baiting, the horrific working conditions in factories, the education of working children, the treatment of women, prisoners, and the insane, cruelty to animals—all these issues were also in the sights of Wilberforce and others behind the "proclamation societies" which began forming to support and extend the influence of a document, issued by the king at the behest of Wilberforce and his allies, called "The Proclamation for the Encouragement of Piety and Virtue and for the Preventing of Vice, Profaneness, and Immorality." This document, usually issued by the king or queen as an empty formality, was converted by Wilberforce and an army of others into a genuine legislative, social, and cultural reform movement. Wilberforce did not originate any of these ideas, and he did not carry them

---

24   Ibid. 97.

out alone; the stories of countless reformers of this time who gave a voice to the voiceless and confronted the conscience of the British Empire with uncomfortable truths might fill volumes. But Wilberforce, who had wanted to spend his time and his opportunities as a Member of Parliament better, was beginning to find a unique niche as one who could bring truth and power, compassion and action, together.

The second of his great tasks was to become the one most often associated with his name, although in this Wilberforce's role was even more that of one who followed and worked with many others. A growing coalition of reformers, both inside and outside politics, was already beginning to arm and mobilize itself for a legal, legislative, and grassroots attack on the slave trade. Indeed, although the exact details and the order and extent of everyone's involvement remain disputed and uncertain, it is clear that several fervent abolitionists deliberately sought out Wilberforce to cultivate his interest in their cause and to enlist his leadership and support. They recognized in him the man who could be the face and voice of their movement in Parliament—a man who could make people listen.

Wilberforce had in fact expressed concerns about and opposition to the slave trade long before his conversion, and he belonged to a political circle that generally favored reform and was disposed to condemn or at least to critique a trade that was already the subject of growing global controversy. But the "crash course" in the slave trade on which Wilberforce now embarked, with characteristic thoroughness, through his reading and research and through his new friends, was to focus the remainder of his political career on a battle to end the slave trade, and slavery itself, in the increasingly vast part of the globe controlled by the British Empire.

The horrifying scale of the Atlantic slave trade, and the widespread and tenacious defense of it that Wilberforce would encounter, both stemmed from the situation of the British Empire in Wilberforce's time. The British Empire, rapidly rising toward the zenith of its power and wealth, and aggressively determined to defend its overseas empire against other European powers (particularly its nemesis France), was fueled at least as much by trade and commerce as by military might. The old adage "the flag follows trade" is the perfect description of an empire which grew in an almost haphazard way by developing military, diplomatic, and legal justifications for claiming and defending vast swathes of territory that had been explored and organized not by armies but by trading companies. The explosive growth of the middle class in England after the Industrial Revolution created a voracious market for coffee, tea, chocolate, and sugar—exotic luxuries a generation or two before, now often considered staple necessities in even the poorest families. But the worldwide trade in these goods and the improved standard of living at home, of which Britain was so proud, had a dark side. It was the slave trade that provided laborers for the plantations and sugar refineries, especially in Britain's extensive possessions in the West Indies. Behind the cup of tea or the spoonful of sugar which might be the one bright spot in the day of a starving child, one who worked ten to fourteen hours a day in the factories and slept at night on the streets or in a filthy, overcrowded, unheated tenement, there lay a dark secret. It was a saga of almost unbelievable suffering and brutality that few, if any, in England could even begin to imagine.

While Spain and Portugal, the first to explore and exploit the newly discovered Americas, had been the first European powers to fling open the doors of the African slave trade, and while all the major European naval powers participated heavily in it during the roughly three hundred years in which it flourished, it was Britain that, in the words of Isabelle Aguet, "had the advantage in this frenzied race," importing in a single year (1786) up to 38,000 slaves into the Western Hemisphere.[25] As Aguet explains, it is impossible to know how many men, women, and children were the victims of the trade, but "It is undoubtedly the largest scale emigration that has ever taken place across the seas," and it seems likely that at least twelve million Africans must have been brought west to cultivate the sugar colonies alone.[26]

The staggering numbers of people involved suggest not merely the scale of the trade but also the barbaric conditions enslaved people inevitably suffered during a transportation process driven and constrained only by profit. The greater the number of people who could be captured, rounded up, purchased, transported, and sold at one time, the greater the economic benefit to every layer of the system—the slave traders, the ship owners, the insurance companies, the captains, the landed gentry who owned the plantations, the shops that sold the sugar. Only treatment sufficiently harsh to reduce the price of too large a percentage of the shipment could deter those who made their livings and built their fortunes in the trade, and with the supply of victims from the African interior seeming all but unlimited, the illnesses and deaths of many prisoners could be written off as the cost of doing business.

For the countless millions of Africans devoured by the insatiable monster that was the slave trade, the nightmare often began with a small scale, lightning-fast raid in which they were kidnapped by men—often African or Arab—who darted out of the forest to

25   Aguet, Isabelle. Trans. Bonnie Christen, *A Pictorial History of the Slave Trade*. Geneva, 1971. Page 11.
26   Ibid. 13.

seize unwary men, women, and children tending their gardens or going for water. During their journey to the coast, they were often shackled and driven ruthlessly through wilderness as unfamiliar and terrifying to them as the interior of North America seemed to the first New England settlers, through kingdoms and villages whose languages they did not know. The main slave routes to the coast were lined, and its rivers polluted, with the bodies of those who died of illness or who grew too weak to keep up and were left to die, or killed by the traders.

Once they reached the coast, the imprisoned were housed in the stifling heat and stench of overcrowded holding areas, often in the terrible slave-holding fortresses that still dot the "slave coast" of Africa. They stayed here until they were purchased from the land-based traders by those who would transport them across the Atlantic, hoping to make a profit by selling them to the plantations of the New World for far more than they had to pay the traders. Often these—the hard-faced men who forced terrified and disoriented Africans into boats and rowed them out to the dreaded ships—were the first white-faced Europeans the enslaved had seen. Despite the horrors of their journey across Africa and their imprisonment in the ports, however, the terror and despair of those catching their last glimpse of the continent on which they were born were so great that sometimes, as they were carried in chains toward the ships, they threw themselves into the sea to drown or to be shot by the slavers, rather than face the future in store for them. One slaver complained, "The Negroes are so willful and loth to leave their own country, that they have often leap'd out of the canoos (sic), boat and ship, into the sea, and kept under water till they were drowned, to avoid being taken up and saved by our boats, which pursued them; they having a more dreadful apprehension of Barbados than we can have of hell."[27]

Whatever the fears and rumors that drove such desperate acts, the reality on board the slave ships could only have been far worse. As surviving drawings make clear, overcrowding alone made the conditions on many slave ships almost unspeakable. One English slave ship, probably typical of many if not most, packed so many slaves into the space between its decks (allowing a height of only five feet nine inches) that when they were lying down there was not an inch of space between them. On another ship, the space between the decks was only four and a half feet high, meaning that even if the chains and shackles that bound them together had permitted it, few if any slaves could have stood upright. Ventilation in the stinking darkness came only from the portholes,

27   Howard, Thomas, Ed. *Black Voyage: Eyewitness Accounts of the Atlantic Slave Trade*. Ed. Thomas Howard. Boston. Little, Brown, and Co. 1971. Page 81.

except during the brief daily periods when the captives were allowed on deck for exercise (often enforced dancing), fresh air, and to empty their waste buckets.[28] Men were usually chained during the entire voyage; women were usually not chained, but a far worse fate awaited them as they were routinely raped by the sailors. The food and water given the slaves were usually no worse than those supplied to the crew, because the profit of the voyage depended on minimizing deaths when possible. But when storms or other accidents caused food and water to run short, slaves were sometimes thrown overboard. And even under the best conditions, disease—from dysentery to smallpox—ravaged the slave ships, killing countless men, women, and children in the confined spaces. "What the smallpox spar'd, [diarrhea] swept off, to our great regret," complained one captain, "after all our pains and care to give them their messes in due order and season, keeping their lodgings as clean and sweet as possible, and enduring so much misery and stench so long among a parcel of creatures nastier than swine, and after all our expectations to be defeated by their mortality."[29] As this shocking commentary suggests, the slave trade was well known as dangerous, difficult, risky, and unpleasant—its brutalizing effect on the white men who worked it would become a major argument for its eventual abolition. Piracy, disease, storm, and the ever-present fear of slave revolts made the trade notorious for its dangers. Their own misery and fear often fueled unimaginable sadism by captains and crew, who inflicted ferocious torture on any of the prisoners who seemed to offer the slightest resistance. Yet the desire to realize a profit on the voyage guaranteed that they would minimize deaths among their human cargo in every way they could.

The slaves who survived their terrible voyage and were sold to the sugar plantations faced an equally grim fate. After yet another terrible scene of loss and parting, in which families, couples, or friends who might have been shipped together were wrenched apart, sobbing, never to see one another again, the slaves were, in most cases, taken to work on the plantations of the British West Indies or southern North America. Those on the plantations and in the sugar refineries worked in brutal and dangerous conditions, exposed to many diseases to which they had little or no immunity. One report estimated that about a third of the new arrivals would die during the first three months, and that their working life could not be expected to last longer than fifteen years.[30] "There is nothing more miserable than the condition of these people," wrote a priest. "Their food consists of plant roots; their houses resemble dens . . . their furniture consists of several

---

28   Aguet 59-65.
29   Howard 87.
30   Aguet 103.

gourds . . . their work is almost continuous . . . twenty lashes with the whip for the slightest mistake."[31] In addition to the terrible heat and the parasites and diseases of their new home, slaves were in danger from the working conditions of the sugar refineries, where such perils as dangerous machinery, fire, excessive heat, and huge boiling vats of liquid made every step of the refining process a dangerous one.

Long before Wilberforce joined a coalition working to end the slave trade, voices had been raised in protest. When the cause was brought to Wilberforce's attention, a growing alliance in Britain was seeking to garner enough support to stand up to the powerful West India lobby. Just as today we might buy an attractive T-shirt without the question of where it came from or who made it even crossing our minds, so many in Britain purchased sugar in the shops without being aware of the lives lost to supply it, or enjoyed comfortable lives on country estates without realizing what it meant that some of their wealth was drawn from holdings in the West Indies. If the public could be awakened to outrage, then perhaps the three-hundred-year-old trade in slaves could be ended.

The Battle Begins

At the foot of the famous "Wilberforce Oak" on the estate of William Pitt, in the spring of 1787, Wilberforce and Pitt discussed Wilberforce's plans to introduce a bill against the slave trade in the House of Commons. Over the next couple of years, Wilberforce plunged into his new role as the spearhead of the anti-slavery moment, functioning as both the student and the leader of those who had been organizing against it. After the usual slow but methodical turning of the wheels of the legislative machinery, the historic day arrived on May 12, 1789, when Wilberforce was to argue before the House of Commons for a bill that would outlaw the slave trade. In the throes of one of his periodic bouts of severe ill health (probably colitis), Wilberforce felt so exhausted and so ill that he was unable to prepare his speech as he would have liked, or even to decide exactly what he would say. But when he rose to address the House, Wilberforce, "by Divine grace" as he wrote in his diary, found the strength to speak powerfully and unforgettably for three and a half hours, electrifying his hearers. The slave trade was not, Wilberforce urged, something happening far away at the hands of a few unpleasant men—it was something the whole nation was responsible for. Delicately, Wilberforce sought to shift blame away from the scapegoat slave traders—who, after all, were engaged in a trade made both lawful and profitable by the British nation— and onto the national conscience, without so directly or so harshly condemning the many

---

31   Ibid. 107.

in his audience who funded the trade and owned the plantations that his bill would be doomed to certain failure. Steeped in the research that had consumed so much of his time for the past two to three years, Wilberforce, even without the preparation he would have liked, was able to pile facts upon statistics upon sources, methodically countering every argument used by the defenders of slavery. One by one he stripped away the excuses used in support of the trade; one by one he brought forward the shocking statistics. Wilberforce concluded by declaring that Britain could no longer evade responsibility: "we can no longer plead ignorance, we cannot evade it, it is now an object placed before us; we may spurn it, we may kick it out of our way, but we cannot turn aside so as to avoid seeing it."[32]

The response, proclaimed by supporting voices in Parliament and by newspapers across the country, was enthusiastic. The death knell of the slave trade had been sounded, some believed—and indeed, Wilberforce had set in motion a train of events that would one day end slavery in the British Empire. It would only take twenty years.

Over the next two decades, Wilberforce would fight the slave trade in Parliament. Always he had fervent supporters, but as the battle dragged on, he lost many of them to death. Sometimes the bill would be tantalizingly close to passage—particularly gut-wrenching was the vote in 1796, when his bill was defeated by only four votes, and ten or twelve of Wilberforce's supporters missed the vote, including several who had accepted free opera tickets from the bill's opponents.[33] Other times the goal receded into the distance, and it seemed to many, including Wilberforce, that it could not be reached in his lifetime. John Wesley wrote to Wilberforce at the end of his own life, offering encouragement, but also a sobering assessment of the hard fight ahead:

Unless the divine power has raised you up . . . I do not see how you can go through your glorious enterprise in opposing that execrable villainy, which is the scandal of religion, of England, and of human nature. Unless God has raised you up for this very thing, you will be worn out by the opposition of men and devils. But if God be for you, who can be against you? . . . Go on, in the name of God and in the power of His might . . .

And another supporter told Wilberforce, "You, sir, will stand in the British parliament . . . with the whole force of truth with every rational argument, and with all the powers of moving eloquence on your side, and all to no purpose."[34]

The powerful West Indies lobby had arguments of their own. They argued not only that the British colonial economy would collapse without the slave trade but also that

32 Tomkins, Stephen. *William Wilberforce: A Biography*. Grand Rapids, MI. Eerdmans. 2007. Page 83.
33 Belmonte Paperback 134.
34 Tomkins 92-93.

slaves traveled across the Atlantic in comfort and were always treated humanely. Many also argued that the conditions in which Africans lived in their own homes were far worse than those on the plantations, and that their lives were much better after they were enslaved. The endless delaying tactics possible through the cumbersome apparatus of the legislature, with its committees and recesses and motions and hearings, offered seemingly unlimited opportunities for stalling and maneuvering, as Wilberforce's annual proposal of another abolition bill became a kind of tradition in the House. A slave revolt in the West Indies resurrected fears of violence and instability if the bonds of slavery were loosened even a little. And perhaps most damaging of all, the war with France, which soon consumed so much of the resources and attention of the British Empire, made opposing the slave trade seem dangerous and unpatriotic. The defense of the overseas empire was seen as key to the war effort, and the slave trade, with the rest of Britain's maritime commerce, was seen as a vital source and training ground for the seamen who would power her navy.

At least twice, Wilberforce came close to withdrawing from the political battle against the slave trade, wondering if it was for someone else, and not for him, to lead the cause to eventual victory. His health continued very poor, and his attacks of exhaustion and agonizing abdominal pain were so severe that he assumed he would not live long. His eyesight continued to deteriorate, and the side effects of the opium he was prescribed to alleviate his stomach pain were also severe. The ferocious public and personal accusations and ridicule he faced were beyond anything the younger Wilberforce, so driven by a desire for reputation, could have imagined. He drove himself relentlessly in his work, both when Parliament was in session and when it was not. And rather than gaining ground, the abolitionists had to face the reality that the slave trade grew and flourished more and more during the first ten to fifteen years of their battle against it. It seemed to grow more entrenched, more ingrained in the national economy, more unassailable, more triumphant, each year. The knowledge weighed relentlessly on Wilberforce and his comrades that as they struggled in vain year after year, countless thousands of lives continued to be destroyed and ended by the slave trade.

In the spring of 1795 and again in the summer of 1796, Wilberforce experienced exhaustion and illness that amounted to virtual collapse, and it was during the summer of 1796, he seriously considered retirement from political life, feeling at the end of his strength. Five years later, in 1801, he again considered stepping down from his role as leader of the abolition party, but this time not from any desire to do so. With a selflessness rare both in politicians and in the leaders of causes, Wilberforce offered the leadership of the cause to another politician, the new Prime Minister, Henry Addington. Addington's role in the peace negotiations with France seemed to Wilberforce to offer a possibility for Addington to press for the abolition of the slave trade. Wilberforce had been trying for fifteen years; perhaps Addington could do better. "[L]est this momentous business, which Providence seems in some sort to have committed to my care, should suffer from my mismanagement," Wilberforce wrote to Addington:

> I have determined to lay before you in writing a few thoughts . . . . It is not . . . without emotion that I relinquish the idea of being myself the active and chief agent in terminating this greatest of all human evils; but you will readily believe me when I say that any unpleasant sensations on this head vanish at once before the prospect of effecting the desired object . . . I should look on with joy, if the Disposer of all human events . . .should further honour you by making you His agent in dispensing to the world this greatest and most extended of all earthly benefits . . . [35]

However, Addington was not only a weak and inexperienced politician who would achieve little as prime minister but also, apparently, not inclined to make abolition of the slave trade a priority. He made no attempt to make the abolitionist cause his own, and Wilberforce found himself still at the head of the movement. Another five years of trying and failing lay before him.

Friendship, Love and Marriage, and Family Life

Two things renewed Wilberforce's perseverance and gave him fresh hope during the twenty-year battle. One was the encouragement and support of Christians he respected who urged him to bear up under the repeated blows of the seemingly hopeless struggle, and who reminded him that this task, whether destined for success or failure, seemed to be appointed to him. A letter from John Newton, Wilberforce's mentor as a young man and a passionate opponent for the trade in which he himself had spent so many years of his early life, arrived at an especially crucial time, when Wilberforce was seriously considering retirement after his 1797 crushing defeat and ensuing physical breakdown. Newton sympathized with Wilberforce's longing to withdraw into private life, but reminded him of the many things he had achieved in Parliament, and of the wonderful opportunity still represented by his having a voice there. In closing, he reminded Wilberforce of a Biblical hero who also lived and worked in a hostile environment:

---

35   Belmonte Paperback 144-145.

It is true that you live in the midst of difficulties and snares, and you need a double guard of watchfulness and prayer. But since you know both your need of help, and where to look for it, I may say to you, as Darius to Daniel, "Thy God, whom thou servest continually is able to preserve and deliver thee . . . .Indeed the great point for our comfort in life is to have a well-grounded persuasion that we are where, all things considered, we ought to be . . . The promise, "My grace is sufficient for thee," is necessary to support us in the smoothest scenes, and is equally able to support us in the most difficult. Happy the man who has a deep impression of our Lord's words, "Without Me you can do nothing"—who feels with the Apostle . . . likewise a heartfelt dependence upon the Saviour, through whom we can both do and bear all things that are [part of] the post allotted us. He is always near. He knows our wants, our dangers, our feelings, and our fears . . . With his wisdom for our guide, his power, for our protection, his fullness for our supply, and proposing his glory for our chief end, and placing our happiness in his favour, in communion with him, and communications from Him, we shall be able to "withstand in the evil day, and having done all to stand."[36]

A second source of great and unexpected encouragement and joy for Wilberforce came when he fell head over heels in love, at the age of thirty-seven, with a woman seventeen years his junior. After a whirlwind courtship which had come just when Wilberforce's fortunes, health, and spirits seemed at their lowest ebb, and during which he both amused and annoyed his friends by bubbling over with enthusiasm and devotion, he married her. Their family would soon include six children, and Wilberforce found that he loved family life, and was unfailingly delighted and refreshed by spending time with his wife and children, surrounded by an ever-changing collection of animals, by his beloved flower gardens outside and books inside, and by a procession of visitors. Having a happy home, full of the laughter of children, as a refuge fueled Wilberforce's renewed commitment to the battle against the slave trade.

The tide, at last, began to turn. Wilberforce and other committed abolitionists kept the issue relentlessly before Parliament, waiting for world events and the rise and fall of statesmen to give them an opening. New circumstances created new possibilities; new allies arose to replace those who would not live to see the victory. Finally, on February 23, 1807, a bill to abolish the slave trade passed the House of Commons, 283 votes to sixteen. As Tomkins writes, "The twenty-year struggle for Wilberforce . . . had consumed a fortune in time and money; it had, in some cases, threatened wealth and reputation; it

---

36   Ibid. 137-138.

had taken eleven bills from Wilberforce plus more from the others, and it was finished."[37] Wilberforce sat, stunned, with tears rolling down his face.

The triumph was one of historic proportions, but for decades to come, and for countless thousands of men, women, and children, it did little to bring the end of the horrors of slavery, as Wilberforce and so many others had hoped it would. A brutal era of slave smuggling now began, and even the British naval ships seeking to enforce the new ban on the slave trade sometimes inadvertently sank ships packed with helpless, shackled slaves. Even on paper, the new law did nothing for the millions of slaves already living and working on the plantations, an increasing number of whom were born into slavery in the New World. A long, hard fight to outlaw slavery itself was just beginning. Wilberforce and others had hoped that outlawing the slave trade would not only be an irrevocable step toward the abolition of slavery itself but would also cause slave owners to treat their slaves more humanely. Surely, once they could no longer be replaced, slaves would be considered too valuable to treat with brutality. However, not only did an illicit trade in human beings continue but many owners also turned ferociously on their slaves, angered by opposition and terrified of a slave revolt.

Yet the tide had turned, and slowly but surely, over the next three decades, a tireless army of abolitionists worked to keep the horrors of slavery before the eyes of the nation and on its conscience. Wilberforce remained a passionate supporter of the abolition movement all his life, even after his retirement from Parliament in 1825 at the age of sixty-six, but during his final years of failing health, it was more his wishes, his prayers, and his reputation than any active participation that still fueled the movement now led by younger men. He also continued to pour his time, energy, and money into countless other causes and individuals. The sense that he could and should have accomplished so much more continued to weigh on Wilberforce from time to time. He wrote to a friend at the time of his retirement from Parliament:

> I am filled with the deepest compunction for the consciousness of my having made so poor a use of the talents committed to my stewardship . . . We alone know ourselves the opportunities we have enjoyed, and the comparative use we have made of them . . . I am but too conscious of numerous and great sins of omission, many opportunities of doing good whether not at all or very inadequately improved.[38]

---

37 Tomkins 171.
38 Metaxas 266.

Later Years and Death

Wilberforce's family remained a lifelong joy to him, but the reckless financial decisions of one of his sons, who fled the country to avoid debtor's prison, brought ruin to the entire family. Wilberforce and his wife were forced to sell their beloved home, and to spend their remaining years as guests in the homes of others—often those of two of their sons, and sometimes those of friends. Cheerful and thankful, however, Wilberforce's only recorded comment is that he enjoyed the time with his adult sons and the chance to know their families and lives better.

John Newton, the former slave captain, had seen in the young William Wilberforce the man who could bring an end to the British slave trade, and Newton had lived barely long enough to hear the news of the 1807 victory on his death bed. Now Wilberforce, himself passing the torch of leadership to another generation, would hear of the passage of a bill abolishing slavery on July 26, 1833, just two days before his own death.

Wilberforce was buried in Westminster Abbey, and was celebrated and mourned around the world. Crowds of slaves and former slaves gathered to commemorate him, and the leading men of Europe offered tributes. The leading orators of the day vied with one another in eulogizing his achievements. But the memorial Wilberforce himself would have found most fitting came at midnight on July 31, 1834, when the law abolishing slavery came into force, a year after Wilberforce's death. Eight hundred thousand slaves in the British West Indies were free. Throughout the islands, many climbed the hills and sat together, their faces toward the ocean, to watch the historic sunrise.[39] Wilberforce had not lived to see the dawn he had worked for and believed in all his adult life, but he died knowing it was coming, and no doubt he celebrated it as, and where, he would most have wished to do.

---

39   Ibid. 277.

CHAPTER 7

George Mueller

RECKLESS TRUST

Their eyes, bright with hunger, looked out of pinched young faces that seemed old. Their bones showed through soiled and stained clothes that were too thin to resist the biting cold. Their skeletal hands were grimy and calloused. Many could neither read nor write. Some had never been taught a skill for which they could be paid—except perhaps for theft. They were destined for life on the streets, or early death in the factories. As orphans, they had nowhere to go and no one to turn to. The hardscrabble life of beggars, thieves, and prostitutes was often all they had to look forward to.

The conscience of the nation was uneasy about them. Some pitied them, while others saw them as a source of moral contagion and social degradation. In one way or another, many were troubled by this grim by-product of the industrial revolution, and many felt that something ought to be done. But one man felt differently. He felt that *he*, personally, ought to do something—although he had no guaranteed regular income. And George Mueller had never needed anyone to lead the way for him when he saw the will of God clearly.

Childhood and Education

Although he would be known for his work in England, George Mueller was born in Germany. He was the favorite child of a wealthy and indulgent father—a situation that would be harmful to many children, and one that was disastrous for George. He learned at a very young age to devote as much of his time and energy as he possibly could to his own amusement, and to that end he learned to lie, cheat, and steal without hesitation and with increasing skill. When George was eleven, his father, whose ambition was that his son become a Lutheran minister, sent the boy to a school where he could be prepared for university. Here George found gambling and novels far more to his taste than study, and he quickly added heavy drinking to his expensive habits. In fact, on the night of his mother's death, the fourteen-year-old George was staggering through the streets drunk, and playing cards with his friends. Even when he met with a minister for confession the day before his confirmation and first communion, he—a future minister—handed over one-twelfth of the money his father had supplied to pay the confirmation fee, keeping the rest to spend himself.[1]

It would have been hard to tell from the outside, but the young George Mueller was not entirely without the occasional twinge of conscience, or even the occasional thought of turning over a new leaf. In fact, after the service at which he observed his confirmation and first communion, the young man who had stolen from a priest the day before spent the afternoon walking alone in the fields, making ambitious plans to reform—to drink and steal less, to study more, to make a fresh start. But the teenager was already caught in a futile cycle of broken resolutions, and already finding it impossible to make a lasting change in his life, Mueller remembered that "it all came to nothing and I still grew worse."[2] In fact, while spending two weeks with his aunt shortly afterward, Mueller not only spent time "frequenting taverns [and] forming resolutions to become different, yet breaking them almost as fast as they were made;" he actually wasted all the money he had been given for his trip and was so hungry that he stole a piece of bread from a soldier staying in the house, something he recognized even at the time as a new low point in his selfishness and dishonesty toward others.[3]

Mueller went so far as to ask his father if he could change schools, planning to make a fresh start and hoping that, in new surroundings and away from his wild friends, it would be easier. But of course it was not; he continued to waste money and drink heavily from his arrival at the new school. And when his father recklessly left George in sole charge of a house being renovated, with the responsibilities of studying under a tutor and collecting debts and rents due to his father, the entire lack of supervision and the ceaseless flow of money proved the complete undoing of the young man's resolution. He soon embarked on his most ambitious fraud yet, collecting money from his father's debtors, giving receipts for only part of the amount, and telling his father the full sum had not been paid—while, of course, spending the money on partying with his friends.

1   Pierson, Arthur T. *George Mueller of Bristol and His Witness to a Prayer-Hearing God*. NY: Fleming. 1899. Page 19-20.
2   Mueller, George. *Autobiography of George Mueller. Third Edition*. Ed. G. Fred Bergin. Lifeline Philippines. 1914. Page 2.
3   Ibid. 3.

The life George was living was bound to end in real trouble sooner or later, and thanks to increasing recklessness it was sooner. When the now sixteen-year-old George escaped from a second hotel in short succession without paying his bill—having spent all his money—he was arrested and jailed. It was a real shock for the spoiled, privileged young man; in an account written decades later Mueller recalled the very literal coarse bread and water, supplemented only by vegetables in the evening, that he was served here, and the close confines of the cell in which he was at first kept alone. Soon, however, he was joined by several cellmates to whom—proud of his exploits and eager to fit in—the boy boasted not only of crimes he had actually committed but also of some he made up for the occasion.[4]

It was almost a month before money arrived from his father, and George Mueller was released. Now, at last, the disgraced and defrauded father was truly angry as never before, and he belatedly placed George under constant rigorous supervision until he could be sent to a new, much stricter school. Meanwhile, George was to pursue his own studies and also to tutor younger students. Determined to win back his father's easygoing approval, George at last did completely change his habits and appearance:

> I now endeavoured, by diligence in study, to regain the favor of my father. My habits were, as to outward appearances, exemplary. I made my progress in my own studies, benefited my pupils, and was soon liked by everybody around me, and in a short time my father had forgotten all. But all this time I was in heart as bad as ever; for I was still in secret habitually guilty of great sins.[5]

The relieved father thought George was over his wild phase at last, but the only lesson George Mueller had learned was the same one he had been practicing since he was a little boy: the trick is not to get caught, and living a double life is a lot more fun than being hungry or going to jail. Focused on his schoolwork for the first time, the naturally intelligent Mueller made great progress in every academic subject, but he was also learning a lesson in hypocrisy.

Mueller's father soon realized that his son was not the completely transformed man he must have hoped, because when he was sent to take the entrance examinations to the strict school his father had chosen, Mueller went instead to another school where discipline was more relaxed and where he had several friends. He was accepted there and, as Mueller would later record, "never told my father a word of all this deception, till the

4   Ibid. 4.
5   Ibid. 5.

day before my departure, which obliged me to invent a whole chain of lies."[6] His father was then, of course, furious, but as so many times before he gave into George's pleas and let him go to the school he had chosen, where he would finish his high school education and from which he would go straight to the university.

To outward appearances Mueller's reformation continued; he was bright and studied hard, and he soon found that the rigorous curriculum kept him hard at work fourteen to sixteen hours a day. His natural intelligence was at last combined with discipline, and he received an excellent education in mathematics, literature, Greek, Hebrew, Latin, and other languages. But he had always been smart, and he had always been capable of great exertion. He hadn't really become any more honest; he was just figuring out that there were better ways for a young man of his privilege and ability to get whatever he wanted than wasting money and playing cards. "I had now grown so wicked," Mueller recalled, "that I could habitually tell lies without blushing." This enabled him to stage a dramatic pretense of having been robbed to get out of paying a debt and to gain money from his friends,[7] and later, as a university student, to plan a trip with a group of friends which involved forged passwords and documents and a great deal of debt, and which George managed so skillfully that he spent far less of his own money than any of the others, without his friends' suspecting the deception.[8]

University

George Mueller finished his preparatory education with excellent grades and entered the university, where he would study to become a Lutheran minister—a profession which could offer him a secure and comfortable way to make a living. He made yet another set of doomed resolutions on starting college. It really was time, he now told himself, to get his life in order. If he did not study hard and earn high grades, he would not be eligible for a really good position after school, and, in any case, he admitted to himself that he was unlikely to be anyone's first choice for a pastor at the moment. Here was another fresh start, with another fresh group of friends, and it was time to get serious. But of course, the almost complete independence of his life at university—still being supplied with money by his father but with almost no supervision whatsoever—was fatal to this

---

6 Ibid. 5.
7 Ibid. 6.
8 Harvey, Bonnie. *George Mueller: Man of Faith. Heroes of the Faith Series*. Uhrichsville, OH: Barbour. 1998. Page 15.

plan. Soon Mueller was cheating his friends, wasting all his money and having to pawn his clothes, and always needing to beg and borrow funds.

Yet one thing was different: George Mueller was no longer enjoying himself. He had, he would later recall, "a desire to renounce this wretched life, for I had no enjoyment in it, and had sense enough left to see that the end one day or other would be miserable, for I should never get a living."[9] But Mueller's realization that the life he was living could only bring him pain and hardship came too late. He had made enough failed resolutions by now to begin to understand that he was not strong enough to shake off the habits he had formed. The self-indulgence and deception he had once believed he controlled now controlled him, and he could see no way to freedom.

Conversion

One afternoon when George was twenty, he went with a friend to an informal Christian meeting held in the home of a local tradesman. Everything about the simple meeting and the warmth of the people who welcomed him made a deep impression on George, but it was the sight of a man kneeling to pray that most deeply stirred the boy who would one day be famous as a man of prayer. "I had never either seen anyone on his knees, nor had I ever prayed myself on my knees," Mueller recalled. At the close of the meeting another man—a tradesman with little education—prayed. Mueller was struck with the realization that he, the well-educated soon-to-be clergyman, could never have prayed as well as this virtually illiterate man. "The whole made a deep impression on me," he concluded. After this meeting, without any idea why, George Mueller felt hope, calm, and happiness that were completely unfamiliar to him. All the pleasures and wild adventures they had shared, everything that had filled their lives up till now, seemed, he told his friend, "as nothing in comparison with this evening."[10]

It was the beginning of a radically new chapter in his life. There was to be another of these weekly meetings the next Saturday, but, Mueller would recall "the next day, and Monday, and once or twice besides, I went again to the house of this brother, where I read the Scriptures with him . . . for it was too long for me to wait till Saturday came again."[11] Although he had been raised in the Lutheran church, had excelled in his studies as a divinity student, and was soon to be a minister, George Mueller would later write, "I had no Bible and had not read one for years . . . I had never heard the gospel preached. I had

---

9   Mueller 7.
10   Ibid. 10.
11   Ibid. 10.

never met with a person who told me that he meant, by the help of God, to live according to the Holy Scriptures. In short, I had not the least idea that there were any persons really different from myself."[12] Now, all that was changed. Mueller had found people profoundly different from himself, and he attended the little meeting regularly, irresistibly drawn to whatever made them different. Here he understood the gospel for the first time, and put his faith in Christ. Over the next few months, the young man who had made so many failed resolutions found that for the first time in his life he was able to begin shedding, one by one, the habits and influences that had seemed so inextricably woven into the fabric of his life—the drinking, the lying, the companions he knew were a destructive influence. "What all my own resolutions could not bring about," Mueller would later write, "I was enabled to do, constrained by the love of Jesus." Just as forgiveness for sins can come only through the blood of Christ, Mueller found, "the individual who desires to get power over sin, must likewise seek it through the blood of Jesus."[13]

A New Start and A New Future

With all his thoughts about his life and future transformed by this new reality, Mueller began almost immediately to think and pray seriously about missionary work— essentially an opposite path to the comfort, financial stability, and social prestige he and his father had planned for him to enjoy as the minister of a prosperous state-sanctioned church. Mueller wrote to his family, telling them of his conversion and new life, and soon he visited his father to ask for his permission to pursue missionary service. Perhaps he expected his father to be pleased at the change in his wild and troublesome son; if so, he was disappointed. Mueller's father was disgusted and angered by this sudden outbreak of religious fanaticism. He wanted his son to settle down to a respectable and profitable career, not to be carried away with enthusiasm for these strange new ideas. Angrily, he reminded George of all the money he had spent on his son's education, hoping that in his old age he might have a comfortable home in the parsonage George would have, thanks to his father's investment. How could all his hopes come to nothing? If his father had been nothing but angry, it might not have been difficult for George Mueller to stand firm, but suddenly, to his dismay, his father began to weep, begging his son to reconsider. This, far more than his father's anger, gave George great pain, but he was unable to give his father the assurance he wanted. Mueller still had two years of university left, but he now felt that he ought to begin paying his own way. After all, it did not seem right to

---

12   Ibid. 9.
13   Ibid. 10.

take his father's money when he had no intention of pursuing the career the money was intended to purchase for him. Taking advantage of his father's generosity and diverting his father's money to his own purposes had characterized the past, but he knew things must be different now. He wanted to be fair to his father, and he needed to feel free to rely on God's guidance and provision alone.

For the first time in his life, George Mueller—who had spent so much of his life scheming and maneuvering to get his hands on plenty of money—found himself in a situation where he felt confident that he must turn away from a reliable source of money, without having any idea what would replace it. And in this formative moment, Mueller saw God open a door in response to his prayers. Through a friend and mentor, Mueller was offered a steady job teaching German to a group of Americans who had arrived to study at the university, and for the next two years, Mueller finished his degree and supported himself by teaching German. His fragile faith was greatly strengthened by this very prompt, tangible answer to a specific prayer, and by seeing that God could and would provide in His own way for the young man who, in the old days, never seemed to have enough money no matter how he pleaded, schemed, borrowed, and stole.

This financial provision in answer to prayer was not the only way in which Mueller's remaining university years foreshadowed the major themes of his future life and ministry. He also had the opportunity during this time of receiving two months' free lodging on the grounds of a well-known orphanage, founded a century earlier by A. H. Francke, a German Christian who had depended entirely upon God for the financial survival of the ministry. Though the young George Mueller was years away from the first thought of founding an orphanage of his own, Francke's story would later make a profound impact on Mueller's future.

Mueller also spent more and more of his time preaching in the churches to which he was invited as a visiting speaker, and he carried gospel tracts in his pockets whenever he went out and looked for opportunities to share with his fellow students and with others the gospel of Christ's redemption—something he felt he had spent most of his life without ever hearing clearly. A concern for the souls around him and a commitment to praying for them characterized Mueller from his very earliest days as a believer—nor did he find it difficult to identify with the drunks, criminals, and other social "failures" many prosperous professing Christians looked down on with fascinated horror, as if they were another species altogether. Mueller's past taught him that financial privilege, social standing, and a good education might conceal greed, dishonesty, and drunkenness, but might not even restrain, and certainly could not cure them. His own failures had prepared him in ways he had not yet glimpsed for a life spent largely in ministry to those at the very bottom of the social ladder.

Struggling and Failing

Despite his sincerity and enthusiasm, in some ways Mueller did not yet have much to offer the many with whom he eagerly shared his new faith. In fact, the periods of temptation, discouragement, and failure he experienced during his first years as a Christian were just as foundational to his future as the bright moments of joy and victory, and the lessons they taught him would prove just as vital.

Before he was a Christian, the young Mueller had proven to himself again and again that he could not reform his character as he would have liked. Even during the times when he got his drinking or spending or other destructive habits under control, the deep-seated hypocrisy of his motives, and of his attitudes toward other people, seemed only to gain a stronger hold over him. He had already seen that his "second birth" into new life as a Christian, and the power of the indwelling Holy Spirit in his life, could produce changes in his life he had never been able to achieve through will power or strategy or any number of fresh starts. But he realized now in his overworked and isolated final years as a student that he could still fail in the same dismally familiar ways if he relied on the self-confident determination that had failed him so often in the past, and if he fell back on the same habits and neglected what he called the "means of grace" that could nurture and sustain his newborn spiritual life.

Driving himself relentlessly to write and study for up to fourteen hours a day, Mueller grew exhausted and depressed, and on several occasions found himself turning once again to the old comfort of alcohol, while for "many days . . . prayer was entirely given up," and he also found himself worried and discouraged about money. But, Mueller would later write, "How good was the Lord!" for the overtired, discouraged, and dangerously isolated young man found it impossible to drift back into the old channels. Again and again, he found that God's grace pursued him whether he pursued it or not. The old comfort he had found in alcohol, and the old ability to convince himself he was not overdoing things, were gone:

> For whilst in my ungodly days I had drunk once about five quarts of strong beer in one afternoon . . . I could now take only two or three glasses before the

wickedness of my conduct was brought before me, and my conscience told me that I drank merely for the sake of drinking, and thus I gave it up.[14]

His former ability to harden and accustom himself to things he knew were wrong had also forsaken him, Mueller would later write, for "I was still so weak that I fell repeatedly into open sins, yet could not continue in them, nay, not even for a few days, without sorrow of heart, confession before God, and fleeing to the blood of the Lamb."[15]

Even his attempt to borrow money from a wealthy philanthropist brought an unexpected and badly needed message to the struggling young man. Anxious to help an impoverished relative, and to pay off—at long last—the last of his debt for the disastrous and dishonest Switzerland trip, Mueller wrote to the rich and titled lady of whose generosity to other individuals and causes he had heard. In the letter he asked her to lend him the money and also, as an afterthought, shared the gospel with her and briefly told his own story of salvation. After hearing nothing by the time a reply could certainly have been expected, Mueller found himself growing both depressed and bitter—in his own words, "very wretched," largely due to physical exhaustion. "What have I now gained by becoming a Christian?" Mueller asked himself, and he wandered about the dark, cold January streets, trying in vain to cheer himself up by wasting money he could not afford on a piece of cake in a confectioner's shop.

But that afternoon a packet arrived in the mail, containing the sum of money he had requested, and also a letter from a completely different person, entirely unknown to Mueller, in whose hands his original and mistakenly addressed note had ended up. The letter reported that, in fact, the lady to whom Mueller had addressed his letter was not the philanthropist he had wanted to reach, nor had she ever been at the address he used. But the unknown writer continued:

> But that I may lessen in some measure the difficulties in which you seem to be, I send you the enclosed small sum, for which you may thank, not the unknown giver, but the Lord, who turneth the hearts like rivers of water. Hold fast the faith which God has given you by His Holy Spirit; it is the most precious treasure in this life, and it contains in itself true happiness. Only seek by watching and prayer more and more to be delivered from all vanity and self-complacency, by which even the true believer may be ensnared when he least expects it. Let it be your chief aim to be more and more humble, faithful, and quiet. May we not belong to those who say and write continually, "Lord, Lord" but who have

---

14   Ibid. 19.
15   Ibid. 16-17.

Him not deeply in their hearts. Christianity consists not in words, but in power. There must be life in us. For therefore, God loved us first that we might love Him in return; and that living we might receive power to be faithful to Him, and to conquer ourselves, the world, distress, and death. May His Spirit strengthen you for this, that you may be an able messenger of His Gospel!

The anonymous letter was signed, "An Adoring Worshipper of the Saviour, Jesus Christ."[16] Mueller would write decades later:

I saw in some measure, at the time when I received this letter, how much I needed such a faithful, and, at the same time, loving word of admonition; but I have seen it more fully since. Self-complacency, and a want of quietness, and saying and writing more frequently "Lord, Lord" than acknowledging Him by my life as such. These were the evils against which at that time I particularly needed to be cautioned, and up to this day I am still much, very much, lacking in these points, though the Lord . . . has done much for me . . . since that time.[17]

The need for authentic fellowship with other believers was one of the great lessons Mueller learned at this time, a period during which he would sometimes walk fifteen miles to hear an encouraging, compelling sermon that really taught the Word of God, because the opportunity arose so seldom. Mueller also cherished not only the informal meetings he still attended at the home where he had first heard the gospel but also meetings of a group of Christian students who encouraged and prayed for one another. Mueller learned that when he shared honestly with his friends in this group about his coldness of heart and the sins into which he had fallen again, their prayers and encouragement renewed his trust in God. He also found that when, as happened several times, he avoided meeting them because he dreaded being asked about his spiritual life, it was a very bad sign of the state into which he had drifted. "'Forsake not the assembling of yourselves together' is a very important exhortation," Mueller would later write, quoting Hebrews. "Even if we should not derive any special benefit at the time, so far as we are conscious, we may be kept from much harm. And very frequently the beginning of coldness of heart is nourished by keeping away from the meetings of the saints."[18]

Mueller would also grow to recognize as both dangerous and wrong the punishing pace he kept, and his neglect of food, sleep, exercise, and other necessities of physical health. Throughout his life, Mueller would often discern in the relentless, driving pace

---

16 Ibid. 18.
17 Ibid. 18.
18 Ibid. 20.

kept by exhausted men and women the same failure he himself had fallen into—a failure to trust God's care of him, and a failure to cultivate the right priorities. A true understanding of God's faithfulness to guide and provide for His children, Mueller would come to believe, should give Christians the freedom to carve out the times of rest, sleep, and prayer they need to guard their health. During these early years, Mueller would later feel, he laid himself open to unnecessary temptation and discouragement by being reckless with his physical health, and driving himself into exhaustion.

Another dangerous lack Mueller would later identify in his own life during this time was a lack of reading the Bible—a habit he had never been taught and which does not seem to have even occurred to him during these early years as a Christian. He did indeed lay aside the novels he had once devoured, and read eagerly all the religious books he could get his hands on—tracts, commentaries, devotionals, biographies, and whatever else came along. Some of them were helpful, but all of them failed to "endear the Scriptures to me," Mueller believed. Looking back, he recognized clearly how much of his weakness as a new Christian was caused by this deficit, as damaging as the lack of water to a new seedling. He also recognized how irrational his neglect was, in view of his professed belief that the Bible was truly the Word of God. A better chain of reasoning, he would later write, would have been:

> God Himself has condescended to become an author, and I am ignorant about that precious book, which His Holy Spirit has caused to be written through the instrumentality of His servants, and it contains that which I ought to know, and the knowledge of which will lead me to true happiness; therefore I ought to read again and again this most precious book, this book of books, most earnestly, most prayerfully, and with much meditation, and in this practice I ought to continue all the days of my life. For I was aware, though I read it but little, that I knew scarcely anything of it.

Yet the dedicated student who had mastered several languages and who for several years had thought nothing of studying for twelve or fourteen hours a day to understand mathematics or literature or theology was, for the first several years of his Christian life, intimidated and frustrated by the Bible, and as a result he avoided it:

> [I]nstead of acting thus, and being led by my ignorance of the Word of God to study it more, my difficulty in understanding it and the little enjoyment I had in it, made me careless of reading it (for much prayerful reading of the Word, gives not merely more knowledge, but increases the delight we have in reading it);

and thus, like many believers, I practically preferred . . . the works of uninspired men to the Oracles of the living God. The consequence was that I remained a babe, both in knowledge and grace . . . And as I neglected the Word, I was for nearly four years so ignorant, that I did not clearly know even the fundamental points of our holy faith. And this lack of knowledge most sadly kept me back from walking steadily in the ways of God. For it is the truth that makes us free . . . by delivering us from the slavery of the lust of the flesh, the lust of the eyes, and the pride of life . . . . If the reader understands very little of the Word of God, he ought to read it very much; for the Spirit explains the Word by the Word. And if he enjoys the reading of the Word little, that is just the reason why he should read it much; for the frequent reading of the Scriptures creates a delight in them, so that the more we read them, the more we desire to do so.[19]

Graduation and Plans for the Future

Despite his struggles, Mueller still felt drawn to foreign missions, and was committed to spending his life on something more important than his own comfort and prosperity. "With all my weakness," he would recall years later, "I had a great desire to live wholly for God."[20] His first plan, influenced by the suggestion of a mentor and by the example of a missionary whose story made a great impact on Mueller, was to serve as a missionary to the Jews of Eastern Europe. A plan of going to Bucharest was disrupted by the outbreak of war in Eastern Europe, but soon he was offered the opportunity to serve as a missionary among the Jews of Poland, replacing the very missionary whose example had affected Mueller so powerfully. There seemed no reason not to at least pursue this opportunity, and Mueller began to move in that direction.

The first obstacle was the mandatory three years of military service required of every young Prussian man, but this problem was unexpectedly resolved when Mueller suffered a broken blood vessel of the stomach. This emergency caused a life-threatening illness that required immediate treatment, undermined Mueller's health for years to come, and produced an official exemption from military service for the sick young man. Mueller had to spend some time in Berlin for treatment, and while there he had the chance to visit and preach often at both a poorhouse and a prison—another preparation, although he could not know it, for the ministry awaiting him.

When he was well enough and the paperwork for his military exemption was complete, Mueller sailed for London, where the English mission agency that would be sending him

---

19   Ibid. 20-21.
20   Ibid. 23.

to Poland had asked him to spend several months in training, preparation, and getting to know his future leaders and coworkers. Mueller had at first been very disappointed to learn he would be expected to spend this time in London. He felt, understandably, that he had already spent a very long time studying hard, and he was eager to go straight to his new home and begin his new ministry, rather than finding himself a student once again. But he accepted the necessity as the will of God, and arrived in England resigned to spending several months there. He would in fact spend the rest of his life.

Early Days in England

George Mueller arrived in London in March of 1829, and immediately began his seminary studies in Hebrew, as well as trying to improve his spoken English. But he was still recovering from what had been a life-threatening illness, and in May he had such a severe relapse that it seemed he would not survive. For at least two weeks, he lay sick in a room he was not expected to leave again. When, after all, he began to recover, he was urged to spend some time in the country by the sea to regain his health, and so traveled into the beautiful countryside of Devonshire to breathe the sea air and to find his strength again among the green fields. Though Mueller didn't realize it, God was answering his prayers for guidance and opportunity, for it was here and not in London that the foundations of Mueller's future work were being laid. It was here that Mueller met his close friend and future partner for many decades, Henry Craik; it was here that he first visited Ebenezer Chapel where he would find a wife and a calling; it was here that his relationship with the Bible was transformed.

During his recovery, Mueller determined to try an experiment. He laid aside the commentaries he had been studying and spent time "simply reading the Word of God and studying it. The result of this was that the first evening I shut myself into my room to give myself to prayer and meditation over the Scriptures, I learned more in a few hours than I had done during a period of several months previously . . . I received real strength for my soul in doing so."[21] For the rest of his life, his love for the Word of God would shape and undergird Mueller's days. The immediacy and intimacy of his relationship with the Bible would become characteristic of a man who would later estimate that he had probably read through the entire Bible two hundred times in his life, and who, in his old age when there were fewer demands on his time, often read it through four times in a year. He considered it especially important to read regularly through the entirety of both the Old and New

---

21   Ibid. 33.

Testaments because otherwise, all readers inevitably tend to read the same favorite portions again and again in isolation from their context, and to neglect other, equally important passages. He also stressed the importance of meditating on and praying through the passages read, and adopted a lifelong practice of reading from both the Old and New Testaments in the morning, and meditating throughout the day on what he had read.

With both his perspective on the future and his devotional life completely transformed by an illness he had not expected to survive, Mueller returned to the London seminary. Here he shared his newfound joy in the Scriptures with his friends, meeting with a group of fellow students from six to eight each morning to pray, read the Bible together, and share what they had learned from the reading. He also resumed his grueling study of Hebrew, eager to complete his training and begin his ministry, but almost immediately, his health began to break down under the strain. Mueller began to realize that his body would never be the same again and that it would no longer stand the strain of twelve- to fourteen-hour days of study. Convinced now that he would probably not live long enough to complete his studies and work among the Jews of Poland, Mueller felt a growing urgency to make his remaining time count, and petitioned the missionary agency to let him begin active ministry right away. While waiting to hear back from them, Mueller began to visit the predominantly Jewish areas of London to meet with and witness to Jewish men and boys.

The London mission agency with which Mueller had planned to work was slow in finding an assignment for him, and during the delay Mueller came to feel that he should not be so dependent on an organization to direct him, and should look only to God for guidance and for financial provision. He told the mission agency he would like to serve without any salary, anywhere he could be of use. The mission agency no longer felt that this unconventional young man was a good fit for them, and the connection was eventually severed. Once again Mueller was free to go wherever God might send him—and once again he could depend only on God's guidance and faithfulness for some way to put bread on the table. England was to have been a stepping stone to Poland, but with no more connection to the agency that was going to send him there, Mueller was at loose ends in London.

Marriage and Ministry at Ebenezer Chapel

Ebenezer Chapel, the very church Mueller had visited during his illnesses and where he had already formed a strong friendship with Henry Craik, now asked Mueller to be their pastor, despite the reluctance of some members to adjust to his foreign accent and culture. Seeing this as the next, indeed the only, open door God had shown him, Mueller accepted. He would return to the church and the community he had visited as a convalescent, there to make his first home and begin his first ministry as someone who was, at long last, no longer a student.

Not only did he find a home and an opportunity at Ebenezer but he also found love. Mueller, who had been praying for the virtuous wife Proverbs describes as a gift from the Lord, fell in love with and married his first wife, Mary Groves, a woman who shared his commitment to absolute trust in God. This became obvious immediately, for about a month after the wedding, Mueller, who had been growing more and more uncomfortable with the idea of receiving a regular salary for his ministry, announced to the church that he would no longer do so. Much of his concern came from the fact that the pastor's salary was largely funded by pew rents, a system which favored the rich who could afford comfortable seats during church services and burdened the poor who might not be able to afford a seat at all. But Mueller also felt that if he was doing work God had directed him to do, God could supply his needs with or without a set salary, and Mueller recognized in himself a tendency to place in the comforting rhythm of a paycheck the faith he ought to place in God alone. Instead, he asked that a box be installed in which contributions to his support could be anonymously dropped. Through the first years of their marriage, Mueller and his wife became more and more convinced that God's direction for them was to rid themselves of any temptation to rely on anyone or anything but Him.

Soon, the stories for which George Mueller is famous began to accumulate, as time after time God provided money for the young couple in many startling ways, often just in the nick of time. Often the couple had literally no money, but always, when there was a pressing need for food or some other expense arose, the provision would appear. Once, Mueller would remember, he had the equivalent of about two dollars, and he and Mary prayed for money. They waited for several hours, and then a lady arrived at their house and demanded, "Do you want money?" Mueller's heartbeat must have quickened, but he was determined not to ask for money, and he replied truthfully, "I told the brethren, dear sister, when I gave up my salary, that I would for the future tell the Lord only about my wants."

"But He has told me to give you some money," the woman replied, pulling the money out of her purse.[22]

---

22   Ibid. 47-48.

Another time, the Muellers lacked enough food for the day. As they sat down to lunch, Mueller prayed for "our daily bread," meaning quite literally, as his wife knew, that he asked God for enough food for their evening meal. While he was praying, there was a knock at the door, and in came a woman (quite poor herself) who had brought part of her own dinner to share with the pastor's family, and some money from another woman in the church.[23]

The practices that would be foundational to Mueller's handling of money for the rest of his life were all established during this time: the refusal to incur debt of any kind so that no money rightfully belonging to someone else might be risked by the choices he made; the practice of giving away extra money rather than saving it for the future; the commitment to praying rather than sharing his financial needs with others; and the habit of recording the minutiae of his financial transactions in order to strengthen his own faith and that of others by telling the story of God's faithfulness. Through his first year without a salary, Mueller kept a careful record of every penny coming into or going out of his little household, and he wrote of this record: "Now the truth is whilst we have not had even as much as a single penny left, or so as to have the last bread on the table, and not as much as was needed to buy another loaf, yet never have we had to sit down to a meal without our good Lord having provided nourishing food for us." In fact, Mueller realized at the end of the year (1831) that the money he and his wife received amounted to a total more than double the salary he had refused— though much had been given away.[24]

Even the crisis of Mary Mueller's life-threatening illness after the stillbirth of the couple's first child—an illness which lasted six weeks and brought an avalanche of unanticipated expenses—strengthened the couple's confidence that it was faith, not carelessness or selfishness, that prompted their decision to reject a regular salary. Both of the medical attendants who nursed Mary Mueller through her dangerous illness refused to accept a penny for their services, but many medicines and special foods and other provisions for the recovering invalid were abundantly supplied through the unsolicited gifts that came in response to prayer.

The loss of his first child and the near loss of his wife also made Mueller aware of unsuspected selfishness and carelessness in his own life. Although everyone who knew the couple had witnessed his delight in Mary and their happiness together, the

---

23 Harvey 39-40.
24 Ibid. 41.

young husband realized through this brush with tragedy that he had much room to grow in his valuing and cherishing the blessing of a wife and children, and feeling the true weight of his responsibilities as a husband. He had, he realized, not rejoiced as he should have at the prospect of being entrusted with a child, but had thought more frequently of the burden or the inconvenience of this added responsibility—and he had not grasped the reality of the ease with which he might lose his precious Mary, and of the true dangers of childbirth which claimed many lives in the early nineteenth century. He had not prayed for his wife as he should have, Mueller realized. Never again would he take for granted the treasure of this courageous woman who so fully embraced the unpredictable life of faith and service to which he felt called. Mueller would emerge from this experience with a new sense of awe and thankfulness at the gift of his beloved wife, and when at last they were blessed with a child he was ready to welcome fatherhood with delight. He also gained a new awareness of the subtle selfishness that can so easily creep into even the sincerest desires, and the need to pray for victory over this selfishness and carelessness. And even as he realized more fully the value of the precious treasure he entrusted to God in his wife and children, he also felt renewed confidence in God's faithfulness to guard the treasure with far more tender care than he ever could. A new joy, a new seriousness, and a new depth of tenderness grew in the happy home of the pastor of Ebenezer Chapel as Mary recovered her strength.[25]

Bristol

After two and a half years at this little church, however, Mueller began to grow restless. He felt more and more drawn to his opportunities to speak in other congregations, and less and less settled at Ebenezer. He felt that his work there was done, and his heart was stirred by an invitation from his friend Henry Craik to join him in his work in Bristol, a teeming city on the coast. Shortly after the Muellers began to pray about this possible change, Mueller was invited by a small Bristol congregation, Gideon Chapel, to be their pastor. Thus, at the age of twenty-six, Mueller and his wife left behind the sweet air and green fields of the countryside, and the tight-knit community of a small town. They moved to the city in which he would spend most of the rest of his life, and took up the leadership of a small congregation, and the work of sharing the gospel with the people who lived and worked in vast, grimy Bristol.

---

25   Pierson 74-75.

The arrival of the Muellers in Bristol was shortly followed by a cholera epidemic which ravaged the city. Cholera was the scourge of nineteenth-century European cities which, in the wake of the Industrial Revolution, had ballooned in population, catastrophically overloading the medieval infrastructure of cities such as London, Paris, and Bristol—cities where torrents of people flowed into overcrowded slums that had been built for exponentially smaller numbers of occupants. Bristol, for example, had been home to an estimated 27,000 in 1700, while by 1802, around thirty years before the Muellers' arrival, the still-expanding population had numbered around 330,000.[26]

Such overcrowding, combined with an approach to sewage management which often amounted to little more than emptying raw sewage into ditches, streams, and rivers, gave rise to the terrifying outbreaks of cholera—a waterborne illness that spreads most easily when drinking water is contaminated with infected sewage—that haunted Europe throughout the early nineteenth century.

Class prejudices associated cholera with the supposed unsanitary lifestyles and moral degeneracy of the poor, in whose neglected and overcrowded areas of the city cholera raged with greater frequency and severity than among the wealthy who had access to clean water. These assumptions lent weight to the predominant scientific theory that cholera was an airborne disease, bred in the noticeably stinking slums. This blend of scientific error and cultural prejudice not only retarded the eventual discovery of cholera's true cause but also fueled the vicious spread of a disease whose dehydrated victims could be relieved only by drinking more of the same contaminated water that had sickened them. Cholera was also horrifically easy to spread from patient to caregiver. The very hands of the exhausted, terrified mothers, devoted siblings, and grieving spouses who nursed the sick spread the infection through families and neighborhoods as they offered water to the victims' desperate thirst and tried to keep beds, bodies, and rooms clean.

The mystery and misinformation surrounding the true cause of cholera made an especially terrifying disease because of its seemingly unpredictable spread, its high death toll, and the appalling speed with which it struck. A cholera victim could be dead twenty-four hours after the very first mild sensation of minor indigestion or an uneasy stomach. A household could be decimated in a weekend. The eerie feeling that you might see a friend in the market or at the pub one day, and hear three days later that he was dead,

---

26 "Industrial Change in Bristol Since 1800." Accessed May 30, 2022. www.humanities.uwe.ac.uk/bhr/Main/industry/intro_industry.htm.

spread fear with a speed equaled only by the deadly bacillus itself. "Our neighbor Mrs. Williams, a few yards from us, was attacked about 3 this morning, and died about 3 this afternoon," wrote Mueller's colleague Henry Craik. "The bell is incessantly tolling; it is an awful time."[27]

The new pastors, George Mueller and Henry Craik, threw themselves into ministering to the victims of the epidemic, visiting the sick and dying to pray and to share the hope of the gospel, bringing what relief they could. "I have never realized so much the nearness of death," Mueller wrote. "Just now, ten in the evening, the funeral bell is ringing, and has been ringing the greater part of the evening. It rings almost all the day. Into Thine hands, O Lord, I commend myself."[28] Not only, however, did both Craik and Mueller remain healthy, but George and Mary Mueller's second baby (and only child to survive infancy), a daughter named Lydia, was also born into the midst of this terror, almost exactly at the halfway point of a three-month epidemic. She was born at a time when both parents knew that she might easily be swept away by the epidemic, and that it was just as likely she might lose one or both of her parents to it. Yet the cholera epidemic only made it clearer than ever that God either preserves life or takes it away, and the Muellers were able to welcome the daughter who would survive to bring such joy to their home in the coming years. (A little boy born several years later would not survive early childhood.)

Whether in spite or because of the terrible epidemic that had welcomed the two new pastors of Gideon and Bethesda Chapels (one was George Mueller's congregation and one Henry Craik's), both the numerical and the spiritual growth of the two congregations and their impact on the communities around them were immediate and striking. In the shadow of cholera, people were forced to confront mortality and the question of eternity, and many came to faith in Christ. Mueller reported that the "inquirers' meetings" held for those who wanted to know more about the gospel were "so largely attended that though they sometimes lasted for more than four hours, it was frequently the case that many had to be sent away for lack of time and strength on the part of the two workers."[29] And this was the case despite the practice both Mueller and Craik had instituted of set times to be available for private meetings and counseling with individuals.

---

27   Steer, Roger. *George Mueller: Delighted in God! History Makers series.* Christian Focus Publishing. Tain, UK. Reprinted 2012. Page 47.
28   Harvey 46-47.
29   Ibid. 48.

Despite the obvious fruitfulness and almost limitless opportunity of his new home and ministry in Bristol, however, Mueller had never—and never would—cease to think often of the needs of the rest of the world, and to pray and wonder about taking the gospel to places where it was virtually unknown. Thus, the sudden invitation to both the Mueller and Craik families to join missionary work in Bagdad presented Mueller with a tempting opportunity and a very difficult choice. Both couples spent countless hours in prayer, and discussion, unable to lean one way or the other and waiting on some clear direction from God. Gradually, however, the intense poverty of the teeming city around him was growing more and more real to George Mueller, and he felt both a growing burden for these hordes of desperate human beings, and a growing recognition of the many ways in which he and his family were uniquely prepared and positioned to serve and reach them. His feeling of being called to and settled in Bristol gradually grew, and eventually both Craik and Mueller separately felt peace in turning down the Bagdad opportunity, however alluring they found it. For the next decades of his life, George Mueller would faithfully visit many foreign lands in his daily prayers, but his own feet would be planted in Bristol—both in his little church, and in the Dickensian slums where the new urban poor of the Industrial Revolution struggled for survival, for decency, and for hope.

The Scriptural Knowledge Institution

Still acutely conscious, however, of the overwhelming spiritual needs not only of Bristol but also of the wide world, in 1834 Mueller and Craik established a society to found day schools and Sunday schools for both children and adults, to distribute Bibles, and to send financial aid to foreign missions. "The Scriptural Knowledge Institution, for Home and Abroad," would become an important aspect of Craik's and Mueller's ministry and legacy, and would have a worldwide impact outlasting its founders. Mueller continued the adventure of faith he had been living by agreeing with Craik that the society would never ask for patronage and never go into debt, and would trust God to stir the hearts of those He would have to provide financial support. The goals of the organization would include supporting missionaries overseas, selling inexpensive Bibles and New Testaments to those wishing to own them, supporting day schools where adults could learn basic literacy and be taught the Bible, and other activities focused on sharing the gospel. But it would also focus on the children of Bristol, through Bible classes specially geared to younger listeners, and through day schools offering rudimentary education to children who spent their days on the streets or in the factories.

Concern for Orphans

It was through these day schools that the seed of an idea first took root in Mueller's mind. The swarms of orphan children who crowded the slums and almshouses, the victims of history and of the appalling callousness castigated by Dickens during this same period, needed so much more—so much more than a few hours of kindness and instruction before they were thrown back into the cesspool of poverty and crime. It was hard to know which children faced the most terrible hardship—the employed or the beggars, those navigating a precarious life on the streets or those living on the harsh, demoralizing "charity" of the workhouses. Mueller was not alone in recoiling from the horror of seeing the poverty and desperation of countless children—Charles Dickens' novel *Oliver Twist* would famously awaken the public conscience to the plight of orphans shortly after Mueller began his work focused specifically on orphans. But the nation was still overwhelmed by the exploding population of orphans and street children produced by the Industrial Revolution—children whose pinched, malnourished faces have come down to us in photographs, and who often bore the scars of horrifying industrial accidents in the dangerous mines and factories where they might work ten hours a day for barely enough money to buy food. The national conscience was slowly awakening to a sense of responsibility for these desperate children, but as Mueller's biographer writes, "in the whole of England and Wales it is possible to trace a dozen orphanages which date back to the 1830s or earlier. They were all small and there was none in Bristol."[30] Furthermore, many of the orphanages which did exist were designed to provide for well-to-do, "respectable" children of documented parentage left orphans by death. For the countless born to or abandoned by desperate unmarried mothers, drunken fathers, or starving, illiterate widows, for the many whose parents were disabled or killed by the dangerous work of the mines and factories, for those who suffered the diseases and deformities of malnutrition and poverty, there was no welcome anywhere.[31]

Mueller had been deeply moved by the desperation of the many child beggars in Bristol when he first arrived there, and he consistently channeled as much money as he could toward offering them some relief. The plight of a young boy who, for a time, attended one of Mueller's day schools but was then sent away to the poorhouse struck Mueller particularly. And during the days and weeks when he was thinking more and more of the possibility of founding an orphan's home of some kind, Mueller stumbled

---

30   Steer 54.
31   Ibid. 54-55.

once again upon the biography of A. H. Franke, the German founder of the orphanage in which Mueller had briefly stayed as a student. Franke had built several private orphan homes relying entirely upon unsolicited donations and trusting God to provide, just as Mueller himself had done in the founding of the Scriptural Knowledge Institute. The rediscovery of Franke's story seemed like confirmation to Mueller, who had been devoting more and more time, thought, and prayer to the possibility of founding an orphanage. The very day after reading the book, Mueller wrote in his diary, "To-day I have had it very much impressed on my heart, no longer merely to think about the establishment of an Orphan-House, but actually to set about it . . . "[32] As he continued to pray and plan, Mueller records that he was struck by Psalm 81:10: "Open thy mouth wide, and I will fill it." Even to consider starting an orphanage, with no money, no experience, and no help, was to open his mouth very wide indeed. But Mueller knew God could fill it.

It is difficult for modern readers to grasp how revolutionary Mueller's plan was—as Steer notes, "private orphan homes were regarded as revolutionary experiments,"[33] and, as we have seen, they were undertaken not for the benefit of the truly desperate, but for the comparatively privileged. The children Mueller hoped to reach were widely assumed to belong in the workhouse—they were often seen as tainted or infected with moral as well as physical contagion. Having been brought up to drink, swear, steal, and engage in all the unspeakable vices middle-class English families did not want to imagine their own sheltered and carefully nurtured children capable of, they were viewed with horror as well as with compassion. They not only *had* a problem; they *were* a problem. As Dickens' Ebenezer Scrooge so memorably pointed out, the prisons and the workhouses were seen by some as adequate provision for those who could not or would not earn their keep. Mueller's own history uniquely suited him to realize, not only that wealthy and privileged children were capable of the same sins the orphans were suspected of and condemned for, but also that the grace and compassion of God overflowed all limits set by human fear or prejudice.

Proving the Faithfulness of God

Mueller's concern was not only for the desperate orphans, however. It was also for the many Christians he knew in Bristol who seemed to be struggling just as much as their non-Christian neighbors, swept along by the relentless competitive struggle for economic survival. Those who came out on top of the expanding capitalist economy

---

32   Ibid. 55.
33   Ibid. 54.

could be just as much its victims as those who ended up on the bottom. Mueller was struck by a conversation he had with one man who worked sixteen hours a day and found that both his physical and spiritual health were suffering badly under the strain. Mueller urged him to consider working fewer hours so that his health might improve and he might have the time he needed for prayer and Bible reading. The man's response was, "But if I work less, I do not earn enough for the support of my family. Even now, whilst I work so much, I have scarcely enough. The wages are so low that I must work hard in order to obtain what I need." Mueller replied, "My dear brother, it is not your work which supports your family, but the Lord; and He who has fed you and your family when you could not work at all, on account of illness, would surely provide for you and yours, if, for the sake of obtaining food for your inner man, you were to work only for so many hours a day, as would allow you proper time [for private prayer and study]. And is it not the case now, that you begin the work of the day after having had only a few hurried minutes for prayer; and when you leave off your work in the evening, and mean then to read a little of the word of God, are you not too much worn out in body and mind, to enjoy it, and do you not often fall asleep . . . ?" Mueller could read in his friend's face that he agreed with the advice, but did not believe it was possible to follow it. "How should I get on?" he asked doubtfully. "How should I get on if I carried out your advice?" Mueller realized that his friend did not really believe he could trust God to take care of his family, and Mueller found himself wishing that he could point to some concrete example "that would act as visible proof that our God and Father is the same faithful God as ever he was; as willing as ever to prove Himself to be the living God, in our day as formerly, to all who put their trust in Him."[34] How sad it was if the church had furnished this man with no such living examples—and how many might be strengthened and blessed if such an example were to be lived out in their own neighborhood, before their very eyes.

Mueller also knew men who professed to be Christians but who succumbed to the relentless temptations of doing business with less than perfect honesty in order to compete in the ruthless environment of nineteenth-century capitalism. They carried a wearing burden of guilt over this contrast between their professed beliefs and their practice, but defended themselves by arguing that if they truly committed with no reservation to conducting their business lives according to Biblical principles they would never survive in the real world, and their families would starve. Such men too, Mueller felt, needed both the rebuke and the encouragement of seeing God faithfully provide

34   Ibid. 57.

in the daily financial and practical details of an operation committed entirely to His direction and provision.[35] Perhaps Mueller's own formative experiences with money, and his memories of being so controlled by it and so desperate for it in his early years that every good resolution or pang of conscience was swept away by his fear of being without it, played a part in giving him eyes to see how the peace and the testimony of his fellow Christians were being eroded by the instincts and assumptions of the commercial city in which they lived. In any case, Mueller longed not only to see God meet the needs of the desperate poor left behind by the booming Bristol business world, but also to see the Christian church embracing and embodying a robust confidence in a real God Who intervened in real lives and solved real problems. As Mueller himself summed up:

> I certainly did from my heart desire to be used by God to benefit the bodies of poor children, bereaved of both parents, and seek, in other respects, with the help of God, to do them good for this life;—I also particularly longed to be used by God in getting the dear orphans trained up in the fear of God;—but still, the first and primary object of the work was that God might be magnified by the fact, that the orphans under my care are provided, with all they need, only by *prayer* and *faith*, without anyone being asked by me or my fellow-labourers, whereby it may be seen that GOD IS FAITHFUL STILL and HEARS PRAYER STILL. (emphasis original)[36]

Plans for the First Orphanage

Mueller began to pray that God would open the way if it was right to proceed with the establishment of an orphanage. In the next couple of weeks, Mueller received the first gift of money for the orphanage—one shilling. He was also given a large wardrobe.[37] And almost immediately after Craik and Mueller shared the orphanage plan with their churches in December of 1835, two people volunteered to serve in the orphanage once it came into being. For the rest of the winter, gifts poured in steadily—gifts of money, furniture, dishes, and everything else that might be of use. A house was rented, and an opening date was set for April 1836.

Mueller had decided that this first home would welcome girls between the ages of seven and twelve who might find a permanent home there until, in their teens, they were able to find jobs in domestic service. This population was especially vulnerable in an

---

35 Ibid. 57-58.
36 Mueller 81.
37 Harvey 65-66.

economy where even the lowest jobs in household service were often unavailable to those without training or references, and where prostitution often seemed the only alternative.

But when at last the house was prepared and furnished, the staff engaged, and everything ready, not a single child had applied for admission. Mueller realized that for months he had labored in prayer over every aspect of the new orphanage, from the repairs on the building to the women to staff it to the money to buy food, but had never once thought of asking God to send the children who would live in it! So vast and so obvious was the need all around him that he had simply assumed there would be orphans to fill the new home. It was a reminder Mueller would never forget that he could and should ask God directly and specifically for every decision and every need. He prayed that the children God wanted the new home to care for might be sent, and he received the first application the next day. Over the succeeding month, he would hear from forty-two children seeking admission.[38]

Establishment and Growth of the Orphan Homes

A second house, soon filled with younger children of both sexes, followed less than a year after the opening of the first, and about ten months after that, in October of 1837, a third house opened, this one for boys. At the end of 1837, there were 81 children in the three homes, cared for by nine volunteer workers. The orphanage continued to grow, and in 1846 Mueller would purchase land outside the crowded city on which to build a house. Here the children could have space for a playground and a garden, away from the pollution of the city, and with no danger of inconveniencing neighbors as they had begun to do. In June of 1849, the children were able to move from the three houses in town to the newly finished, much larger building designed and built especially for them. The money for the land, the building, and the much larger expenses had all been supplied in answer to Mueller's daily prayers for 607 days.[39]

And the rest is history. A second house would follow the first, then a third, a fourth, and finally a fifth in 1870, thirty-five years after Mueller first began to pray that God would supply enough money to open an orphanage. During this period of more than three decades, Mueller had seen with increasing joy and confidence the money, the staff, and everything else needed for the orphan homes supplied in answer to prayer, without borrowing a cent and without fundraising of any kind. Sometimes the supply

---

38   Harvey 66.
39   Mueller 258-259.

was spectacular and overwhelming—like the time the owner of the land Mueller wished to buy for the first orphan house awoke at three AM and lay awake for two hours, during which time he felt compelled to offer Mueller the land for 120 pounds an acre instead of 200; or the gift of two thousand pounds that came in just before building began; or the gift of a thousand pounds of rice.[40] Other times it was on the smallest imaginable scale, like the time a single penny was needed to purchase dinner and a single penny tumbled out of the collection box, or the time Mueller received twelve shillings and sixpence for the sale of rags and bones, noting "As a steward of public money, I feel it right that even those articles should be turned into money; nor could we expect answers to our prayers if knowingly there were any waste allowed in connection with the work."[41] Often there were astonishing stories of God's faithfulness and generosity behind the gifts—a tiny legacy of money, all he had, left to the home that had sheltered him by one of the orphan boys who knew he was dying, or virtually her entire life savings donated by a poor seamstress who assured Mueller she could trust God for enough to live on during her remaining years. The gifts came from anonymous strangers and faithful friends, from around the world and from down the street, from those who had no idea why they felt compelled to send the money and from those who joined Mueller and the other volunteers in praying faithfully for the needs of the orphanages. Sometimes there were seasons of abundance, and sometimes there were seasons of long, hard, uncertainty, when again and again, day after day, for months at a time, there was not enough for the day's needs at the start of the day. Indeed, Mueller always emphasized to those who questioned him the importance of persistence in prayer, and the importance of not avoiding the hard times that strengthen and build faith. He accepted as normal days, weeks, years, even decades of asking for the same thing before receiving a visible answer. But always, just in the nick of time, the answer would come. A knock on the door would bring bread or milk for the children; a letter in the mail would bring a gift of money delayed on its way. As biographer Bonnie Harvey records, "Even when he was responsible for feeding two thousand orphans a day by faith, George testified later that no meal was ever more than thirty minutes late!"[42]

During the more than three decades during which the orphanage ministry doubled and redoubled again and again, Mueller continued his ministry at the church where he was a pastor, and with the Institute, including its many day schools for children. Yet one of the most characteristic aspects of Mueller's life was his refusal ever to be too

---

40   Harvey 105; 107.
41   Ibid. 85; 110.
42   Ibid. 70.

busy for the private times of prayer and Bible reading he had found as indispensable to his ministry as to his own spiritual life. Once, in the very early years of the first orphan home, Mueller realized he had begun to find his days too full to spend as much time on his knees as he felt the need to do—overwhelmed as he was by both the opportunities and the incessant needs surrounding him. At this time he was leading a church of about four hundred people, as well as superintending the first two orphanages, each housing thirty children, and participating in the work of the Institute. The thirty-two-year-old Mueller still had no idea of the unimaginable growth of the orphanage ministry that lay ahead, but he already felt an urgent need for wisdom and grace in confronting the opportunities that seemed to be continually opening ahead of him. After a time of struggle, he was at last so convinced of the absolute necessity of his own time for prayer and Bible reading that he began to insist on it more forcefully, telling his friends and coworkers that four hours of work after an hour of prayer would accomplish more than five hours of work without prayer, so that hour of prayer must be each day's first priority.[43] There may never have been a more striking illustration than George Mueller of the truth that a rich devotional life, focused on the Word of God and prayer, feeds and extends a life of grappling with practical needs and pressing social concerns. It does not compete with it.

Nor was Mueller an unworldly dreamer, unaware of the endless practicalities involved in his work. On the contrary, Mueller's incisive, analytical mind and administrative ability were both remarkable—one biographer comments on his consistent attention to detail, his meticulous record-keeping, and his methodical approach to weighing up the pros and cons of a decision.[44] Every ounce of the mental focus and discipline developed so reluctantly during Mueller's student years stood him in good stead as he maintained oversight of a ministry whose size and complexity both grew exponentially throughout his life. Mueller's warmth, patience, and gentleness to those he served and those with whom he worked were equally noticeable—despite his independent approach to ministry, Mueller did not strike those who met or worked with him as exacting, rigid, inflexible, or insistent on his own way. Instead, they commented on his kindness, courtesy, and calm of manner. He seemed less hurried and burdened, rather than more, as his responsibilities grew, and he struck others as warm, lovable, and approachable rather than as intimidating or overbearing.

---

43   Ibid. 69.
44   Steer 234.

Influence and Travel Around the World

Mueller's impact extended far beyond his own ministry. He was distinguished by deep, lifelong friendships with those who found Mueller's friendship and example a source of strength and guidance. His bold ministry of prayer and faith was significant to such pioneering overseas missionaries as William Carey and Hudson Taylor. Mueller gave many the courage to believe that the God who could provide for orphan children in response to prayer and faith could carry on His work around the world, and would not fail those who trusted Him. Mueller did not see the needs of the world or the work of God as divided into opportunities at home and abroad. Rather, he saw God's work in the world as a seamless whole, and believers in every country as praying, giving, and working for the same goals. In the harsh, squalid world of nineteenth-century urban poverty, Mueller's prayers were a living connection between the grace of God and the desperate need of his time. Mueller also left an autobiography which helped countless Christians to a deeper appreciation for God's faithfulness, and challenged those in ministry around the world to a bolder trust in Him.

The final two decades of Mueller's life were strikingly different from but no less demanding than the years of building the orphanages. After the death of his beloved first wife, Mary, Mueller married his second wife, Susannah. He would also live to bury his second wife, but her health was much stronger than Mary's had been, and with her as a companion, Mueller was able to revisit an old dream in his latter years: travel and missionary work around the world. After James Wright, an old and trusted friend and Mueller's son in law, became the director of the orphanages, Mueller, in his seventieth year, set out with Susannah on the first of the seventeen missionary trips around the world that would take him to forty-three countries. During these journeys, Mueller would estimate, he preached thousands of times and spoke to three million people. Never breaking with his settled convictions, Mueller never asked for money or sought to fundraise in any way for these journeys, but instead prayed for God to provide the funds for the trips on which He wanted the Muellers to go.[45] From the USA to India to Australia to Egypt, Mueller's old, restless longing to carry the gospel to distant lands was at last abundantly satisfied.

Final Years in England

Only when he was in his late eighties would Mueller return to England, where, after the death of his beloved second wife, he would spend his few remaining years. Mueller

---

45 Harvey 127.

was known for continuing to rise early each morning for several hours of Bible study; in these years when there were fewer demands on his time Mueller often read the entire Bible through several times each year. The man who, as a young student, had avoided grappling with the Book he did not understand and could not enjoy now found that the Bible grew in wonder and freshness for him as he became, with every passing year, more intimately acquainted with it.

All his life, Mueller's cheerfulness and the joy he found in God amidst the most painful or difficult circumstances had been striking to those who knew him, but it seemed that in the final years of his life his cup of joy was continually running over, and the impression he left on those who spent time with him was of one who had known a life, not of sacrifice or hardship or extraordinary achievement, but of continually feeling overwhelmed by the kindness and generosity of God. "I am a happy old man," Mueller said in another of his last sermons, "yes, indeed, I am a happy old man! I walk about my room, and I say, 'Lord Jesus, I am not alone, for Thou art with me. I have buried my wives and my children, but Thou art left. I am never lonely or desolate with Thee and with Thy smile, which is better than life itself!"[46]

After the years of illness he had struggled through as a young man, Mueller enjoyed unusual strength in his eighties and nineties. Just days before his death, Mueller told a close friend about recent visits to two friends younger than he who were in far worse health. "I came away feeling myself quite young in comparison," Mueller told his friend. "Oh, how very kind and good the Lord has been to me! Now in my ninety-third year, I am still without rheumatism, or an ache or pain, and I can still do my ordinary work at the Orphan Houses with as much comfort to myself as seventy years ago."[47]

The next two days after this conversation Mueller did his usual work. On the third he felt very tired in the morning and had to rest several times as he dressed, but later in the day he reported, "I feel quite myself again," and he led the evening prayer meeting before going up to bed. In the morning he was found beside his bed, having died peacefully and almost instantly, seemingly as he rose to cross the room to his dressing table.

Hundreds who wished to attend Mueller's service were unable to enter the packed chapel where his life and legacy were celebrated, and around seven thousand people crowded into the cemetery for his burial service.[48] His story was told and retold in newspapers across the country, with *The Daily Telegraph* describing him as one who had

---

46   Steer 228.
47   Mueller 706.
48   Steer 231-232.

"robbed the cruel streets of thousands of victims, the gaols of thousands of felons, the workhouse of thousands of helpless waifs." Mueller would have rejoiced to hear in these tributes echo after echo of the answer to his prayer, decades before, that the orphan homes would not only bring hope and relief to desperate children but would also be a striking testimony to the reality and power of God—a testimony that would demand the consideration of even the most skeptical. "In an age of agnosticism and materialism," said the *Bristol Evening News*, "he put to a practical test theories about which many men were content to hold profitless controversy."[49]

Mueller's life had been long, and by the time he died, the national conscience had been awakened and popular views on something to improve the condition of orphans had aligned themselves more and more with Mueller's youthful commitment, which had been so exceptional when he first made it. But at the same time, rationalism and the rejection of traditional Christian orthodoxy had advanced rapidly. It was now fashionable to engage in humanitarian endeavors and to solve social problems; it was less fashionable than ever to believe in or discuss an actual, existing God—neither the embodiment of human benevolence nor the remote designer of a mechanistic universe that now ran very well without him, but a personal God Who intervened in human affairs in response to prayer. The many who wrote tributes to Mueller, however, found it impossible to ignore, explain, or dismiss in any way his unique legacy of prayer and faith. A paper from Liverpool, another major port city, reported that through Mueller's work thousands of children "have been fed, clothed, and educated out of funds, which have poured in without any influential committee or organization, without appeal or advertisement of any sort." "How was this wonder accomplished?" the writer asked. "Mr. Mueller has told the world that it was the result of 'Prayer.' The rationalism of the day will sneer at this declaration, but the facts remain, and remain to be explained. It would be unscientific to belittle historical occurrences when they are difficult to explain, and much juggling would be needed to make the Orphanages on Ashley Down vanish from view."[50]

Mueller died with only just over sixty pounds of cash in his possession, never having changed the habit of giving away, rather than saving up, anything left over after immediate needs and obligations were met. (A biographer notes that during Mueller's life he received approximately 93,000 pounds for his personal expenses, of which he

---

49   Ibid. 232-233.
50   Ibid. 232.

gave away more than 81,000 pounds.)[51] He left a will which closed with a paragraph reflecting his own view of the amazing things God had accomplished through Mueller during his life:

> "I cannot help admiring God's wondrous grace in bringing me to the knowledge of the Lord Jesus when I was an entirely careless and thoughtless young man, and that He has kept me in His fear and truth, allowing me the great honor, for so long a time, of serving Him."[52]

Mueller was anxious, always, that no one should consider him a man of exceptional faith. Rather, he saw himself as a very ordinary believer simply putting to the test what God had made available to all His children. "I beseech you," he wrote, "do not think me an extraordinary believer, having privileges above other of God's dear children, which they cannot have; nor look on my way of acting as something that would not do for other believers. Make but trial! Do but stand still in the hour of trial, and you will see the help of God, if you trust in Him."[53]

---

51 Pierson 298-300; Harvey 156-157.
52 Mueller 717.
53 Ibid. 174-175.

CHAPTER 8

Xi Shengmo

REFUGE AT THE END OF HOPE

The sluggish, heavy smoke coiled out of the pipe like a snake. Once, he could still remember, the sight and the smell of it had brought him delight—pleasure, anticipation, a sense of comfort. Then, later, it had brought only the thought of relief, of escape from the tormented waking nightmares and pain. Now it brought him only feelings of burning shame and bitter, sick despair. He was bound hand and foot by that ribbon of smoke, as if it were a chain. He knew that now. He was poisoned by it, as if it were a cruel serpent whose toxic bite was already killing him—slowly, inexorably, spreading through his body and soul to paralyze and poison and rot. He understood now, as he had not understood in those long-ago days. The man he had once been would have felt nothing but contempt for the man he was now. He would have wiped his shoes after stepping over such a creature in the road. The man he had once been could not have imagined the degradation, the stomach-churning shame, the helplessness, the unrelenting pain he lived with. Now, they were his only realities. Beyond them were only the dreams and hallucinations—the dark, terrifying, cruel ones real and powerful, and the good ones, like the memories of his past life or the thought of his family, pale and faint and distant, impossible to reach. And the worst of it was, there was no escape. He knew that. He could never be free—not now. It was far, far too late for that.

Early Life

Xi Shengmo, as he would eventually be known, was born in 1835, the fourth son of a doctor in a small village in the Western Zhang region of China.[1] Like his brothers, Xi received a good education to prepare him for a career as a scholar, and, ultimately, to

---

1   Wright, G. Doyle. "Xi Shengmo." *Biographical Directory of Chinese Christianity*. Accessed May 30, 2022. bdcconline.net/en/stories/xi-shengmo.

practice both law and traditional Chinese medicine. He was strong-willed, determined, quick-tempered, and exceptionally bright, with an obvious and early talent for leadership. His progress at school, remarkable even among the talented children of parents who valued education and could afford the best, made him his father's favorite son and best hope for the future. Xi distinguished himself by earning his first degree at the age of sixteen and continuing on to further university studies. He was also matched, as was customary, with his first wife, and allotted a fourth of his father's extensive farmland, and the young scholar began his family and his adult life on his own farm as he continued his studies.

Outwardly, then, Xi's early life was one of comparative privilege, early achievement, and happiness. But always there was a darker current flowing beneath the surface of his mind. A keenly intelligent and deeply thoughtful child, Xi was troubled from a very early age by questions about the purpose of life, and especially about death. Was death the end of all human existence, experience, and achievement? If so, what was the redeeming value that gave meaning to life? If not, what was the nature of the life that came after death? Xi did not yet talk much about these questions or about the discontent with life and fear of death that haunted him, but he pondered them in his own mind with increasing seriousness as he grew older. He wanted to know the ultimate truth about the nature of the universe, about good and evil, and about human life. Even as Xi achieved steadily growing success and reputation, life conspired to keep reminding him of his sense of futility and his fear of death. He and his first wife had no children, and she died young, leaving Xi to years of loneliness. He would come to be estranged from all of his brothers, their jealousy, hot temper, and stubbornness, added to his, sparking family conflicts that split the family apart.

The Search

Even after his second, and ultimately very happy, marriage to a beautiful, gentle, and loving young woman, Xi was dissatisfied. But he was a scholar with a keen mind, a decent education, and impressive powers of application and investigation. He determined that he would find the truth—the real meaning of life. Throughout his twenties he searched for answers, even as he cultivated his career and rose to prominence in the community, and even as he hoped for a second chance at a happy family and an end to his loneliness. All the while, behind the scenes, Xi the scholar and the restless seeker after truth was busy looking for answers to the questions that would give him no rest.

In the rich and ancient philosophical heritage of China, Xi found three major belief systems that claimed to offer the answers his restless mind and uneasy heart were searching for. First there was Confucianism, which nourished the scholarly and literary tradition in which he was educated, and which underlay China's culture, legal system, government, and civil service. Students of Confucianism still cannot agree on whether it is best described as a religion, a philosophy, or an ethical system, and its deep roots in and pervasive influence on the history and culture of China only make it more difficult to analyze. In fact, the teacher and writer Confucius—"China's most famous teacher, philosopher, and political theorist"—did not consider himself the founder or originator of the system of thought that would bear his name. Instead, he claimed to be merely a transmitter and a reviver of ancient and traditional knowledge.[2] Born around 551 BC, Confucius emphasized in his teachings—the most influential of which are collected in *The Analects*—the importance of disciplined self-cultivation, virtue, and responsibility in order to achieve full human potential in the larger, holistic context of an orderly world and society. Confucianism nourished a rich, centuries-old scholarly and literary tradition and emphasized the importance of duty, responsibility, virtue, and discipline. These characteristics made it ideal to influence and shape China's governmental and legal tradition and to supply scholar-rulers for leadership and for the vast civil service. If he could have been satisfied to embrace Confucianism wholeheartedly, Xi would have taken great pride in the intellectual ability and relentless self-discipline that enabled him to eventually pass three daunting and extremely prestigious examinations. He would also have hoped for a life of usefulness and respect as a leader of the community and the country. His destiny would be to lead, to enjoy respect and veneration during life and by his descendants after death, and to fit into his appointed place in family and society.

About the more ultimate questions that troubled Xi, however, Confucianism had very little to say. Its teachings were focused, much like those of the Graeco-Roman Stoics, on a virtuous life that adapted itself to the realities of human life and human society, and on developing one's full potential on earth. It was not concerned with, and offered no promises about, the existence or nonexistence of one or more deities, or of a life after death. It was a self-contained system that found the meaning of human life in achievement, education, and filling well one's place in the human family and human society. To the restless and daring questions of a mind like Xi's, with its hunger for a

---

2   Kuiper, Kathleen, ed. *The Culture of China*. Britannica Educational Pub. 2011. Page 63.

larger meaning for the human story, Confucianism had nothing to say. The Confucian tradition offered the prize of being remembered and esteemed by one's descendants for one's learning and achievements as the ultimate reward of a virtuous life, and of scholarly toil and discipline.

Another candidate the young Xi encountered in his quest for meaning and understanding was Buddhism, but to Xi Buddhism offered a dark, haunting specter rather than hope. With his background, Xi experienced Confucianism as the sophisticated, scholarly worldview of the privileged and well-educated, and Buddhism as the dark and terrifying superstition of the poorer villagers. Near Xi's childhood home were two Buddhist temples, and childhood visits to them terrified him. The chilly confines of the temple were filled with strange incense and mysterious chanting of hooded monks, the stone gods seemed strange and remote, and the stone face of the Buddha gazed blankly back at the awe-struck boy. Far worse, in the lower city temple, the terrifying torments of the Buddhist hell were depicted in sculptures that horrified and frightened young Xi. His family did not practice Buddhism, and he did his best to shake off the lingering shadow cast over his mind by his limited exposure to it, but as a young adult he would revisit it in his quest to find the truth. If Confucianism left him dissatisfied because it did not address the question of the nature and destiny of the soul, then Buddhism haunted him because it suggested that the soul might, after all, survive death, and that perhaps the achievements of the proud Confucian scholar might mean nothing in that mysterious future life.

Finally, Xi investigated the claims of Taoism, the third belief system familiar to him, hoping that here he might find the knowledge, the hope, and the peace that continued to elude his restless mind. Taoism was as old as Confucianism, and, while an infinitely complex understanding of the world, emphasized the balance or harmony of forces (it gives us the yin and yang symbol) and the importance of aligning oneself with the inner, natural moral direction of the universe. Its practice, especially among the less educated people surrounding Xi, also involved a great deal of ritual and magic, and it offered the promise of escaping suffering and achieving one's desires in life through performing the correct rituals. Perhaps most importantly, Taoism offered the elusive prize of immortality.

Xi plunged into a serious study of Taoism, but instead of finding the health, happiness, prosperity, and good fortune he hoped to discover there, he grew more and more restless and depressed, and his health began to disintegrate, exacerbated by his stress, depression, and long hours of study. Ultimately, Xi became captivated by the "Golden Pill," a Taoist group that was the best known of many cult-like secret societies in Xi's area during this period.[3] The Golden Pill supposedly offered immortality through its mystical practices and bodily health through its special breathing exercises, but it did not bring Xi the peace he sought, and the breathing exercises failed to strengthen his failing health. The feeling grew on Xi that he had opened every door he knew of without finding what he sought. He was running out of places to look for the peace and rest that still eluded him, and he was suffering from a persistent cough, the symptom of some unidentified chronic illness he couldn't shake.

Opium

The answer that would come so close to destroying him was proposed by well-meaning friends: opium. Opium was already becoming the terrible curse of China. An especially devastating epidemic of addiction ravaged the country in the wake of the Opium Wars, which had been fought by the British Empire largely to force China not to ban the flood of imported opium from British India—despite the warning of Prime Minister Gladstone that he feared the judgment of God on his country in the wake of this greedy and cynical policy, with its horrific cost in ruined lives and families.

But opium was also seen as a source not only of pain relief but also of relaxation, sleep, the lifting of depression, even enlightenment. Xi was both restless and reckless. He was adrift and unhappy, and he was a man of action, with a strong will and a driving energy, not one to drift through life from day to day without risking drastic action. Instead, he was a man who would always tend to take bold steps—whether advancing his career, achieving high honors as a student, searching for ultimate truth, or, at last, demanding relief for his troubled mind. He sampled opium, and found that, at first, it brought him a sense of transcendence, of hope, of confidence, that he had failed to find in any other way. But of course, it brought in its wake a terrible lassitude and depression, one that so intensified Xi's malaise that he was driven back to opium almost immediately. Its grip on him strengthened with alarming rapidity.

Over the next decade, opium would destroy Xi, inch by inch. As his farm, his family, and his reputation fell into disrepair and sank under his neglect, Xi's gradual disintegration was agonizingly public, unfolding against the backdrop of a national

---

3   Austin. Alvyn. *China's Millions: The China Inland Mission and Late Quing Society, 1832-1905*.Grand Rapids, MI. Eerdman's. 2007. Page 164.

epidemic which transformed men and women into withered wrecks begging in the ditches and besides the roads, all over China. Nothing else could have so completely and so cruelly humiliated the gifted, self-reliant scholar who had once been a leader of men, envied and respected by many. Now, Xi realized, there was no difference between him and the terrible ghosts of the opium epidemic that haunted the countryside.

Just when it seemed that no worse curse could descend upon the Chinese inland, a severe drought and resulting famine plunged much of the country into starvation, costing countless lives. Xi's desperation was increased by the horrors of the famine that, along with the opium epidemic, ravaged his whole province. Xi, still regarded as a leader among the local farmers, was continually besieged with requests for advice, wisdom, and help he could not give. Whenever he set foot outside his own house, he looked into pinched, emaciated faces and hollow, despairing eyes like his own. The famine was so severe that even cannibalism haunted the province. Between them, opium and Xi's Taoist quest for immortality had left him a shadow of a man, devoured by his own hungers.

The Essay Contest

Had it not been for the desperation and shame that had stripped away the lingering shreds of his self-respect, Xi would in all likelihood have refused to investigate the teachings of the British missionaries, no matter what the incentive. Like many Chinese, Xi correctly blamed the British Empire for the "black mud" of opium that was eating out the heart of China, and it was with suspicion and hostility that Xi first heard of the teachings of the new religious sect introduced by Englishmen—already doubly suspect as Western foreigners and as citizens of the country whose greed and arrogance had flooded China with opium. From what he could learn about the teachings of this sect—Christianity—Xi could only consider it foolish, contemptible, hardly worth the time of a scholar to investigate. Here and there, he knew, the uneducated common people were drawn to this foreign faith, but a scholar such as he knew better than to believe in the ideas of a personal God, answered prayer, and other foolish notions. And furthermore, terrible rumors circulated throughout the province about the mysterious foreigners. Other white men who had come to China had had motives that were only too transparent—greed, arrogance, a lust for power. These men, whose activities were more mysterious and whose motives were harder to understand, only seemed the more sinister because it was not clear why they were here or what they wanted. Xi's involvement with the Taoist mystery cult with its incantations and secret words put him especially on his guard against the sinister powers he imagined this foreign magic might have.

Thus it took a clever trap to ensnare Xi into first meeting the English Christians. David Hill, an English missionary, had labored and prayed for years for a way to reach the scholarly class of the province—the learned Confucian literary men who were so contemptuous and so suspicious of Christianity. How could they be persuaded to read the Bible, to investigate the Christian scriptures as they did so many other books, so many other philosophical traditions? It was like searching for some way over, around, or through a blank stone wall. Where was the door?

At last, Hill had his inspired idea. He would reach these learned men in exactly the way that was most familiar to them—most respectful, most aware of their cultural and scholarly tradition, as natural to them as breathing. He would hold an essay contest. He would offer prizes, both the monetary value and the prestige of which would appeal to many in such hard times. The prizes would be for the best scholarly and literary essays written on carefully chosen themes in the Christian Scriptures. It would be an invitation to the scholars of the province to bring real questions and sincere consideration to the message of Christianity—to study its text as they had studied so many others. It was an invitation in the native language of a proud and ancient tradition.

Excitement spread as the missionaries circulated the invitations to their contest—the deadline, the address, the requirements, and topics for the essays. Suspicion and hospitality remained the prevailing attitudes toward their work, but this was different—an academic exercise that simply offered an opportunity for men of great ability and achievement to do what they did best—to exercise their craft on a new topic and to earn badly needed money and distinction in the process.

Even so, Xi was initially reluctant to participate—a fact that demonstrates not only the depth of his hostility and mistrust toward the Christians but also the apathy, listlessness, and cynicism into which years of illness, poverty, disillusionment, and addiction had driven him. Yet as he and his neighbors gathered around to read the notice, first one and then another urged him to enter. Indeed, several people urged Xi to write an essay in their names. The prize money was alluring, and no actual contact with the missionaries seemed necessary, other than picking up the prize in person if it were actually won. At last, Xi decided to write four essays, under four different names—one his own, and three in those of friends or neighbors who had asked his help.

This meant that Xi would not only have to dust off his neglected skills as a scholar and critic but also to investigate the teachings of Christianity thoroughly and compare it with other belief systems. The topics to choose from were:

1) *The Source of True Doctrine, or the Right Way.* The great origin of the Right Way is said (by Chinese sages) to be from Heaven. The sages of antiquity, both in China and in the West, "inquired into the lucid degrees of Heaven." But the traditions of the Right Way were not transmitted. Later, ancients composed scriptures and precepts, supplementing books of ceremony and music. They spoke of transmigration, rewards, immortality, and so forth. Now again one meets with those who proclaim a Right Way. If one inquires whether it is from Heaven, or of men, what definite evidence is there to decide its source?

2) *The Regulation of the Heart.* The Confucianist desires to make his faults few; the Buddhist to conquer his passions; and the Taoist seeks to obtain the elixir of immortality. The Mohammedan acknowledges only one God. And all attach supreme importance to rectifying the heart. But what is High Heaven's method for the Regulation of the Heart?

3) *On Prayer.* Man's virtue is limited; the grace of Heaven is infinite. How should those who wish to receive the favour of Heaven, sincerely seek that they may obtain it, and avoid calamity?

4) *Rewards and Punishments.* That good is to be rewarded and evil punished is a great principle with wise rulers. God loves all men; and, to lead us into the way of virtue, rewards and punishes the people of every age. How does He offer happiness in place of retribution, in order to lead men to avoid the sufferings of hell and gain the blessedness of heaven?

5) *Images of the Gods.* Is it permissible that those who worship the Supreme Ruler and follow the right way of Yao and Shun [ancient Chinese rulers] should bow down before idols?

6) *On Opium.* Those who wish to see the opium evil conquered, and thus to carry out the wise desires of the Government, know well the injury caused by the drug. What good methods are there for stopping the cultivation of opium, restricting its use, and curing the craving it causes?[4]

---

4   Taylor, Geraldine (Mrs. Howard). *Pastor His: Confucian Scholar and Christian*. London. Overseas Missionary Fellowship. Reprinted 1977. Pages 38-39.

So Xi set to work, his old brilliance and discipline coming to his aid as he embarked upon his careful study of the Bible and other Christian literature (copies of which were supplied along with the contest packet.) Once more, just as he had so many years before, Xi sat alone late into the night, reading, analyzing, thinking, writing. The big questions about life, death, immortality, and ultimate truth that he had once pursued with all his might, then given up any hope of answering—questions that were only dulled by the opium to which he had turned instead in his quest for peace—arose before him, once again forcing his mind along forgotten paths and gripping his conscience, his intellect, and his imagination.

Yet while Xi had once brought to his studies a real hope of finding truth, of finding meaning and peace, he now felt only despair. He knew he was a good scholar, and was likely to win one of the prizes, but he felt certain that whatever the Right Way of Heaven might be, it was not for him, the hopeless prisoner of opium who had sunk into disgrace, neglected his family and his profession, thrown his life away. The proud, stubborn scholar had learned at last the harsh lesson he had found so difficult to accept; knowing the right thing to do, and wanting badly and trying hard to do it, were not always enough. For men like him, bound hand and foot by choices and behaviors they hated but could not shake off, there could be no hope. No one and nothing could turn back the clock, restoring the ruined lives and the lost years. No one and nothing could change a heart, a mind, and a will into what it ought to be. One could be like Xi, a man whose scholarly brilliance had enabled him opportunities to seek truth as few can do, a man who could articulate, as few can do, what was the right and wise way to live one's life, what one owed to oneself and one's ancestors and one's family and one's community—yet a man whose family starved in rags while he lay, day after day, year after year, stupefied with a drug he hated and knew was killing him. One could see clearly the gap between those two realities, yet be absolutely powerless to close or cross the chasm. No amount of reading or writing about the Christian God or the hope of heaven he offered could change that.

It is a mark of Xi's brilliance that now, after neglecting scholarship and abusing opium for more than a decade, he won, under different names, all four of the prizes offered by the missionaries. One hundred twenty essays were submitted, carefully read, arranged, and selected by native Chinese scholars first, and the finalists submitted to David Hill and his coworker. And of the 120, the four best were all Xi's—although, of course, the two missionaries had no idea they had been written by the same man. Xi, after years of financial failure and poverty, had won a remarkably large sum of money—even if some of it was destined for the neighbors on whose behalf he had written.

Meeting David Hill

The problem now was how to collect the prize money with as little contact as he could possibly have with the English missionaries—preferably without meeting them at all. In fact, Xi sent a messenger in his place to receive the prize, unwilling to set foot in David Hill's home or to see his face if he could possibly avoid it. But David Hill very respectfully insisted on the requirement that the author of the essays claim his prize in person. Xi would have to come to David Hill's home and be introduced to him.

Xi came, on his guard, distrusting the tea that was served to him, distrusting the seeming courtesy of his host, distrusting even the eyes of his host which might be casting a spell on him as so many people warned the foreigners could do. Yet Hill's courtesy and respect disarmed him, and at last they sat together, drinking tea, making small talk. Hill asked nothing of Xi, and Xi left, feeling that he had survived his first—almost certainly his only—contact with an English Christian with no ill effects, and with no entangling obligations whatsoever. He returned home in triumph, a much richer man, celebrated once again by his friends and neighbors.

At the Home of the "Foreign Devils"

David Hill let several days go by before he called upon his new friend with an unexpected request: He, David Hill, badly needed to advance his own education in Chinese classics, to better understand its language and literature, so complex, so beautiful, so ancient, so different from his own. He needed a teacher, and he needed a native speaker to help write and translate his gospel tracts. Now, thanks to the contest, he had met one of the greatest minds the province had produced in a generation, exactly the man he needed to instruct him in China's rich literary tradition. Would Xi accept a job as a live-in tutor and translator who would stay in Hill's home for a time, help him to translate tracts and other materials, and give him one-on-one lessons every day? His hesitation and suspicion much reduced by two visits with the very respectful and unassuming Hill—and perhaps by the fact that in such an arrangement he, Xi, would be the one in a position of power and influence, rather than the other way around—Xi agreed.

His study of the Christian Bible had opened Xi's mind to the possibility that there might be much truth in this new faith. But it had only left him more convinced that such things as conquering the evil in one's own heart or having a confident hope of

Heaven after death—let alone escaping the prison of opium addiction—were impossible, and no amount of knowledge or truth could make them otherwise. It was his new life in the Hills' home that gave Xi, for the first time in his life, the glimpse of a new possibility: people who were really different, whose hearts and daily lives and families and homes were really changed, because of some real power that had come into their lives. Xi was a quick, keen observer. He was a deeply insightful, if now a somewhat cynical, man, one whose ability to read others made him a natural leader who could usually get his own way. He was prompt and accurate in assessing people and situations. Now he lived with David Hill, and every day, his observation sharpened by suspicion as well as curiosity, he studied Hill, his family, his fellow missionaries, and the Chinese Christians who were often at his home. He held himself apart, having no desire to be identified with or mistaken for the strange group of foreigners and predominantly lower-class, uneducated Chinese. He walked and sat in the garden, often smoking his opium pipe, when he and Hill were not working. He did not ask questions, or share his thoughts, but always, he watched. There was in Hill something he had sought in vain all his life—some organic connection between his beliefs and his life, his words and his actions, something that gave him a kind of hope and a kind of rest Xi had decided could not exist. What was it?

It was natural that Xi—ever the scholar, and still reluctant to share his thoughts with anyone, much less this foreigner—should turn to a book for answers. To better understand what it was that gave David Hill the wholeness and the peace that permeated his life, Xi turned to the Chinese New Testament that was seldom out of Hill's reach. Xi had seen that Hill turned to it again and again, seeming to draw strength from its pages. Of course after writing his essays and studying with Hill, Xi was beginning to know the basic outlines of what it contained, but he wanted to understand what gave it such a hold over Hill's mind and heart and life, and why Hill seemed to find joy and refreshment in it. Xi began to read the book on his own time.

It was the stories of Jesus Christ that struck him most powerfully and moved him most deeply. Gradually, as he read with greater and greater eagerness and attention, Xi began to see Jesus Christ not as another virtuous man or another wise teacher, but as something completely different—someone who must, indeed, be God as he had claimed to be. As his fascination with the stories increased, however, so too did Xi's terrible guilt. He could no longer force out of his mind all the failures he had long recognized in his own life and heart. What could he, a man whose own terrible choices had destroyed him and those around him, ever have to do with this Jesus who now so clearly stood apart from the philosophies and stories in which Xi had sought the meaning of life?

Still he did not speak to Hill, or anyone else, but he read hungrily, desperate for hope as a drowning man is desperate for the air. And at last it became clear to Xi that Jesus Christ had not merely set an example no one could possibly hope to follow, but had paid with his death for the sins of those who hope in him, and had offered every sinner—even Xi himself—the life and hope that come from being united with the triumphant, risen Christ. In floods of tears, Xi knelt in prayer, all alone, giving thanks for the forgiveness and new life he knew God had given him.

"[A]lone in that quiet room," writes a biographer,

> the living, present, personal Jesus was so wonderfully revealed to him by the Holy Ghost, that he was ever afterwards as one who had seen the Lord . . . He saw Him then, not only as his Saviour but also as his absolute Owner, his Master, his Lord. And to the first, glad wondering consciousness—He has redeemed me, succeeded the deeper, more adoring conviction—He has enthralled me: I am forever his.[5]

So great and so immediate was the change in Xi that he sought out the Chinese Christians he had previously despised and avoided as so far below him in class, wealth, and education, and joyfully announced himself a fellow Christian. He also eagerly begged to join the little church at once, identifying himself with them publicly as he had been so determined not to do. The missionaries urged caution, wanting to be sure that Xi had been truly born again, not simply influenced by his new surroundings or captivated by an emotional experience that would fade and leave him again in darkness. But Xi assured them that there could be no going back, and the Christians welcomed him among them.

It may have been especially necessary for Xi to have this unforgettable, transcendent experience of the presence of Christ, because a dark and terrible ordeal lay ahead of him. Xi seems to have known immediately that he must give up opium—that he could not serve both Christ and the drug that had enslaved him. He did not doubt, at least not in his mind and heart, that the power of Christ and the indwelling Holy Spirit could do for him what nothing had been able to do, and make it possible for him to leave opium behind forever. He knew how few people ever succeeded in breaking the chains of the addiction,

---

5   Ibid. 47-48.

and he knew the terrible suffering it would entail. Yet it is characteristic of Xi that he did not begin to gradually limit or reduce his opium consumption, as doctors today usually urge. To him, it seemed that either he still needed opium or he didn't—either it still had a hold on him, or he could walk away from it. So he simply stopped one day, after a severe addiction of at least ten years. He decided that he would never go back, and that he must pray for the mercy of God to survive what lay ahead.

Xi would never forget the agonizing ordeal of the next terrible days. Today, we understand better than either the doctors or the patients of the nineteenth century what addiction is, how it works, and why it is so destructive, but the experience of withdrawal from opium and its derivatives has always been, and remains, one of the cruelest and most difficult a human being can face. His biographer describes Xi's ordeal:

> As hour after hour went by, his craving for the poison became more intense than the urgency of hunger or thirst. Acute anguish seemed to rend the body asunder, accompanied by faintness and exhaustion that nothing could relieve. Water streamed from the eyes and nostrils. Extreme depression overwhelmed him. Giddiness came on, with shivering, and aching pains, or burning thirst. For seven days and nights he scarcely tasted food, and was quite unable to sleep. Sitting or lying, he could get no rest. The agony became almost unbearable . . . Mr. Hill and others did what they could to help him. Medicines were given in larger doses, and native as well as foreign drugs were tried, but all without avail. Prayer was constantly made on his behalf, and Xi himself, as far as he was able, cast himself upon the Lord . . . In his most suffering moments, he would frequently groan out aloud: "Though I die, I will never touch it again!"[6]

At last, the desperate man felt, all in a moment, that his prayers were answered, and that the struggle was over. He believed that a spiritual battle had been won by the Spirit of God over the powers of evil.

Xi would always feel that, because of the ministry he would later have to hundreds of those addicted to opium, it was necessary and valuable for him to experience the days of agony, the desperation, and the mercy of God in just the way he did. He would be able to assure his fellow sufferers that God could deliver them from opium, but also he would never underestimate the torment they endured and he could pray for them as he could never have done without surviving his own struggle with opium. He would always be grateful for, and make use of, all that both Western and Chinese medicine could do

---

6   Ibid. 51-52.

to relieve the symptoms of withdrawal and to help patients make it to the other side of the dark valley, but he also remained convinced that there was a spiritual, perhaps a demonic, aspect to addiction, and that ultimately it was only the power of God that could be trusted for deliverance.

Xi's own deliverance was complete. Though he was in his mid-forties when he gave up opium, and though he would spend much of the rest of his life surrounded by opium addicts, he would never again touch the drug he had once believed he could not live without.

Xi now made a visit to his home, and then returned to spend two months with David Hill, now as both a student and a teacher, and also, increasingly, as a friend. Xi's transformation was immediately obvious to his family and neighbors, but at first it only confirmed their worst fears: the once-great scholar had been bewitched by some mysterious foreign spell, just as so many had feared might happen to anyone who spent too much time with the English. The more Xi tried to tell them about Christ, or about his own experience, or about the Scriptures, the more certain his hometown became that he was under the sinister control of some dark force. When he insisted upon removing and destroying all the idols from his home, they had no more doubt that he had lost his mind. His wife noticed a great change for the better in his temper, his attitude, and his treatment of her—but still, such a great change was troubling even when it was for the better. Xi left many questions and raised eyebrows behind him when he returned for several crucial more weeks with David Hill and the missionaries and Chinese Christians. It would take much more time, after his return, to convince those who had known him longest that the change made in his life was more to be celebrated than to be feared.

Xi's remaining months with David Hill, his colleagues, and the small Chinese church Xi had joined were foundational to his future life and ministry. David Hill's departure from the province was already planned, and the two new friends and colleagues both knew they had only a short time to cultivate the friendship that had come to mean so much to both of them. Xi was to return to his village as the only Christian there, hoping to take with him the good news of what Christ had done for him. He would be during the succeeding years very isolated, compared with these precious months of fellowship and discipleship in Hill's home and the little church there. Also, Xi would find leadership and responsibility descending on him very quickly, and these months of putting deep roots into the Word of God, the life of prayer, and the fellowship of other Christians would prove essential to him.

Xi's parting from Hill was one of great sadness, but he knew it was time for him to return to the family, the life, and the village his opium addiction had devastated, and his conversion had filled with suspicion. His great desire was to spend the rest of his life sharing the hope of the gospel with others, but he knew he would have to begin that task by proving to those who had known him all his life that it had truly changed him—that his addiction was over, his character transformed, and his mind clear and not under a mysterious foreign spell. Just as he had watched David Hill months before, trying to understand what was different about him, looking for inconsistencies, so everyone he knew best would be watching him.

"A New Man in a New World"

It was, indeed, considered by many an even greater shame that a talented scholar such as Xi should have succumbed to the enticements of the foreigners than that he should have sunk into opium addiction, and his neighbors wondered that so proud and learned a man should have fallen into a trap that usually ensnared the poor and the illiterate. They could see that his opium use was completely at an end, and that the many hours he used to devote to it were now spent in prayer, Bible study, and work on his long-neglected farm. But this was not reassuring—it was bad enough that he should engage in the mysterious rites of this new foreign religion, but that might be understandable; what a disgrace it was to see a prominent scholar such as Xi engaged in manual labor in his own fields, like a common worker! No one questioned that the farm had fallen into sad disrepair and his family under the double blows of the famine and Xi's enslavement to opium, and the improvement in his land was striking to all. But still, it was disturbing to see that Xi, of all people, no longer considered himself above such work. At least there was no sign of the foreign money which many believed the missionaries must have bribed him with—on the contrary, everyone could see Xi working hard to climb out of a financial pit and meet his family's needs. He continued to talk enthusiastically to anyone who would listen about his new beliefs, and to try explaining what had transformed him from a despairing, cynical addict to an undeniably happy, responsible, hard-working man. But his neighbors would need a little time to decide what to make of the change in him, and only then would they be ready to listen.

Meanwhile, it was Xi's own family that saw the greatest change in him, and that could see soonest and most clearly how much better it was for the head of the household to be under the influence of the new sect, however mysterious and embarrassing it might be, than under the influence of opium. The transformation of Xi's character would be gradual, but the immediate change in him was already astonishing, especially to his wife and mother. So much more patient, so much more cheerful and gentle, so much more considerate and respectful was this new Xi than he had ever been before—even before the opium had turned him into such a dark, moody, unreliable man during the past several years. Also, they were struck by his eagerness to share and explain his new beliefs—something very new in the traditional Chinese scholar who had never thought of trying to teach any of his learning to mere women. Whatever he had come to believe now was something he considered important for women, too, to understand. They hardly knew at first what to make of this.

Then Xi reached out to his more extended family, showing a humility, a willingness to ask forgiveness, and an eagerness to make peace that had never before been characteristic of him. He sought out the elderly stepmother who had been turned out of the home years before and left to a life of poverty and neglect, asking her forgiveness and begging her to return home and see what a different man he had become. He also took what was, in such a small community, the dauntingly public step of asking the forgiveness of his brothers, from whom he had been so long estranged after a family quarrel. The old Xi might perhaps have considered accepting the apology of one of these brothers if it were made humbly, but it would have been unthinkable for him to humiliate himself in public by seeking out his brothers, who had been far from blame in the quarrel, to ask for their forgiveness and seek for peace in the family. This, however, Xi now did. And indeed, nothing but ridicule on all sides greeted his first efforts. But he persevered, continuing to reach out to his brothers and work for reconciliation, until, little by little, his relationships with them were restored and they were on friendly terms.

Such steps of humility and kindness, together with the passage of time during which Xi continued to live free of opium, to work hard, to make amends, and to talk about the gospel of Christ with all who would listen, made gradual but steady inroads into the suspicion of his family and neighbors, and the times of family worship at Xi's house included not only his family but also interested friends and neighbors. Over the first year or two of his new life, Xi would see his beloved wife, his mother, and many of his friends put their faith in Christ.

Gradually his reputation grew throughout the province, attracting respect from some, ridicule from some, persecution from some, and an enthusiastic welcome from others. He found that first a trickle, then a stream, and soon a flood of requests for financial help, for prayer, for healing, for legal help, for hope for opium addicts, for advice, and for the preaching of the gospel found their way to him from all over the province. Most astonishingly, he was eventually asked to serve as the headman of his village—a final proof that, if his neighbors still thought him odd, they no longer considered him bewitched or demon-possessed. Because offering sacrifices to the idols of the village was a key part of this role, Xi considered himself automatically disqualified, and he pointed this out to the elders who asked him to serve. To his surprise, they replied that they considered his religion a private matter of conscience that would have no bearing on his fitness to serve. Xi pointed out that his service to Jesus Christ consumed his time and energy and said he did not believe he would be able to invest the time they needed in a leader. Again and again he refused, and again and again they urged him. Finally, Xi said he would consent to serve on two conditions: First, he himself would not under any circumstances participate in the worship of or sacrifice to the idols, and second, that during his leadership the whole village would cease the worship of the idols—bringing them no sacrifices, holding no ceremonies in their honor, even closing their temple. Xi assumed that this stipulation would put an end to any consideration of him in the role of headman, and at first it seemed he was quite right. The delegation of village authorities were appalled and exclaimed that it was entirely out of the question to abandon the village gods. Xi simply assured them that, in that case, he certainly could not consider serving. The authorities left, and it seemed for a little while that the matter was closed, but shortly after his neighbors called on Xi again. Astonishingly, they had decided to agree to his terms.

Xi took his responsibilities very seriously and approached his position with much prayer. He did his best for the village, and at the end of the year, they were so pleased with his leadership, and the village had prospered so much, that he was unanimously reelected. The same thing was repeated the following year, so that Xi served three consecutive years and was urged to serve again at the end of them, although by then he felt obliged to decline because his responsibilities as an evangelist and his work with opium addicts had grown so demanding. Upon giving up the office, Xi urged his fellow villagers to consider the village idols as "quite starved to death" after three years without food—during which no misfortune or punishment had been visited on the village. Surely there was no need to begin feeding them again!

A House Always Full

In the meanwhile, Xi found a very different kind of responsibility and opportunity in his own home. No sooner had Xi and his wife and mother found their farm beginning to prosper once again, and their family worship meetings filled with others eager to learn more about the Christianity that had delivered Xi from addiction and despair, than the farm began to fill with visitors—those who needed work, medical help, financial help, or help giving up opium, some who were Christians, some who wanted to learn about Christianity, and some who had no interest in Christianity but were desperate enough to seek help or hope from Xi, his family, and his growing group of fellow new Chinese Christians. Some of the visitors were temporary; others Xi gave work on his property or invited to stay for longer periods, because of their own needs, the help they could give to others, or both. Many traveled long distances to seek Xi's advice or teaching and needed to stay for several days before undertaking the return journey. Because of the widespread hostility toward and frequent persecution of Christians in the province, many who identified themselves as Christians and joined the church faced unemployment and poverty—they might lose their jobs or their homes or their land. And even if they did not, those who refused to grow and sell opium incurred a major loss in income.

The province was recovering from the worst ravages of the famine, but there was still great need, and Xi and his wife felt from the first that generosity and hospitality were key elements of the Christian life, and vital to opening hearts and minds to the gospel. A British missionary would later write that Xi

> considers the whole of his time, and influence, and means must, as a matter of course, be at the feet of the Lord Jesus. We [missionaries] never told him that. He said, 'Why, the Lord has redeemed me; He shed His blood, He spared nothing in working out my redemption; therefore I consider that granary of mine, full of rice, is for the use of the brothers and sisters, if they need it.'[7]

By using their resources to serve others, Xi and his family could help to overcome the perception that Christianity was a foreigners' scheme, or a way to make money.

---

7   Austin 259.

They would show their neighbors that Christianity could be vibrantly and authentically Chinese, and that Christ offered hope to those who had no other hope.

Xi's biographer summarizes the gradual, organic development of this earliest phase of Xi's ministry:

> The world that had grown up around [Xi and his wife] was becoming increasingly complex. More and more the Christians from neighbouring villages, brought to the Lord through their efforts, looked to them for help and teaching. The mission station in the city was fully ten miles away, and though younger men walked over on Sunday for the services . . . old people, and most of the women and children found the double journey more than they could manage. This means that they must be cared for nearer home. And in many cases the help needed was for body as well as soul . . . Suffering and impoverished, many of the converts were in need of temporary succor, and Xi's resources were taxed to the utmost . . . Inquirers coming from a distance frequently had to be entertained for a few days in that Christian household that they might see in practice the truths they were being taught. Believers gathering from miles around for Sunday services were often weary, and too far from home to go back between the meetings for their mid-day meal. Some brought flour, bread, and other provisions; some had little or nothing to bring; all needed the use of kitchen and guest-hall . . . Then benches for the meetings had to be provided; oil for the lamps; hot water for perpetual tea-drinking, without which nothing can be done in China . . . [8]

As more and more people came and went, or came and stayed, Xi and his wife found themselves not only sheltering, feeding, and guiding the infant church but also offering support and teaching to the leaders of churches springing up in other parts of the province. They were overjoyed to see the progress of the gospel and the changed lives around them, and felt a weighty responsibility to serve those who came to them hungry for hope and help and truth and support. Xi often thought of Christ's words in the Gospel of John, that His sheep "will go in and out and find pasture." If they were the keepers of these sheep, Xi felt, they must be faithful to offer safe pasture.

The Hall of the Joyful Sound

The problem was, they were rapidly running out of money, food, and other supplies. Xi's farm was supporting more people than it ever had before, and finances were stretched to the breaking point. Xi and his wife prayed, talked, wondered, and prayed again about

---

8   Taylor 84-85.

where the supplies would come from. Meanwhile, many of the people seeking Xi's help continued to be those, with whom China was flooded, who longed for freedom from opium. The longing for escape from addiction continued to be one of the main things driving interest in and openness to the gospel, and many sought Xi's understanding, compassion, and prayer in their struggle to give up opium.

Thus, when a small drugstore became available for purchase, Xi and his wife saw it as an answer to their prayers. By selling herbs and medications and practicing Chinese medicine, as he was qualified to do, Xi would earn an income to support the work of evangelism and hospitality growing up in his home. And by combining spiritual and medical help with his own story of addiction and recovery, Xi would be able to offer even more hope and more help to a greater number of those addicted to opium.

Thus, in 1881, what was essentially a medical mission, entirely local and without any Western connections, opened. It would provide employment and would supply small but steady profits for the next two decades. It offered a welcoming atmosphere and was called The Hall of the Joyful Sound.[9]

The Opium Refuges

Soon, from these two points—the medicine shop in the village and Xi's own family farm—there spread not only Xi's growing ministry of evangelism and discipleship but also the aspect of his ministry for which he is especially remembered: the opium refuges. Among those who became Christians in response to hearing the gospel from Xi were several who, like him, had been opium addicts, and as with Xi's own story, the undeniable and dramatic change in them, and the possibility of some real hope for the scourge of China that so many longed in vain to defeat, became a powerful and compelling testimony to the reality of the gospel, forcing even the skeptical and reluctant to give serious consideration to their message. Xi and others began to open "refuges" for those who wanted to give up opium. Here they could stay and receive medical attention, prayer, compassion, and support while they endured the agonies of withdrawal from opium, and here they could find the support to recover and rebuild their lives without opium, even when, as often happened, the same medical conditions that might have driven them to opium in the first place remained or were made even worse. At a time when China was flooded with desperate and impoverished addicts,

9 Ibid. 87.

Xi, a man who had himself found hope and freedom after years of crippling addiction, was a spokesman for Christ who compelled attention. There could be no greater proof of the reality of the compassion, hope, and freedom offered by the gospel than this man who had gone from sinking helplessly into addiction and poverty, dragging his family down with him, to a tireless, generous, helper and rescuer of others.

Xi was the ideal leader of the network of opium refuges (although of course many other Chinese Christians were involved in founding, leading, and running the multiplying refuges), because he combined three extraordinary qualifications: he was a doctor of traditional Chinese medicine, he had himself endured the agonies of breaking off the use of opium and could therefore offer both compassion and hope, and he had a genuine passion for offering to as many others as possible the hope and healing he had found in Christ. The opium refuges were fueled not only by Xi's conviction that true freedom from opium could often come only through the supernatural power of God in answer to prayer but also by a deeply realistic commitment to helping those seeking freedom through every step of what could be a slow and difficult process. Xi and the others who served in the refuges sat up at night by the beds of those in the throes of withdrawal, prayed for them, performed the most menial household tasks as necessary to provide a safe and welcoming environment, and offered work, support, medical help, and structure to those learning to live new lives without the drug that, in many cases, had already cost them their homes, families, or livelihoods.

In the earliest days of the first refuge, Fan, Xi's friend and a fellow former addict and early convict to Christianity, used to obtain medical supplies from Western missionaries to ease the agonies of those who came to stay with him to break their addictions. But the day came when there were several desperate patients in the refuge, no more Western medicines remaining, and no Western missionary within reach. Xi urged Fan to join him in praying for the sufferers, and he also prayed specifically that he might be able to create, himself, from the traditional Chinese ingredients available to him something that would ease and strengthen those enduring the same ordeal he remembered so well. From this came Xi's own medicines, probably primarily herbal, especially created to help those giving up opium. In the coming years, Xi would himself carefully prepare batches of the little pills to distribute to the opium refuges, setting aside time for prayer and fasting before creating each batch and asking God to make the medicines beneficial to those seeking freedom from opium. As Xi and the work of the refuges grew, he would inevitably be offered money for the recipe, but he was horrified by the idea of making a profit from the sufferings of those desperate to be free of opium. He refused to sell.

When Xi said goodbye to David Hill and left the mission station five years earlier, he had been alone. Of all the people he had known his entire life, excepting only those he had met at the mission station in the previous few months, he was the only Christian, and he was surrounded by watchful eyes, assessing whether his previous opium addiction or his new bewitchment would prove to be the most dangerous and destructive. The speed and scope of the change Xi had helped to spark since then can hardly be overstated. A biographer summarizes:

> Thus, at the close of 1884, little more than five years from the time of his conversion, Xi was the leader of an already quite extended work. Eight or ten "Refuges" had been established: from Tengtsun south of his own home, to Chaocheng city forty miles to the north; and in villages and hamlets all along the line, little companies of believers were meeting regularly for worship.[10]

Not only the farmland, and not only the medicine shop but also another unexpected answer to prayer provided funds for the needs of this growing ministry. It was fitting that, at one of their periods of greatest financial need when all funds were exhausted, Xi and his family and coworkers learned of another writing contest—this one for poetry, on Christian themes, with a cash prize. The scholar Xi took up his pen once again, and not only earned the desperately needed prize money but also created many beautiful, original Chinese Christian hymns for the infant church. While he would always be best known—as well as most criticized—for his work with the opium refuges, Xi's work as a hymn writer and Bible teacher were at least equally essential to the establishment and growth of the Chinese church. Xi's educational background did not cut him off from communicating effectively with the surrounding farmers, not all of whom were literate. Rather, he had a gift for bringing Biblical truths alive for them, making it clear that God had spoken not only to the mysterious foreigners but also to China. One historian notes that Xi "could preach a sermon on St. Paul's shipwreck with such emotion that tears streamed down his cheeks like an old-fashioned marketplace storyteller, making it come alive" to an audience who, in most cases, spent their lives in a landlocked province surrounded by mountains and had never seen the sea.[11]

---

10 Ibid. 143.
11 Austin 258.

Reaching the Cities

After beginning in the rural villages of the province, the outreach of Xi and his coworkers had also begun to reach the large cities of the region. At first, this had seemed an impossible undertaking—the lump sum of funds that would be necessary to find premises and start operations in the city simply did not exist, and the whole project of opening a refuge among strangers in the sophisticated city, where hostility to and contempt for Christianity would be even greater, seemed exponentially more difficult than the organic popping up of refuges in homes or on land belonging to believers who opened their homes to communities they already knew, or where their families had ties. But when two Chinese Christians arrived in Chaocheng, the first city in which a refuge was founded, with nothing but enough supplies to sustain them for a few days and a small supply of Xi's pills, praying for some toehold in the city, they were astonished to find that their reputation had preceded them, and that the notoriously hostile city authorities were ready to welcome them. Not only that but they were also ready to offer premises and some funding for this "benevolent work" which offered some hope to the city's countless opium addicts. Thus the first city refuge was opened and became a pattern for others. Xi next felt a great burden for Hochow. For months he and his wife prayed for this vast, beautiful city where Christianity was almost entirely unknown. One day Xi's wife pointed out that they had prayed so long for Hochow—was it not time to take action? Could they not simply send men to open a refuge, as had been done at Chaocheng? It would take, Xi replied, about thirty thousand cash to start such a work, and he not only did not have the money in hand but had already sold or given away all the possessions that could be spared from the busy household. They must continue to pray, waiting for God to provide.

Shortly afterward, Xi's wife came to him one morning after their time of prayer, a small package in her hands. "I think perhaps God has answered our prayers," she told her husband. Xi unwrapped the handkerchief, and his eyes filled with tears as he saw his own wedding gift to his wife—all the hair ornaments and jewelry that marked her as a married Chinese woman. "I can do without these," she urged. "Let HoChow have the gospel."[12] With this sacrifice, the second city refuge was opened, soon to become a bustling haven for hundreds in search of help.

Xi tried never to turn away anyone seeking help, and all were welcome to seek relief at the refuges without being Christians, or having any interest at all in Christianity.

---

12   Taylor 144.

Nevertheless, the refuges were known to be run by Christians and to rely on prayer and the power of God to help those seeking to be free of opium, so while many did not become Christians, and many who claimed Christianity for a time later abandoned their profession, many did accept the gospel. Around each of the refuges, evangelism, church planting, and other ministry appeared like sparks thrown out by a spreading fire. Often, the establishment of an opium refuge would be followed by the establishment of a church.

Xi had now many fellow Christians and fellow leaders among the Chinese Christians, and he also formed and maintained close friendships with, and worked in partnership with, several missionaries from the China Inland Mission, to which David Hill had belonged and through which Xi himself had first heard the gospel. Xi was only one of many extraordinary leaders during a time in which the gospel was spreading rapidly in inland China. But as one of the first, and one of the most prominent, Christian leaders in the province, and as the point of contact between so many far-flung ministries, Xi was seen as a key Christian leader whether he wanted to be or not, and he was like the hub at which the spokes of a wheel connect, or like the intersection where many roads cross. He found that he must be always on guard against both pride, and excessive busyness. Like George Mueller, Xi found that as his responsibilities and the demands on his time increased exponentially, he had no choice but to spend more, not less, time in prayer for God's guidance and provision. Xi never lost sight of the truth that if God Himself did not do the great work of opening eyes and saving souls, and of building and healing lives, it could not and would not be done. So Xi became known as a man of prayer, who jealously guarded countless hours for prayer and fasting.

Dispute and Mediation in Pantali

Xi prayed not only for others but also for himself, well aware that his native pride, temper, stubbornness, and take-charge attitude were always with him, and that he must continually ask God for the humility and gentleness that had once been so foreign to him. Many times, especially in his early years as a Christian, the old Xi appeared—fiery, impatient, domineering. But as Xi prayed faithfully, he became known as one who could be, at least at times, a humble peacemaker—no longer one who strode into any situation and took charge, but one who could point others to the gentleness and humility of Christ. In one especially memorable instance, Xi was called in to mediate a dispute that had developed between two brothers, both Christians—both, in fact, leaders among the small, tightly knit new church. So urgent was the situation that Xi, donning his fur-lined coat, traveled through the snow and the frigid winter air and over the rough mountain roads to reach Pantali, where the small group of Christians was in trouble.

The quarrel had already turned so ugly that virtually the entire village had gathered around the two brothers as they shouted and argued in front of everyone. Some found themselves taking sides, and drawn into the conflict; others were spectators of the disgraceful scene of the two Christian leaders hurling insults and accusations. Then the younger brother, in the heat of anger, threw a chopper at the other. This violent act, which happened in full view of the village, could obviously have ended in the brother's death, and instead ended up injuring a bystander—one who was interested in learning more about Christianity—whose leg was badly wounded. However horrifying the scene would be considered by anyone, it was, if possible, even worse in the cultural context of rural China, where it was unthinkable for a younger brother to raise his hand against the older brother to whom he owed reverence—and where there was already so much suspicion and hostility toward Christianity to be overcome.

The scene that greeted the exhausted and chilled Xi when he arrived was worse than anything he could have imagined. The two brothers had resumed their quarrel with redoubled ferocity, the friends of the injured man were enraged and vociferously demanding compensation, and almost the entire village was now embroiled in the poisonous conflict. One can only imagine the pain and distress—perhaps the despair— that must have struck Xi like a physical blow as he saw the two leaders of the fledgling Christian community spreading violence, cruelty, and rage among the villagers where they had so recently been preaching the love of Christ. Nearby, neglected by all, shocked and in pain, was the injured man. Shouts of rage filled the air, echoing back from the snowy mountains. It seemed indeed, as a biographer writes, as if "Satan had triumphed; and there was no telling to what proportions the trouble might grow."[13]

Every eye turned to Xi as he arrived on the scene. The warring parties waited to see what he would say. The air crackled with tension. Xi knew the situation was like a powder keg, ready to go up at the slightest spark. The wrong word now, the wrong tone, the wrong glance—that would be all it would take to add fuel to the blazing conflict.

Xi did the one thing no one expected—something that the old Xi could never have done. He turned in silence and walked away, leaving the angry crowd staring after him.

13   Ibid. 125.

He disappeared, and for some time no one knew where he was. All alone, he knelt in desperate prayer for wisdom and for the healing grace of God. He knew better than to attempt to reason with the inflamed mob. There was nothing anyone could have said or done, at that moment, which would not make the situation worse. Xi also knew that if there was to be any hope of recovery from this, it must be a supernatural hope—something from outside the hopeless tangle of old grudges, simmering feuds, unforgivable injury, words said that could never be taken back. Nowhere in that bleak village, chilled by the winter cold and heated only by anger and hatred, was any hope to be found. Xi sought for hope in the only place he knew it could be found.

The surprise and suspense of the crowd distracted them from their quarrel, and an awkward, waiting pause succeeded as everyone wondered what Xi would do. Then he reappeared, walking back toward the group. Now, at last, he would speak—but to whom, and what would he say? Everyone watched and waited, and again he surprised them. He walked right through the group to the wounded man, who had been neglected by everyone and was in considerable pain. Kneeling down, Xi asked permission to treat the man's injury, and, given permission, began to treat the wound, speaking calmly, quietly, and only to the patient. The bystanders began to grow calmer, and to show signs of feeling ashamed of themselves and of the damage done by their quarrel. They were quiet now, watching Xi, listening to his quiet voice.

Once the crowd had quieted, once Xi had first the ear and then the sympathy of his audience, he began to speak of the great sadness he felt over the day's events, and to acknowledge to the village what a great shame it was to him and to all Christians that they had disgraced the gospel of Christ in this way. He identified himself fully with his fellow Christians, taking upon himself the regret, the grief, the shame, and the sense of responsibility for terrible failure and defeat. The crowd listened as if spellbound. Gradually, Xi began to speak less to the whole crowd, and more specifically to his fellow Christians—although the rest of the crowd continued to listen. As Xi's biographer writes:

> Little by little he went on, still making himself one with the offenders, until he could speak more directly to the Christians and lift the whole matter on to a different plane. Not against each other or their fellow-villagers only was this sin, but against the One who loved them best, and whom in their deepest hearts they truly loved.[14]

---

14 Ibid. 126.

Now, at last, Xi addressed the two brothers—leaders among the Christians of the region—directly. He spoke to both as if he, too, were their brother, and urged them to consider the triumph of Satan in such a display, and the shame they had brought upon the name of Christ and the message that could alone offer hope to the valley. Xi could now freely say that both had been greatly wrong, and he could point out how the mercy of God had saved them from the sin of taking a human life. He urged each one to acknowledge his own wrongdoing and beg his brother's forgiveness. "Go thank the Lord upon your knees for saving you from untold misery and remorse," Xi told the younger brother. "Had not [G]od turned that blow aside, your brother's death might even now be at your door."[15]

Xi then addressed the whole crowd again, publicly thanking Koh, the unfortunate victim of the injury, and pointing out that, without intending to, he had saved a life, and prevented a far greater conflict from engulfing the whole community. The crowd was now both respectful and responsive, giving Xi their full attention and murmuring agreement with him.

One very important detail still remained, however. No compensation had been provided to the injured man, as must, according to custom, be done. Xi might have told the two brothers to make sure they provided this restitution, but instead he surprised the crowd again. Leaving the village he went to a nearby pawnshop, pawned his fur-lined coat—his only protection against the winter cold with a long return journey still ahead of him—and, returning, put the money into the hands of the injured man.

Now at last, as he prepared to leave, Xi was moved to open tears, and he begged the two brothers in particular and the other Christians in general to rebuild unity and maintain peace. Seeing their beloved and respected leader standing cold without his coat and weeping with grief they had caused, the two brothers were both, alike, entirely humbled and broken, stricken with remorse. In answer to prayer, Xi had been guided to act and speak in a way that had accomplished what had seemed utterly impossible, and the unity and testimony of the little church was healed as he could hardly have dared to imagine. As he left, the Christians, who could not afford to replace the cost of his coat, expressed their distress, guilt, and concern at his facing the cold mountain journey through their fault, but he assured them "God has called me to bear your burdens, and care for you as my own children. I must do it, because I love you and have you in my heart, and cannot help it."

---

15   Ibid. 127.

Not only did the church in Pantari recover but it also grew and thrived, and soon a refuge was opened there to minister to the opium users who came there seeking help. Not only so, but Taylor notes:

> [T]he Chang brothers never went back. They grew in usefulness as years went on. One of them, the offender on this occasion, became much valued as a deacon of the church, and the other, who was first a deacon and then an elder, subsequently labored for some years as a missionary . . .[16]

The outcome was something the old Xi, so proud, stubborn, and domineering before he became a Christian, could no more have imagined than he could have achieved it. Xi was still a leader of men, and he was still and always distinguished by what one close colleague called "strenuous warfare against evil in himself and others . . . [which] made him . . . over-severe in his rebuking and exhorting,"[17] but he was a kind of leader the arrogant, domineering scholar of his younger days would not even have recognized, and the change in him from year to year, as he grew in gentleness, humility, respect for others, and willingness to admit his own failures was striking to everyone who came in contact with him, even his harshest critics.

Controversy, Persecution, and Perseverance

Xi would need all his growing humility and all his desire for unity as the years continued, and as the churches and refuges blossomed around him, for the most bitter test of the young Christian church in Shansi province was still to come. And it, like this memorable incident, would involve bitter division and hostility from within, rather than the persecution from without which had already failed so often to slow the growth of the church—although persecution, too, continued, and the storm of opposition which would, in a few short years, break in the horrific bloodshed of the Boxer Rebellion was already gathering. Fan, one of Xi's oldest friends and earliest partners in the establishment of opium refuges, turned against his former mentor with vicious accusations of self-aggrandizement, hurling accusations (for which he would, years later, apologize) at Xi in public, and rallying an opposition party which split the infant church of Shansi into rival factions.

Some of these tensions were no doubt inevitable "growing pains" of a ministry and a network of churches which had sprung up so quickly, and which included such a mix of

---

16   Ibid. 128.
17   Austin 456.

true believers, religious seekers, hangers-on, and opportunists. Some of them were the fault of Fan and others who would, in some cases, ultimately repent of their conduct. Yet others were undoubtedly worsened by Xi's tendency to trust others too quickly, to give orders too readily, and to act too impulsively and too independently. There was at least a grain, and sometimes more than a grain, of truth in most of the attacks made on him— that he functioned too independently; that he was too quick to take charge; that he was too quick to appoint new converts and newly recovered addicts to important positions; that he sometimes made decisions too quickly; that he disregarded wise advice; that some of the forty to fifty refuges he founded and entrusted to others fell into corruption and disrepute; that his charismatic personality and the healings and exorcisms he performed attracted the superstitious and opportunistic to make false professions and later abandon Christianity. As one colleague, an admirer and friend yet also a clear-eyed critic of Xi would say:

> His was rather an extreme case, because all the circumstances were extreme. Here was a man of exceptional force of character and organizing power, and whose education and position gave him weight; then, a man of exceptionally deep spiritual life; and. further, circumstances had been such that he had never had missionary supervision, but really he had been left practically alone [during the first five or six years of his ministry]."[18]

Yet for the fifteen years of his Christian life—from his conversion at the age of forty-five to his death at sixty—Xi grew gentler and humbler, his passion and energy mellowed and tempered by maturity, hard experience, and much prayer. While his addiction to opium had been eradicated during a couple of weeks, his stubborn streak, his independence, and his haste in reacting to both problems and opportunities were harder diseases to treat—and Xi knew it. But the growth in humility and gentleness was as steady and undeniable as it was gradual. Xi's opium refuges grew to number close to fifty; the number of those who sought help there or at Xi's home, now called "Middle Eden," grew to number many hundreds. But perhaps this growth of patience, kindness, and humility was the most remarkable transformation of all, when one considers how rare it actually is for a man in his mid-forties, who continues to be given great influence and acclaim, to grow away from, rather than further into, such sins as anger, inflexibility, and self-confidence.

---

18   Ibid. 258.

The period of division and conflict sparked by Fan, was itself, in fact, an important time of deepening and humbling for Xi, and marked a turning point in his ministry and character. He became less independent and more willing to value—though not always to act upon—advice from the missionaries. He grew in an attitude of dependence on prayer and in careful study of and obedience to the Bible. He learned to wait for God to resolve problems, rather than resolving them himself.

In one instance, the opposition party simply took over the property of the church and opium refuge, driving out its rightful owners. Xi and other leaders agreed to do nothing at all to regain their property, but simply to leave its new owners in possession, even though it took many weeks of searching and failure to find new premises to rent. In the end, without opposition to fuel it, this particular faction simply fizzled out, and the church and refuge were able to reopen, having resorted only to prayer to see their rights restored.[19] Such experiences were an invaluable preparation for a test a few years later, when Xi had begun urging the infant church to give up the use of lawsuits and appeals to the mandarins to enforce their property rights, noting that squabbles over money and property were bringing the church into disrepute. Scarcely had Xi published his urging to the whole province for Christians not to resort to the law to defend their rights when a neighbor, perhaps seizing the opportunity, coolly appropriated a particularly fertile piece of Xi's farm by moving the boundary markers and adding it to his own. His only response to a visit from Xi, asking that the matter be put right, was a storm of threats and abuse. Xi, after the hard experiences of the past few years, found that he was able to say, "It is my Master's land. I hold it only for His service. If He wants to use it thus, to illustrate the spirit of the Gospel—let it go."[20] And indeed, the land was never returned.

Thus, gradually, after what one friend and colleague called his "humbling experiences," Xi showed what a biographer calls "a great change, most noticeable to those who had known him from the beginning. Not to override others, but to bear their burdens; not to rule, but to serve, had become his ideal."[21] When, as continually happened, his old habits reappeared, Xi grew quicker to ask forgiveness. A missionary who was Xi's friend and colleague remembered one occasion when a deacon from one of the rural inland churches was visiting Xi for advice and help after having, through

19   Taylor 209-211.
20   Ibid. 280.
21   Ibid. 267.

a series of poor decisions, involved his church in what the missionary called "quite a tangle." Xi kept asking questions, trying to help the man see where he had gone wrong, but the man "could not be made to see it" and kept defending his own actions. "As [the visiting deacon] went over his view of the matter, again and again, Xi had hard work to keep his temper," wrote the missionary. "[Once] more, as patiently as possible, [Xi] put the whole case before the man, and said: "Now really, do you think that was the wisest thing to do?"

When the man once again defended his decision as if he hadn't heard a word, Xi at last spoke sharply, startling the visitor and "shaking his complacency not a little." Instantly, Xi regretted it. "Oh," he said, "let us pray. We must ask forgiveness." And then, as the tears came into his eyes, "Truly, I am nothing. I am unfit to shepherd the flock of God."

The incident was "very characteristic of his attitude during those riper years," wrote the missionary, who worked with Xi for ten years and saw the change in him firsthand.[22]

On another occasion, two Christian leaders who served at the same opium refuge found themselves bitterly at odds, each blaming the other for months of failure, wrongdoing, and misunderstanding. At last the two went straight to "Middle Eden," Xi's own home, to get a hearing from him and "have it out" with one another. The seriousness of the breach between them was obvious to everyone as soon as they arrived, and the reaction of others staying at the center made it obvious how damaging the rift could be if it were publicly aired and people began to take sides.

Xi's response would once have been forceful and hasty, but now, in his later years of ministry, he responded by asking the two men to wait while he spent three days in fasting and prayer over their situation. During the three days, he took special care to make sure that each was waited on carefully and treated with great attention and respect, but no reference to their disagreement was made. Finally, at the end of the three days of waiting on God, Xi called the two men into his room and urged them each to own and apologize for his own fault. "The blame is chiefly mine," he said. "If I had been more prayerful and considerate of your welfare, I should probably never have put you in the same Refuge. I feel that in this matter, I have sinned against God, as well as against you both. Shall we not forgive each other, and seek His forgiveness?"[23] Thus, after his "humbling experiences," Xi increasingly grew to recognize himself the same mistakes and

---

22   Ibid. 286-287.
23   Ibid. 288.

failures others saw in him, and he cultivated a readiness to repent and seek forgiveness. Such moments represented, perhaps, an even greater victory over the old Xi than his deliverance from opium addiction.

Final Days, Death, and Legacy

Xi's final illness, seemingly heart-related and either caused or greatly exacerbated by his grinding schedule of traveling, struck about six months before he died, leaving him mostly bedridden and with rapidly dwindling strength. He had time to put his affairs in order and to consolidate and make arrangements for the network of opium refuges, as best he could. "The Lord is taking away my strength," Xi said. "It must be because my work is done."[24] He died on February 19, 1896.

Xi's life, ministry, and legacy were and are those of a pioneer—a dramatic, polarizing, larger than life personality whose flaws and failures, gifts and victories, mistakes and achievements, all cast long shadows. When he became a Christian at the age of forty-five, the number of Chinese Christians in his province could be counted on one hand. When he died fifteen years later there were many hundreds—yet shortly after his death opium, persecution, and the terrible Boxer rebellion decimated the churches. Through his opium refuges poured many who would ultimately go back to the drug—yet also many who found there the freedom they had found nowhere else. He could be exacting and domineering toward others—yet he could also be far too quick to trust those who were inexperienced or insincere. He was not an easy man to work with, but he labored for unity, forgiveness, and reconciliation whenever and wherever he found friction between fellow Christians, and he grew, with every passing year, quicker to repent and take the blame upon himself. He was noted for sensational healings and exorcisms, especially in his early years as a Christian, believing that God might act miraculously in answer to prayer as Xi believed He had when Xi was struggling to escape his opium addiction. Yet Xi also embraced the most menial and unappealing tasks of waiting on and caring for outcasts and addicts.

Ultimately, Xi experienced, modeled, and shared with others an authentically and naturally Chinese Christianity—not a westernized transplant, but genuine, spontaneous encounter between the gospel of Christ and the rich, ancient culture of China. Xi had found Christ to be his only hope—a hope beyond hope, when he had believed that all was lost for him. He embraced the sacrificial mission of sharing

---

24   Taylor 291.

that hope with his countrymen and women, and he poured himself out like water to achieve that mission.

One of the many beautiful hymns Xi wrote in Chinese for his fellow Chinese Christians captured his desire and the legacy he left to a church which, during the next hundred years, would face horrific persecution:

> *When Thou wouldst pour the living stream,*
>
> *Then I would be the earthen cup,*
>
> *Filled to the brim and sparkling clear,*
>
> *The fountain Thou and living spring.*
>
> *Flow Thou through me, the vessel weak,*
>
> *That thirsty souls may taste Thy grace.*[25]

---

25 Austin 354.

CHAPTER 9
Pandita Ramabai
THE GOD WHO SEES

She had known the story for as long as she could remember. Krishna had once reigned over his people from the island city that was created in one night of gold and precious stones. When Krishna left the earth the city had sunk beneath the Arabian sea, but his golden palace still remains, invisible to eyes polluted by sin. The pilgrim who purifies his life of sin and meets all the requirements set forth in the Puranas can visit Dwarka and, looking out to sea, can see the golden turrets rise glittering from the waves.

If anyone could hope to see Krishna's palace of gold, it would surely be her father, a man who had devoted his life to studying and teaching the sacred Hindu texts, a man who had spent all his wealth in generosity and now traveled from shrine to shrine making offerings to the gods and supporting himself and his family by the gifts of those who paid to hear him read the Hindu scriptures. As the sun began to sink toward the horizon, he and his children gathered with an eager crowd of hundreds of thousands of pilgrims to watch for the appearance of the palace of Krishna, flashing with jewels. So huge and so eager was the crowd that many were trampled to death as the crowd surged forward, each hoping for a glimpse of the palace. "I see, I see!" cried some in the crowd. All the more convinced that she would see, too, Ramabai stood with her father and mother watching, waiting, never doubting the palace would appear. But the sun went down, and sunset faded into twilight, and she saw nothing.

For the first time in her life, the teenage girl doubted the religion on which her family's life was built. She confessed to her religious teacher, who told her that she must pray harder, work harder, suffer, and sacrifice more, and one day the gods would reward her.[1] She tried to believe him. And in the years that lay ahead, her family would suffer and sacrifice more than any of them could imagine.

---

1   Miller, Basil. *Pandita Ramabai: India's Christian Pilgrim*. Grand Rapids, MI. Zondervan. 1949. Page 12

Family and Childhood

The girl who would one day be called Pandita Ramabai was born on April 23, 1858, the sixth (and third surviving) child of a very remarkable man. Her father was a Brahman, a member of the very highest caste of traditional Hinduism. He stood at the pinnacle every devout Hindu wished to reach in the cycle of reincarnation, from which one had the opportunity to reach the final union with Brahma after death. Most people would suffer through millions of years of suffering, in life after reincarnated life, before accumulating enough merit to be born a Brahman man, for only he had any hope of escaping the cruel cycle of reincarnation and, at last, achieving oneness with God after death. Ramabai's mother also belonged to this caste, of course—a Brahman should never marry outside of his or her caste. But women, traditionally, were not considered full participants in the spiritual life of the Brahman and were not allowed, much less taught, to read the Hindu scriptures and other literature in the very difficult Sanskrit language that was seen as the sacred ancient language of India.

This is where Ramabai's father, Ananta, differed from his colleagues: at great personal cost: he instructed not only his sons but also his wife and his daughters, in Sanskrit and in all the literature of Hinduism. The idea had first come to him when, as a very young man, he studied under a guru, or teacher, who was also teaching Sanskrit to an Indian princess. As he saw how the princess mastered the language in which all the great sacred literature of India was preserved, Ananta decided that one day he would teach the women of his own family to read and study Sanskrit.

He returned home fired with his new idea, but both his mother and his first wife refused to study with him—whether from lack of desire or from fear, it is impossible now to know. For years Ananta lived, worked, and studied in great wealth and privilege under the patronage of great rulers, but it was not until he was forty-two years old, a widower, and met and married his second wife that Ananta could begin the work he had set his heart on—teaching the women in his family to read and love the treasured literature of Hinduism.

Once again, however, he immediately faced opposition. When he returned from a religious pilgrimage with his new wife and announced his plans to educate her in Sanskrit, the hostility from his family and community was so intense that Ananta was driven from his own home. He built a wilderness retreat for his new bride, high on a mountain surrounded by jungle. The man who had lived and studied in courts and palaces and enjoyed prestige and riches wherever he went was now, by comparison, almost an outcast. Yet here he would make his dream come true; he would make his new wife a true companion in the study of the Hindu scriptures.

As the years passed, he did just that, and as, later on, children joined the family, he instructed them as well. This little family in the middle of the jungle received one of the finest educations India had to offer. In fact, as the word gradually spread, students and scholars sought out the great man from all over India. Wealth poured into the beautiful home he had made for his family in the jungle, as princes and nobles sent lavish gifts to the scholar.

It was in this period of his life that Ananta's sixth child, a daughter he named Ramabai, was born. But she was to have no memory of this fairy-tale existence in the beautiful jungle retreat where scholars from across India counted themselves privileged to study under her father. She was only about six months old when her family left their home for good. Despite his fame and the money that had flowed through his hands, Ananta had been reduced to poverty by the famously generous hospitality he lavished on all who came to stay with him. As a biographer writes, "Ananta's generosity and the conniving thievery of evil men brought him to dire need. He lost his possessions and his jungle home. Virtually all his wealth was dissipated by this generosity."[2]

For the second time in his life, Ananta had lost the home where he planned to raise his family. Now destitute, though also beloved and famous across India, he decided that he and his family would become full-time traveling pilgrims, journeying from shrine to shrine. Ananta was growing old, and he would spend the remainder of his days in holy pilgrimages. He would trust to the gods and to the generosity of his people to support his wife and three children, including the infant Ramabai, as they traveled from place to place, and he would be able to show his family all the greatest shrines in India.

Upon returning to this more public life, the first obstacle he encountered was a familiar one: opposition to his reforming views on teaching the language and literature of Hinduism to women. Ananta was actually put on trial by his fellow Brahmans for teaching Sanskrit to women. Unintimidated, the great scholar seized his opportunity. He could match his knowledge of the Hindu scriptures against that of any man on earth, and in his trial he did just that, so skillfully quoting and expounding all the passages that justified his position that, in the end, he won the trial. His beliefs and practices were vindicated. He would now be not only a famous scholar but also a famous reformer—an "orthodox reformer" as he would be called. In other words, he was one who held all the traditional doctrines of Hindu philosophy but believed in reforming certain practices. In any case, he was now free to embark upon his new life of pilgrimage.

Itinerant Life, Education, and Growing Doubt

Thus Ramabai would grow up on the road, traveling on foot with her family from one holy place to another. Wherever they went the whole family read aloud from the Puranas or other sacred texts, and the donations of those who believed they received great merit from hearing the reading—even though they did not understand the language—bought the food, drinks, clothes, and shelter the family needed. Such merit could help a person atone for sins committed in previous lives and advance him or her higher up the ladder of reincarnation. The little Ramabai had an education in Hinduism that many great scholars and priests might have envied, for she spent her childhood among the faithful visiting the greatest shrines of Hinduism, and as they traveled her father gave her an extraordinary education in Sanskrit and in all the great literature and ancient traditions of India. She had a rare gift for languages, and in addition to excelling in Sanskrit, she learned the languages of the regions her family visited. Thus, as a very young girl, Ramabai was fluent in several languages, an expert on the grammar of Sanskrit and on Hindu literature, and able to recite by heart an incredible eighteen thousand verses from the Puranas. As Ramabai would explain in her autobiography, her parents guarded their children from other subjects of learning:

> [M]y parents did not like us children to come into contact with the outside world. They wanted us to be strictly religious and adhere to their old faith. Learning any other language except Sanskrit was out of the question. Secular education of any kind was looked upon as leading people to worldliness which would prevent them from getting into the way of Moksha, or liberation from everlasting trouble of reincarnation . . .[3]

In particular, any contact with English was forbidden.

But a shadow of doubt had fallen across Ramabai's once wholehearted young faith when the palace of gold failed to appear. The shadow continued to grow over the next few years during which, as a young teenager, she continued to study and read the sacred texts and to join the rest of her family in giving every penny they could spare to temples and priests. On their travels Ramabai and her family had, of course, met people who professed devotion to Hinduism but did not really believe it or live according to its

---

3   Ramabai, Pandita. *A Testimony of our Exhaustible Treasure*. Maharashtra, India. Pandita Ramabai Mukti Mission. 10th edition. 1977. Page 12.

philosophy, but her parents' faith was absolutely genuine. Their entire life was ordered around the quest for salvation. "Our parents had unbounded faith in what the sacred books said," Ramabai would remember.[4] Ramabai had shared in this unbounded faith as a child, and during her teens she struggled to cultivate and bolster her faith, but doubts and questions continued to arise.

It was not until years later, after becoming a Christian, that Ramabai wrote her memories of this period, so that both the lapse of time and her new faith must have colored her recollections to some extent. Yet she retained vivid images of the sights and experiences that began to open cracks in the foundations of her belief. She saw that many of the "Puranikas"—those who, like her family, read the Puranas in public to gain merit for themselves and those who heard them—often offered no explanation of the words they read, words which, because they were in Sanskrit, were entirely unintelligible to their hearers. When they did explain, by telling some of the stories from the texts, they often wildly exaggerated them to make them more dramatic or exciting. "This is not considered sin, since it is done to attract common people's attention, that they may hear the sacred sound, the names of the gods, and some of their deeds, and be purified by this means," Ramabai would write.[5] She saw that many of the religious beggars she encountered—people who gave up everything to live in poverty and travel from shrine to shrine—were "most ignorant and pretend to great sanctity of life, but in reality they are vile, evil and wicked people."[6] She saw how some priests exploited the desperate pilgrims who came to the shrines. She saw people who starved themselves and their families in order to pile offerings before the feet of the gods. She saw "the pilgrims looking so disappointed and downcast on returning home after the pilgrimage . . . The enthusiasm which kindled their hearts as they start from home gradually dies away and not a particle of it is left when they return home."[7] She realized that at many shrines only a small percentage of the pilgrims who crowded the temples would ever even see the images of the gods—at one shrine her family visited she estimated that perhaps seventy thousand of four hundred thousand actually saw the face of the idol, while meanwhile scores of people were trampled to death in the crush.[8] If only she could be sure, as her parents were, that all of the sacrifices and the suffering offered to the gods would be repaid in the end, then it would all be worth it. But sometimes it was hard to be sure.

---

4   Ibid. 15.
5   Ibid. 14.
6   Ibid. 11.
7   Ibid. 15.
8   Ibid. 15.

Famine

The greatest test of Ramabai's faltering faith, and the darkest period of her life, was yet to come. Between her thirteenth and sixteenth years, a terrible famine ravaged India. Ramabai's father was growing old, and his sight would no longer allow him to read, so Ramabai, her sister, and her brother had been doing more and more of the reading. But soon no one had money—or even food—to donate to readers of the sacred texts. Because they had received no secular education or training at all, Ramabai and her siblings began to realize they were unprepared to make their living in any other way. They had no land to farm, no skills for which they could be employed, nothing but their life of earning money by reading the scriptures. Now that they were not being paid to do this, the family began to find themselves in increasingly desperate poverty. They began to sell, one by one, all the items they owned—pots, pans, clothes. It was never enough. They began to grow weaker and weaker from malnutrition. They were too proud to beg, something they had never done and which their father refused to consider. But in any case, India was submerged by a mighty tide of starving beggars. It seemed as if there was not enough money and not enough food anywhere in the land for all of them.

Ramabai's parents' faith did not falter in these desperate years. Instead, they turned to the gods, to the promises of the holy books. They continued to visit shrine after shrine, and despite their desperate need they gave alms and fasted as they prayed to the gods. They prostrated themselves at shrine after shrine, and they offered their increasingly desperate prayers to all the gods through the long hard days and the bitter hungry nights. Ramabai would remember:

> The sacred books declared that if people worshipped the gods in particular ways, gave alms to the Brahmans, repeated the names of certain gods, and also some hymns in their honour, with fasting and performance of penance, the gods and goddesses would appear and talk to the worshippers, and give them whatever they desired. We decided to take this course of meeting our temporal wants. For three years we did nothing but perform these religious acts. At last, all the money which we had was spent but the gods did not help us.[9]

Ramabai's parents and older sister all starved to death within a few months of each other, despite the fact that, at last, Ramabai and her brother cast aside all pride and resorted to begging and looking for manual labor—a disgrace for people of the prestigious Brahman class. They soon grew too weak for manual labor, and their desperate decision

---

9   Ibid. 15.

to break a promise to their dying father—the first to die—that whatever happened they would not beg came too late. By the time Ramabai overcame her horror of breaking her last promise to her father and begged for food, her mother was too weak and ill to eat it. Images of those days were seared forever into the memories of the surviving brother and sister: living for days on a little water and a handful of berries, pits and all; engaging in the manual labor for which they had no aptitude and which was an offense to their caste for a handful of rice; digging grave-like troughs in the dirt to keep warm at night; digging their father's grave and burying him—once one of the greatest minds of India— alone; repeating with growing desperation the prayers and rituals that never seemed to change anything; wandering without hope from one village to another, sharing the road only with other desperate and starving beggars.

The two had entered the famine members of a proud and happy family of five, full of hope for the future and faith in the gods, able to boast that they had never begged, stolen, broken caste, or committed any other offense against their cast or religion. They emerged from it orphaned, ill and starving, disgraced beggars, and having lost all confidence in the religion that had given shape and meaning to their childhoods. They had done all that the gods had asked of them, and waited faithfully to see the promises of the holy books fulfilled. Instead, the heavens had been silent, not only to them but also to their father, a holy man and scholar of the sacred texts who had been famous for his generosity, compassion, integrity, and single-minded devotion.

One scene in particular seemed to sum up the bitter end of Ramabai's descent into doubt, as the moment when Krishna's palace failed to appear above the waves of the Arabian sea captured its beginning. At one shrine she and her brother visited during their famine wanderings, a breathtaking mountain lake in the Himalayas, they saw the seven famous floating mountains of Hindu legend. These mountains were supposed to float toward the visitor who was worthy and sinless to receive his or her adoration. If an unworthy or sinful worshipper appeared, the mountains remained distant, fixed in place. Ramabai and her brother, despite their growing doubts, had continued absolutely faithful in the rituals and requirements of their religion except for being forced to beg and perform manual labor. The two exhausted, grief-stricken pilgrims prostrated themselves at the shore of the lake, and fixed their eyes with a last, flickering hope on the distant mountains. But the mountains did not move. This time, Ramabai and her brother were not prepared to accept the explanations of the priests who guarded the shrine, and who warned the pilgrims earnestly not to set foot in the lake, which, they said, was full of man-eating crocodiles. Not trusting this warning, or perhaps feeling he had little to lose, Ramabai's brother slipped into the lake early one morning before the priests were guarding it, and swam toward the mountains on the horizon. He had had enough of waiting for the gods to come to him; now he would go to them.

When he reached the floating mountains, which pilgrims never approached because the supposedly crocodile-infested lake lay between the mountains and them, he realized that they were skillfully constructed of mud and stone, planted with little trees, and positioned on wooden rafts. Behind them was a boat. If only he and Ramabai had been able to give the guardian priests a large enough offering, he now realized, they would have called upon the mountains to move, and the generous pilgrim would have seen them pushed toward him by means of the boat.

"We had fulfilled all the conditions laid down in the sacred books and kept all the rules as far as our knowledge went," Ramabai wrote years later, "but the gods were not pleased with us and did not appear to us. After years of fruitless service, we began to lose our faith in them, and in the books which prescribed this course and held out the hope of a great reward to the worshippers of the gods."[10]

Travels of the Two Survivors

The two young people had no home other than the roads of India, and they had no identity and way of life other than the Hinduism their parents had loved, so for about three years, they continued following both. "We still continued to keep caste rules, worshipped gods, and studied sacred literature as usual," Ramabai wrote. "But as our faith in our religion had grown cold, we were not quite so strict with regard to obtaining secular education and finding some means of earning an honest livelihood." They no longer trusted the gods entirely to meet their needs and secure their future, but, as good Brahmans, "We wandered from place to place, visiting many temples, bathing in many rivers, fasting and performance penances, worshipping gods, trees, animals, Brahmans, and all that we knew for more than three years after the death of our parents and sister."[11]

Ramabai had traveled the length and breadth of India for as long as she could remember. Now, as a young adult, she experienced and explored its dazzling variety of geography, language, and culture even more deeply and thoroughly. By the end of her three years' travel with her brother, Ramabai estimated that they had traveled about

10   Ibid. 16.
11   Ibid. 16.

four thousand miles on foot.[12] Many born into Ramabai's Brahman caste, especially to a successful and prominent man such as her father had been, might have reached young adulthood knowing virtually nothing of the lives of the poor. Ramabai, on the other hand, despite her faithful keeping of caste by not eating or coming into other close contact with those of lower castes, grew up seeing all around her the millions of India, especially the women. She saw the girls tricked and forced into temple prostitution, the mothers of starving children, the earnest pilgrims who could not hope to escape the brutal cycle of reincarnation until, having endured it again and again, they might at least be born as Brahman men. Above all, her heart went out to the child widows—girls who, at the age of nine or ten, were left as widows and outcasts. She would not forget them.

Arrival in Calcutta

Ramabai's and her brother's directionless wanderings at last brought them, in 1878, to Calcutta, a teeming city where work would surely be easier to find and where they might hope to establish a home. Well-educated, hard-working, high-caste, the children of a famous man, the two quickly began to find their feet in the community of scholarly men and women of their own caste. The years of wandering and desperation were over; Ramabai quickly began to find herself secure and accepted in the prestigious community of Brahmans.

It was during this time and at the suggestion of their Brahman friends that Ramabai and her brother attended, for the first time, a dinner hosted by English Christians. They were shocked to see Brahmans eating with the forbidden English and with Indians of a lower caste, and when the Christians knelt by their chairs to pray Ramabai and her brother believed them to be worshipping the chairs—strange idols even to them who had worshipped so many, of different shapes, all over India. Two men they met there gave Ramabai, as a gift, the Bible they themselves had translated into her language, but though she was delighted with the gift and tried to read it, she found it strange, difficult, and confusing, and gave up trying to understand it.

Calcutta provided work not only for Ramabai's brother but also for her: teaching women their duties as women according to the Shastras, or the laws derived and organized from the Hindu scriptures. It was a vast and daunting task, but Ramabai, with her keen mind and scholarly training, was up for the challenge. She bought a big stack of books

---

12   Ibid. 16.

on Hindu law, and also revisited many of the books she had learned from as a child and read others, such as the Dharma Shastras, for the first time.

Independent Study of Hinduism

This work was the beginning of a new phase in Ramabai's personal grappling with her doubts, and in her search for truth. It was characteristic of her that, instead of rejecting her religion entirely because of the ways it had failed her during the famine, Ramabai instead determined to use the training her father had given her to fearlessly and thoroughly explore its texts and teachings for herself in a whole new way. But as she began to do this, the doubts she had experienced because of her personal experiences and disappointments, and the greed and hypocrisy of some priests and pilgrims, began to take on new life as the perplexing intellectual questions of the scholar. Two issues, in particular, troubled Ramabai deeply. One was the freely admitted existence of countless contradictions among the sprawling canon of Hindu texts. "The Vedas differ from each other; Smrities, that is, books of sacred law, do not agree with one another; the secret of religion is in some hidden place: the only way is that which is followed by great men," Ramabai remembered reading in the Mahabharata, the sacred Hindu epic. After all the sacrifices her father had made to instruct her in sacred literature, and the years during which her parents had so faithfully pointed her toward the holy books for hope and guidance, it was disheartening to face the idea that "the secret of religion is in some hidden place," and that no amount of devoted and disciplined study of sacred texts could lead one to the truth.

The second question that haunted Ramabai, especially after the people she had met and the lives she had witnessed during her famine wanderings, was the bleak prospect offered to women, and to people of lower castes. Her father, of course, had successfully defended and practiced the idea that women might study the Puranas and worship the gods, and perhaps his delight in his daughter's mind and his confidence that she could have a rich, authentic devotional life of her own had insulated her from the full realization of what traditional Hinduism offered women. As she studied in Calcutta and sought to instruct other Hindu women in the duties and hopes their religion laid out for them, she was increasingly horrified by the eternity believed to lie before them. Her years of starvation and traveling had taught her how hard life was for many Indian women in this life, but that might all be worthwhile if it resulted in future blessings from the gods. Instead, she realized, women were offered no prospect of achieving "Moksha" or liberation from the cycle of reincarnation.

The only hope of their getting this much-desired liberation from karma and its results, that is, countless millions of births and deaths and untold suffering, was the worship of their husbands. The husband is said to be the woman's god; there is no other god for her . . . She can have no hope of getting admission into Svarga, the abode of the gods without his pleasure, and if she pleases him in all things, she will have the privilege of going to Svarga as his slave, there to serve him and be one of his wives among the thousands of the Svarga harlots who are presented to him by the gods in exchange for his wife's merit.[13]

A woman's only hope of achieving the far higher existence of Moksha or liberation was to perform such extraordinary and heroic acts of religious devotion that she might win the privilege of being one day reincarnated as a Brahman man. These were the only people allowed to study the most sacred of all Scriptures, the Vedas, which provided the only way to achieve Moksha. These extraordinary acts of religious devotion still consisted almost exclusively in the worship and service of her husband. "The woman has no right to study the Vedas and Vedanta, and without knowing them no one can know the Brahma; without knowing Brahma no one can get liberation, therefore no woman as a woman can get liberation," Ramabai summed up.[14]

Nor was the outlook bleak only for women. Virtually anyone other than one born as a Brahman faced a terrible fate, Ramabai realized. The Shudras, a lower caste, were, like women, not allowed to study the Vedas or perform the religious rituals which alone might achieve Moksha—in fact, a Shudra who accidentally overheard the Vedas being recited was supposed to have his ears filled with liquid lead, while one who had the presumption to learn a verse of it must have boiling hot liquid poured down his throat. "His only hope of getting liberation is in serving the three high castes as their lifelong slave," Ramabai wrote, "then he will earn merit enough to be reincarnated in some higher caste, and in the course of millions of years, he will be born as a Brahman, learn the Vedas and Vedanta, and get knowledge of the Brahma and be amalgamated in it. Such is the hope of final liberation held out . . . to women and to the Shudras."[15] When one considers that this ultimate liberation, or amalgamation of the self into the Brahma, was essentially the loss of individual consciousness in the absolute—in other words, escape from existence with all the inevitable suffering it brings—one begins to sense the horror that began to grow in Ramabai's mind as she studied.

For of course the grim ladder of existence went still lower—there were the "untouchable" people of the lowest caste of all. Ramabai knew that her life during the famine had been

---

13   Ibid. 19.
14   Ibid. 19–20.
15   Ibid. 20.

much like theirs, but always she had considered herself apart from and above them. As she studied their position in orthodox Hinduism, she realized still further the misery of their lives:

> [T]he poor things have no hope of any sort. They are looked upon as being very like the lower species of animals, such as pigs; their very shadow and the sound of their voices are defiling; they have no place in the abode of the gods, and no hope of getting liberation, except that they might perchance be born among the higher castes after having gone through millions of reincarnations. [To achieve this] they should be contented to live in a very degraded condition, serving the high caste people as their bondservants, eating the leavings of their food in dirty broken earthen vessels, wearing filthy rags . . . They may sometimes get the benefit of coming in contact with the shadow of a Brahman, and have a few drops of water from his hand or wet clothes thrown at them, and feel the air which has passed over the sacred persons of Brahmans. These things are beneficial to the low-caste people, but the Brahmans lose much of their own hard-earned merit by letting the low-caste people get these benefits! . . . How very sad their condition is no one who has not seen can realize.[16]

If the whole system of Hindu philosophy, rooted in its scriptures, had held together better for Ramabai she might have found a different perspective on the sufferings of women and the lower castes, and if she had found more hope and comfort to offer the women of her classes she might have been less troubled by the complexities and contradictions she was encountering in her studies. But it increasingly seemed to her that the only thing agreed on all by all texts and traditions was the desperate plight and harsh treatment of women and lower castes, while on everything else there was endless contradiction and confusion. It would be hard enough to choose between truth and hope, but to be offered neither was indeed a blow. Ramabai realized, of course, that the sufferings people experienced in their lives were the result of their sins committed in previous lives, so there was believed to be a kind of overarching justice in the brutal cycle of reincarnation. But the grim realization that even the most desperate and committed search for virtue, truth, and hope would not be rewarded for millions of years, if ever, was a heavy weight to carry. Studying her beliefs on her own for the first time, Ramabai felt her foundations rocked by all she was learning. "I had a vague idea of these doctrines . . . from my childhood," she would write, "but while studying the Dharma Shastras, they presented themselves to my mind with great force; My eyes were being gradually opened . . ." Ramabai did not merely grapple intellectually with

---

her studies, but took seriously their implications for her own life, and as her search for truth intensified her heart darkened.

> II was waking up to my own hopeless condition as a woman, and it was becoming clearer and clearer to me that I had no place anywhere as far as religious consolation was concerned. I became quite dissatisfied with myself. I wanted something more than the Shastras could give me, but I did not know what it was that I wanted.[17]

Ramabai's combination of growing doubt and desperate hope even led her to take, at the urging of a modernizing Brahman reformer, the incredibly bold step of studying the Vedas themselves—the most sacred of Hindu scriptures which were forbidden to women and which she had never even thought of venturing to read. In Hindu tradition, only the Vedas themselves—the most ancient texts—are believed to be directly inspired by the gods. All others, while they are seen as being holy and containing divine truth, are believed to have been written by holy men.[18] Now, tentatively, Ramabai "convinced myself" that a woman might read both the Vedas and the Upanishads. The only result was, in Ramabai's terse summary, "I became more dissatisfied with myself."[19] She had gradually climbed the ladder of Hindu literature from the bottommost rungs considered suitable for women, up into giddier and giddier heights of knowledge protected from the profaning eyes and ears of all but Brahman men. She had followed the stream to its source, but here she stood still thirsty.

Early Achievements, Marriage, Motherhood, and an Encounter with Christianity

Even while all this was going on in her heart and mind, however, Ramabai was achieving extraordinary success. She was becoming, in her early twenties, a figure not only of national but also of international fame, the rising star of a community of highly educated reform-minded Brahman scholars in one of India's leading cities. Even as she herself was growing so deeply disillusioned with the status of women in Hinduism, she was rapidly gaining fame as an inspiring symbol of the new Hindu woman. Ramabai was a gifted communicator, and her lectures for and about Hindu women won both male and female admirers across the city and beyond. Groups of Brahman scholars summoned her to speak before them and to prove

---

17   Ibid. 21.
18   https://www.crystalinks.com/indiascriptures.html   and   https://www.hinduwebsite.com/hinduism/hinduscriptures.asp.
19   Testimony 22.

her knowledge in various tests, marveling at her ability to speak all of India's seven languages with such fluency, and at her grasp of Sanskrit—a language which many believed virtually impossible to speak, but in which Ramabai could throw out extemporaneous poetry on command.[20] It was during this time, and at such a young age, that she was given the title "Pandita" by the Brahman scholars—an honorific which in its masculine form has given us our English word "pundit," but which was, in its original Sanskrit, a rare and prestigious designation accorded to the leading Brahman scholars of the land. By calling this twenty-two-year-old "Pandita," the Brahman scholars were declaring her one of their number.

Just at this time, when she was becoming famous and beloved as a scholar and speaker yet also relinquishing her last hope in the truth of her parents' religion, Ramabai's beloved brother died. Left unprotected and now, at twenty-two, far older than the customary age of marriage, she needed to choose a husband—indeed her dying brother begged her to promise that she would marry as soon as he left her without his protection. It is a measure of her disillusionment with Hinduism and her Brahman heritage that she broke caste by marrying a Shudra, a Bengali attorney of far lower caste than her own. By doing so she cut herself off from the support and acceptance of much of the Brahman community, but she seems to have loved her husband and been very happy with him during their brief marriage in his hometown of Silchar, Assam. Within just two years, however, he would be dead of cholera, leaving her a widow with a baby daughter.

It was during her brief married life that Ramabai, finally at the end of all her hope in her parents' religion and having even cut herself off from traditional Brahmans—the identity that had once met everything to her—first encountered Christianity. She was looking for something to believe in—not only had she lost hope in traditional Hinduism but she also could not find convincing the "reformed" or westernized Brahmanism which sought to reconcile Hinduism with modernity and the west. This belief system, Ramabai recognized, was "not a very definite one," but instead "it is nothing but what a man makes for himself. He chooses and gathers whatever seems good to him from all religions known to him, and prepares a sort of religion for his own use."[21] Ramabai was far more drawn to this gentler and warmer flavor of Hinduism than to Hindu orthodoxy, but her scholar's mind and her hunger for truth could not be satisfied with it. Thus, when a Baptist missionary introduced her to the Bible she was intrigued. She was ready to become a Christian, she told her husband, if, upon investigation, she found it to be

---

21 Testimony 24.

true. She was embarking upon yet another journey of discovery. In the desolate weeks following her husband's death, she pored over a copy of the Gospel of Luke in Bengali. Ramabai, the scholar, had embarked upon the exploration of yet another holy book.

Rootless and alone with her infant daughter, the young widow considered her future, and lived briefly in a few different places before eventually moving to Poona, the capital city of a district and considered the intellectual center of the Chitpawan Brahmans to which she and her family belonged. Here she planned to study English, the language of the west and of the allies of reform. She already recognized that her life's work would involve working to help and educate the women of India, and adding English to the extensive list of languages in which she was fluent would prepare her for that mission.

Ramabai and her daughter took up residence in a rented room, sparing her friends or family the shame of inviting into their homes a woman who had broken caste. She began to study both English and the Bible with a Miss Hurford, an English woman who headed a government training school for women, along with the wife of a Chief Justice who knew Ramabai and offered her the opportunity to join his wife's private lessons.

Ramabai, who had not only mastered numerous languages but was also fluent in the notoriously intricate grammar of Sanskrit, found the English lessons almost too easy. She mastered the language rapidly and almost effortlessly. It was the Bible lessons that absorbed her eager curiosity; she was still seriously considering the claims of Christianity and was ready to give to it the same thorough and enthusiastic study she had given to Hinduism.

Ramabai was also invited by the same Chief Justice to deliver in his home a series of lectures on the sacred literature of India—lectures that soon became popular and led to the founding of a club for Indian women in which they could meet weekly for two purposes: to advance their own education, and to work for the causes of educating women and ending child marriages in India.[22] Soon this society, and Ramabai's lectures, began to attract the attention not only of Indian but also British authorities, propelling Ramabai into even greater fame as an advocate and the leader of a reform movement, not simply a communicator. The English government even set up an Education Commission specifically to investigate the needs of Indian women and girls. Ramabai also advocated tirelessly for women physicians to offer medical care to the women of India.[23] She was becoming a symbol of hope for the women of India, and giving them a voice to which both Indians and Europeans were listening.

Ramabai felt a growing desire to study in England. She not only desired to perfect her English and to continue her study of Christianity but she also recognized that an

---

22   Miller 33–34.
23   Ibid. 34.

English education and English connection would both be invaluable to her future work. Nevertheless, the idea of traveling to England was a tremendously daunting one even to Ramabai, who had made so many hard journeys in her young life. Not only did she have no money for the trip and no way of obtaining it, but she would also face a grueling and dangerous ocean voyage, and then a land whose climate, food, culture, religion, and ways of life would be entirely foreign. Ramabai was used to being a wanderer and used to being an outsider, but if she made this journey, she would experience both to a far greater degree than ever before. "It is such a great step for a Hindu woman to cross the sea," Ramabai wrote.

> One cuts one's self always off from one's people. But the Voice came to me as to Abraham. It seemed to me now very strange how I could have started as I did, with my friend and little child. Throwing myself on God's protection, I went forth as Abraham, not knowing whither I went.[24]

This comparison Ramabai would make years later to the Biblical Abraham aptly captured her feelings of leaving everything she knew and journeying into the unknown.

To raise money for her trip and her education in England, Ramabai published her first of many books: *Morals for Women*. It was both the culmination of her study and teaching over the past several years and the beginning of her future work, and it carried what one biographer calls "a timeless plea for India's womanhood."[25] She also continued to travel and lecture, more extensively and to more extensive audiences than ever before. She formed several branches, in several cities, of the women's society that had grown out of her weekly lectures in Poona. She wrote, and translated, and spoke. She also adopted the first of several child widows she would welcome into her home throughout her life—a twelve-year-old girl, a Brahman like Ramabai, who had been begging on the streets for several years after being thrown out by her husband's family after his death. Pandita had very little herself, but she realized that the rescue of India's child widows would have to be carried out one at a time, not just through writing and speaking.[26]

To England

Pandita Ramabai sailed for England in 1883, where she stayed and studied with a group of religious women, the Anglican "Sisters of Wantage" who were especially known for their

---

24 Ibid. 35.
25 Ibid. 36.
26 Ibid. 36.

work with women who had fallen into prostitution—women whom they offered shelter, training, the hope of the Gospel, and the chance of a new life. As she stayed and studied with them, Ramabai was especially struck by their commitment to and compassion for these women—women who, in orthodox Hinduism, were believed to have fallen so far that they should be treated only with contempt and offered only punishment.

"I had never heard or seen anything of the kind done for this class of women," Ramabai would remember. "I had not heard anyone speaking kindly of them, nor seen anyone making any effort to turn them from the evil path they had chosen in their folly . . . They are considered the greatest sinners, and not worthy of compassion."[27] Ramabai asked the sisters about their attitude toward and treatment of these women. One sister, Ramabai would remember years later, read in response the story of Christ's meeting with the Samaritan woman at the well. "She spoke of the Infinite Love of Christ for sinners," Ramabai wrote.

> He did not despise them but came to save them. I had never read or heard anything like this . . . I realized after reading the 4th chapter of St. John's Gospel, that Christ was truly the Divine Savior He claimed to be, and no one but He could transform and uplift the downtrodden womanhood of India, and of every land.[28]

Ramabai's experience of the authentic compassion, hospitality, and humility of the Sisters, who welcomed her with such love and extended that love even to the outcasts of society, opened a new perspective on her ongoing struggle to understand the differences between Hinduism and Christianity, to find a truth in which her mind could rest. She still had many questions, and she had no real understanding of her own personal need for salvation. But she felt certain that Christianity was true, and she was ready to make a commitment to it even though she knew how costly that commitment would be. "I was intellectually convinced of its truth after reading a book written by Father Goreh, and was baptized in the Church of England in the latter part of 1883," she wrote, despite knowing "that it would displease my friends and my countrymen very much."[29]

Over the ensuing years, Ramabai continued to study Christianity, and to grapple with many questions. She was especially overwhelmed by the many different sects and denominations within Christianity. "No one can have any idea of what my feelings were at finding such a Babel of religions in Christian countries, and at finding how

---

27   Testimony 24–25.
28   Ibid. 26.
29   Ibid. 26.

very different the teaching of each sect was from that of the others," Ramabai would remember.[30] It was all too reminiscent of the infinite complexities and contradictions of Hinduism that had already caused her so much confusion and disillusionment. She was "comparatively happy" with her new Christian identity and beliefs, but years of struggle still lay ahead. "Although I was quite contented with my newly-found religion, so far as I understood it, still I was laboring under great intellectual difficulties, and my heart longed for something better which I had not found."[31]

After spending a year with the Sisters, Ramabai became professor of Sanskrit in the Ladies' College at Cheltenham. While there she continued to fill the gaps in her own education by studying mathematics, science, and English literature. She wanted to learn all she could during her time in England; she was preparing herself in every way she could think of to be as useful as possible to the cause of reform for India's women. At this time she thought that a position within the British government might well offer the greatest opportunity to do that, and the young woman who was already one of the greatest scholars of India was now becoming as accomplished a scholar as possible in the English tradition also.

In 1886 Ramabai was invited to attend the graduation ceremonies for the first Indian women ever to receive the degree of Doctor of Medicine. She was graduating from the Women's Medical College of Pennsylvania, and Ramabai seized the opportunity not only to be present at this historic occasion but also to visit America as well as England. Accompanied by her four-and-a-half-year-old daughter, Ramabai sailed to America (although a year later her daughter traveled back to India with friends, a year ahead of her mother's return).[32] Ramabai made a tremendous sensation in America and received invitations to speak from all across the country, and eventually in Canada as well. Her visit to America not only established many connections and friendships that would be important to her future but also gave her a whole new vision for her future work in India. Instead of working within the system of schools set up by the British colonial government, she would work to establish native schools for Indian women. With her characteristic thoroughness and enthusiasm, Ramabai studied kindergartens and began work on several textbooks to use in instructing the women of her native country. She financed the publication of her textbooks by writing and publishing her second book, still considered by some her most important. *High Caste Hindu Women* introduced western

---

30 Ibid. 27.
31 Ibid. 26–27.
32 Miller 41.

audiences to the abuses women suffered in India, and challenged the best minds of India to take up the challenge of reform.

The book electrified American audiences, and the Ramabai Association, whose members included the most famous names of the time, was formed to support the schools Ramabai would found in India, and especially "with the object of giving education to high caste child widows of India."[33] (High caste widows were in especially dire straits because they were entirely unprepared for any type of manual labor, and because they were forbidden to marry again.)

Ramabai left America in 1888, and in 1889 she arrived in Bombay. After being away for so long, and after learning and experiencing so many new things, Ramabai "felt as if I were going to a strange country and to a strange people."[34] She was now, and would remain for the rest of her life, an international celebrity, treated as a famous person wherever she went.[35] It was time to see how she could use her platform and all her preparation for her fellow Indian women.

The First School Opens

In 1889, her first year back in India, Ramabai published in Marathi an account of her travels in America. The book's theme was that the opportunities and education available to women in America had enabled them to achieve tremendous things and given them much to offer their country, and that the same potential lay with the women of India. The book was hugely successful and became an instant classic.[36]

Ramabai also opened her first widow's home: Sharada Sadan, meaning "Home of Wisdom." She began with two students, but at the end of six months, she had twenty-five. She began at the beginning, teaching the alphabet in Marathi, English, and Sanskrit. In 1891 the school would move to Poona, where living expenses were lower.

Ramabai's early efforts were focused largely on winning over the reform-minded Hindu community. If any young women were to wish, or be allowed, to come to her for an education it was essential that she overcome the mistrust and hostility of the educated and progressive Hindus, many of whom were beginning to look favorably on reforms, including the education of women, but all of whom were mistrustful of contamination by western influences and especially of Christianity. If Ramabai's classes were offered by a respectable Indian woman with an excellent high-caste Hindu background, to

---

33   Ibid. 43.
34   Ibid. 44.
35   Ibid. 45.
36   Ibid. 45.

respectable Indian women who would become the virtuous Hindu women of the future, Hindu reformers were ready to throw the full weight of their support behind her. If, on the other hand, the school turned out to be a conduit for English and especially Christian influences that might undermine the Hindu beliefs and identities of the students, they were ready to turn against it. Everyone knew, of course, that Ramabai had officially become a Christian and had joined the church of England—those who had read her books or heard her lectures would even know that she considered Christ and Christianity the only hope of India's women. But some were willing to give her the chance to prove that she would not try to convert her students.

Thus, instead of any Christian prayers and activities that students were required to participate in, Ramabai simply conducted her own daily prayer and Bible reading time with her daughter in a room with an open door. Anyone who wanted to come in and listen was welcome, but no one was required to be there. Thus, no one could say she was teaching her students Christianity. In spite of this, the opposition she faced ebbed and flowed; there were times when she seemed to be making headway, and times when she believed her school would not be allowed to survive. But the decision that nearly dealt a deathblow to her efforts was Ramabai's own, and it was one she would never regret. Eight years after declaring herself a Christian, Ramabai at last, and for the first time, came to personal faith in Christ, not as an example of virtue and compassion, not as the Savior of the women of India, but as her own Savior.

Salvation

"It was nobody's fault that I had not found Christ," Ramabai wrote. "He must have been preached to me from the beginning." Perhaps the relief of deciding, after such a long, exhausting exploration, that Christianity was true had been so great that for awhile she did not seek anything more. Perhaps her old, deeply ingrained belief in earning salvation by gaining merit had remained foundational to her understanding in ways she did not suspect. She had believed, as she would later recount in her autobiography, that her Christian baptism functioned in the same way as Hindu baptism rituals, washing away her sin just as she and her family had once sought to wash away their sins at temples and shrines. Perhaps, too, she saw Christ as the Savior of those, like the fallen women served by the Sisters, who had destroyed their lives through sin, but felt that she was one of those who had made great sacrifices to live a virtuous life and did not understand how her need for a Savior could be the same as theirs. Ramabai herself pointed out that she had also spent more time reading *about* the Christian Scriptures than reading the Bible itself—and that when this changed, things began to change in her own mind and heart. "The open Bible had been before me, but I had given much of my time to the study of other books about the Bible, and had not studied the Bible itself as I should have done," Ramabai wrote. "Hence my ignorance of many important doctrines taught in it."[37]

After her return to India from America, however, Ramabai laid aside many of the other books she had been studying, and began a new program of regularly reading the Bible itself. "Following this course for about two years, I became very unhappy in my mind," she wrote. "I was dissatisfied with my spiritual condition." During this time she visited Bombay on business, and happened upon a book called *From Death unto Life*. The book was the memoir of a Church of England minister who had been a zealous and devoted servant of the church. One day a woman in his congregation told him that he was "trying to build from the top." In his book, the minister described how this remark caused him to realize that he himself had never been reborn, and that he was building all his good works on a foundation of pride and self-confidence, rather than on a foundation of new life.

"I read his account of his conversation, and work for Christ," Ramabai would remember. "Then I began to consider where I stood, and what my actual need was."

She returned to her Bible reading with a new urgency: "I took the Bible and read portions of it, meditating on the messages which God gave me." Still, she found, "there were so many things I did not understand intellectually." But one thing, at least, was for the first time entirely clear. "One thing I knew by this time, that I needed Christ, and not merely His religion."[38]

"I had failed to see the need of placing my implicit faith in Christ and His atonement in order to become a child of God by being born again of the Holy Spirit, and justified by faith in the Son of God," Ramabai explained later. At the time, nothing was clear except that things were not as they should be—she was not satisfied, she was not ready to stand before God, she had never known the regeneration the Bible described. "I realized that I was not prepared to meet God, that sin had dominion over me, and I was not altogether led by the Spirit of God, and . . . had no witness of the Spirit that I was a child of God."

But what could she do? She had spent her whole life seeking salvation, first as a Hindu, then as a Christian. Always she had been ready for any struggle, any sacrifice. If there was a good deed, she had done it. If there was a ritual of prayer or service, she had been

---

37   Testimony 28.
38   Testimony 29.

eager to perform it. If there was a way to learn more, to think more clearly, to understand better, she had thrown herself into it. She had shrunk from no effort, no discipline, no struggle, no sacrifice. No one had sought for truth, for virtue, for salvation, with more passion and more commitment. Never before had she been helpless. Always, somewhere deep down, she had counted on herself—she had believed that whatever was required, she could do.

Now, everything was different. "My thoughts could not, and did not help me," Ramabai wrote. "I had at last come to an end of myself, and unconditionally surrendered myself to the Saviour; and asked Him to be merciful to me, and to become my Righteousness and Redemption, and to take away all my sin."[39]

There was no truth and no experience that this woman who was master of seven languages desired so greatly to describe, but she found herself almost at a loss for words. She reached for a metaphor: "I do not know if any one of my readers has ever had the experience of being shut up in a room where there was nothing but thick darkness and then groping in it to find something of which he or she was in dire need," Ramabai wrote.

> I can think of no one but the blind man, whose story is giving in St. John chapter nine. He was born blind and remained so for forty years of his life; and then suddenly he found the Mighty One, Who could give him eyesight. Who could have described his joy at seeing the daylight, when there had not been a particle of hope of his ever seeing it? . . . I can give only a faint idea of what I felt when my mental eyes were opened, and when I, who was "sitting in darkness saw Great Light" . . . [40]

Now, at last, Ramabai began to grasp the great chasm between the hope that had failed her and the hope she had found. "How very different the truth of God was from the false idea that I had entertained from my earliest childhood," she wrote. "That was that I must have merit to earn present or future happiness . . ." She had sought merit first as a Hindu; later, although she had not realized it, she had simply continued to seek merit as a Christian. Now she realized that she never had, and never could, merit the love God had lavished upon her in Christ. In her written memories of this experience, she piles up one Bible passage after another, as if they had suddenly sprung to life for her—as if in inexhaustible astonishment: "When we were enemies we were reconciled to God by

39   Testimony 30.
40   Testimony 31.

the death of His Son;" "Herein is love, not that we loved God, but that He loved us, and sent His Son to be the propitiation for our sins;" The kindness and love of God our Savior toward man appeared, not by works of righteousness which we have done, but according to His mercy He saved us." The girl who had stood on the shore, hoping for a glimpse of the shining palace of Krishna, now saw at last that salvation was not something waiting at the end of an unimaginably long, hard, road, but was a gift. "O the love, the unspeakable love of the Father for me, a lost sinner," she wrote. "I had not merited this love, but that was the very reason why He showed it to me."[41]

A New Life, A New Home

Pandita Ramabai had, in one sense, arrived at the end of her journey. But in another sense, her journey was only now beginning—the source and spring of the phenomenon that her women's school would become was now, for the first time, unleashed. Ramabai's new birth in Christ overlapped with her school's move to Poona and the work of preparing the new facility. In the summer of 1892, the new Sharada Sadan held its opening ceremonies, a current group of forty resident students hosting local dignitaries and visiting guests.

The school was in a newly constructed building, set back from the road and screened by trellises. Half of the compound on which it stood bloomed with trees and flowers. Ramabai wanted this place—the first place where many who entered had ever tasted kindness or acceptance—to be a home, a welcoming oasis of beauty and safety. "They come from homes where they have been treated as outcasts, where no love has been bestowed upon them and no comfort provided for them," she said.

> I wish them to see the contrast in all things where love rules. I wish them to become acquainted with as many good people as possible, to learn what the outside world is about from pictures and books and to enjoy the wonderful work of God as they ramble in the garden, study with the microscope and view the heavens from the little veranda on the roof.[42]

It was not surprising that, although Ramabai kept her promise to her Hindu supporters and did not require attendance at any Christian prayer, Bible reading, or other activity, attendance at her "private family prayers" each morning grew and grew. Several of the students became Christians, and some declared their new faith to their families

---

41   Testimony 31–33.
42   Miller 53.

and were baptized. A firestorm of controversy and opposition descended on the school in response to this, and many of the new converts faced severe persecution. So many students were withdrawn from the school that its numbers were almost halved, and Ramabai was attacked in the newspapers.[43] Yet even as opponents attacked the school, they were creating publicity for it, and as some girls were withdrawn, others learned of the school for the first time and traveled there. The storm of hostility also resulted in a new freedom for the school to nail its colors to the mast as a Christian institution. Ramabai felt that she had kept her agreement with the Hindu community; it was they who had turned against the school now that some students had freely chosen to become Christians. "We give them all liberty to keep their caste and customs and have made all arrangements for it," Ramabai wrote.

> They are not prevented from praying to their own gods nor from wearing those gods around their necks if they want to . . . I have not taught the girls any religious form. I was a Christian woman and I had a home of my own and a daughter for whom I thought I must make a home . . . When I had my family worship in my own home, and not in the school hall, some of the girls began to come in, and we gave them freedom to come if they wanted to.[44]

Now that some of the girls had converted and the Hindus had withdrawn their support, it was not possible for the school to be seen as anything but a Christian one. Ramabai now felt free to give it a more explicitly Christian identity, although she would always allow religious freedom. Without the need to secure the support of local Hindu families, Ramabai also felt free to focus new efforts on reaching out to and seeking to rescue the child widows ensnared or forced into temple prostitution.[45]

The Farm

Other circumstances also combined to make this a turning point in Ramabai's ministry. As she looked toward the future expansion of the school, she began hoping for a way to make it at least partially self-supporting. The financial backing of the Hindu community had been withdrawn; the American Ramabai Society was pledged to support the school with funds for ten years. Soon, the school would need a way to support itself. Ramabai thought that perhaps the school should purchase a larger piece of property, out in the country, where it could grow fruit and vegetables and use the income from the

---

43   Ibid. 54–55.
44   Ibid. 57.
45   Ibid. 56–58.

farm to support the school. But then Ramabai's American society rejected her proposal to fund the new endeavor. Without the support of the local Hindus, or the American Christians, Ramabai found herself, for the first time, looking to God alone in a new way. It was a new step in her life of faith that would lay the foundation for a bold new life of dependence on God in the future.

Ramabai and her friend and assistant agreed to pray together that, if it was God's will for the school to purchase land, He would supply the money. She even looked into the possibility of raising the money against her life insurance, but it proved impossible. For two years the women prayed, and gradually the money trickled in. At last, one unforgettable day, the large remaining sum arrived from a group of friends in America. Ramabai was able to purchase her farm in 1895.

"This was the beginning of Pandita Ramabai's life of trust," writes a biographer. "Eventually the farm was planted to orange, lime, and mango trees. The remainder of the hundred acres was cleared gradually and planted to other useful crops."[46]

Also putting down roots, however, was Ramabai's new faith. Around this time she read several Christian biographies—a biography of Amanda Barry Smith, the former slave who became an evangelist, the autobiography of George Mueller, who founded orphanages with no financial backing other than the gifts that came in response to prayer, and the stories of pioneering missionaries Hudson Taylor in China and John Paton in the Pacific islands. What the stories had in common was their testimony to God's faithfulness in supplying financially for huge, seemingly impossible undertakings sustained only by voluntary gifts in answer to prayer. "I wondered after reading their lives," Ramabai wrote, "if it were not possible to trust the Lord in India as in other countries. I wished that there were some missions founded in this country which would be a testimony to the Lord's faithfulness to His people, and that truthfulness to what the Bible says in a practical way."[47] Over the coming years, as the ministry of the original home in Puna expanded and overflowed far beyond its walls in ways the first pupils could never have imagined, Ramabai and its other leaders would increasingly turn to pray and trust in God's faithfulness to provide the money that would fuel its extraordinary achievements. As the school continued to grow, and as more of its students came to faith in Christ, the group of people who prayed faithfully for its needs, both in India and overseas, expanded also.

---

46   Ibid. 60.
47   Ibid. 61.

Famine

The strengthening of Ramabai's faith and that of her fellow Christians at the school came just in time, as did the bold purchase of the farm property with its gardens and fields. The following year, Ramabai's prayer for new students would be answered even as disaster struck India, straining the financial resources not only of Ramabai's ministry but also of every institution in the country, and forcing Ramabai to test the faithfulness of God to the very end. It was the reawakening of that terrible ghost of her childhood: famine.

In the Madhya Pradesh famine of 1896-1897, one of the most severe famines ever to strike India, a conservatively estimated ten to fourteen million people died of starvation or related causes across India. A cholera epidemic flared up to exacerbate the desperate conditions. As desperate girls and women began to make their way to Ramabai, she was determined not to turn any of them away. She even traveled the areas where the famine was most severe, gathering and bringing back with her the women and children—especially child widows—she found starving on the streets and in the forests as she and her family once had. She erected grass huts to house them on the farmland she had purchased. She dug more wells, planted more fruit trees, built more buildings. And above all, she prayed that God would supply the needs of all who came to her. In the famine she survived as a young woman, she had seen the desperate calling upon the Hindu gods and receiving no answer. Now, she knew the God Who would answer, and she knew that only He could give hope to those facing the terrible ordeal she herself had barely survived.

During the year 1897 alone, eighty-five thousand dollars poured into the school and the farm. Ramabai issued no appeals and conducted no fundraising, although she did communicate frequently with her supporters in America, and much was written about her work in journals, magazines, and newspapers around the world. As the money continued to arrive, so did the refugees. Ramabai made a second trip to the hardest-hit regions, and returned from this single trip with more than six hundred women and girls who had nowhere else to go.[48] Some stayed at the home in Poona, now bursting at the seams, while others went to the farm property which was being built and planted even more rapidly under the pressure of the great need. With the great numbers of people gathered there, and with the bright testimony of kindness and generosity the ministry had been able to offer, there was a great response to the evangelistic meetings at which

---

48 Ibid. 64.

Ramabai invited a minister friend to speak. Not only numerical growth but also great spiritual harvest was growing in the midst of the famine.

The Mukti Mission

In 1897 the Mukti Mission was officially dedicated at the new farm property. "Mukti" means salvation, and the name was taken from Isaiah 60:18: "Thou shalt call thy walls Salvation, and thy gates Praise." Born of famine, the Mukti Mission was to be a source of strength and hope to countless people in the decades to come.

The year 1889 was a milestone for the now thirty-one-year-old Pandita Ramabai. The ten years since her return to India—the ten years during which the American Ramabai Association had committed to financially support her work—were over, and she returned to both America and England to revisit her friends and supporters there and to update them on the progress of the work. She could report that the home at Poona had welcomed, sheltered, and educated nearly five hundred women with the over ninety-one thousand dollars the Association had contributed. Her property was valued at sixty thousand dollars. She had also started the Mukti Mission farm, virtually without any contribution from the Association. Several young women had become Christians, and countless others had been rescued from suicide, prostitution, or starvation. During the great national crisis of the famine, Ramabai and her associates had been ideally prepared and positioned, with their farmland, wells, and fruit trees, to offer hope to the desperate victims. The original committee was now disbanded, and a new committee formed to support the Sharada Sadan at Poona, with no cutoff date this time, and also to support and cooperate with the Mukti Mission. Ramabai suggested the name "The Faith, Hope, and Love Association for the Emancipation of the High Caste Child Widows of India," and she urged her supporters, "Do not concentrate your interest in one person, for that person will die and be gone, as many have gone before, but this association must not die. It must be perpetually alive, and how will it live but through faith, hope, and love?"[49] The Association had previously been sending six thousand dollars a year, but now Ramabai asked for twenty thousand a year. "If we had not a single cent in hand, God would shower from heaven the funds we want. Last year God sent thirty thousand dollars. He is as rich today and He will send us twenty thousand dollars, not for one year, or two, or ten, but so long as India and its needs exist."[50]

---

49   Ibid. 68.
50   Ibid. 69.

From America Ramabai returned to England, where she was able to speak at the Keswick Convention, a gathering of Christians from around England. She asked for prayer for a hundred thousand men and a hundred thousand women from among the Christians of India to dedicate themselves to taking the gospel to their fellow Indians. Pandita Ramabai had become a woman with big dreams for her country, and one with a deep and growing faith in a generous and faithful God.

The rest of Pandita Ramabai's life would be dedicated to two great works. The first, only beginning in the wake of the great Madhya Pradesh famine, was the Mukti Mission. Around its founding core of sheltering and educating child widows, the mission would expand in countless directions and in response to other needs. First, immediately upon Ramabai's return to India from her American trip, the mission established a new department especially for rescuing girls from prostitution and preparing them for a new future. An additional twenty-two acres was added to the property for this expansion.[51] New wells were dug, new gardens planted, and new buildings dedicated, including the mission's own church.

Once again, the expanded ministry was no sooner ready than it was desperately needed. Three years after the previous famine, in 1900–1901, the Gujerat famine struck, and again Pandita and her fellow workers at Mukti opened their doors to as many famine victims as they possibly could. Hundreds of women and girls were rescued from starvation, and from the trafficking of unprotected girls and young women by ruthless traders who took advantage of the famine to trick, trap, or force desperate girls into prostitution. So many newcomers sought refuge at the two properties at the Mukti Mission that it had about two thousand residents by the end of this famine. It is impossible to know how long it would have taken Ramabai's ministry to grow from the embattled and controversial school with a fluctuating handful of fewer than forty students, attacked by and cut off from the leaders of the surrounding community, into the unstoppable phenomenon it became, but it is fitting that it was two famines that propelled the ministry to grow to fifty times its size in just five years. The young woman who remembered so well, all her life, the sufferings of her family during the famine of her childhood and who had wandered the length and breadth of India in search of the peace, the safety, and the welcome she never found, was now able to open her arms and her doors to hundreds and thousands of women and children who had no other hope. She hoped that in the aptly named "Mukti" or "Salvation" home, they would find the compassion and faithfulness

---

51   Ibid. 69–70.

of Christ. The famine of her childhood had taken everything from her and driven her to the end of the hope in her parents' holy books that had once sustained her. The famines that assailed India now gave her a unique opportunity to share the new hope she had at last found.

"Think of my mother and remember that it was there I got my inspiration for famine work," Ramabai once said to her daughter. Many felt shock and compassion in response to the ravages of famine, with the epidemics, prostitution, crime, and other horrors they brought in their wake, but Ramabai knew exactly what it was like to starve on the roadsides and in the jungles of India, and she never forgot what her family had suffered. She was able to paint an unforgettable work picture of the terrible need:

> Small streams and rivers have dried up long ago and the large rivers have dwindled down into threads of small streams of water. Large wells too have scarcely any water . . . Large herds of hungry and thirsty cattle move about like armies of ghosts. They have nothing but skin and bone left and fall down dead at any moment . . . The death of cattle means a great loss to the agriculture of this country for years to come.

> But turning from the cattle, we see a more pitiful and heart-rending sight in the human skeletons moving about in search of food. Nearly six millions of people are at work in Government Relief camps, and the number is fast increasing. But there are many more poor people who are too weak to work and too helpless. Many High Caste people who are too proud to work in relief camps are dying in their own homes. Life in relief camps is very hard. The people are asked to break 12 basket-fulls of stone in small pieces . . . The money they earn is not enough even to give them one coarse meal a day . . . Everyone is not able to stand this hard camp life . . . Vast numbers of children and famished old people can be seen picking a few grains from the dirty roads over which carts of grains have passed. They are filling their empty stomachs with sand and small stones in order to escape the pangs of hunger. They are drinking filthy and muddy water, and strike their stomachs and their heads in great agony . . . some of them simply stare at you when you see them,-their poor lightless eyes, so deeply sunk in their sockets, through which their death agonies are expressed, haunt you day and night . . . Numberless such skeletons are lying down everywhere, and dying away without even a groan or sigh, for they have no strength even for that.[52]

---

52 Dongre, R.K. and J.E. Patterson. *Pandita Ramabai: A Life of Faith and Prayer.* Madras, India. The Christian Literature Society. 1963. Pages 20–21.

Despite the overwhelming need, however, Ramabai explained that the mistrust and hostility toward Christianity was such that many were not willing to accept her help— just as her own parents had responded to their spiral into poverty and starvation by redoubling their dedication to the Hindu gods and the promises of the holy books.

> It is hard work to gather and save girls and young women. Their minds have been filled with such a dread toward Christian people that they cannot appreciate the kindness shown to them . . . They cannot understand anyone would be kind to them without some selfish purpose . . . The enemy is very busy in starting bad reports about this work among people around us, . . . And say, 'Why does Ramabai take all these animals to her home; what is she going to do with them? 'Yes, we see, she is taking them to make Christians, and outcastes of them and make money and fill her purse!"

Even when she had persuaded some to return with her, the filthy, diseased, and exhausted famine victims had such a bad smell and were regarded with such horror by others that people were unwilling to share train compartments with them, or to rent houses to them. "But though thus despised and rejected by society," Ramabai wrote, we know that He who came to save the fallen and call sinners to repentance—the Man acquainted with sorrows and the Friend of the poor sinners—is with us . . . .We consider it a great privilege to be counted worthy to be despised by the world like our Master and thank God for His goodness."[53]

The explosive growth of the Mukti Mission and the hundreds of women and children who flooded into it during the two famines are even more striking because during both of them, Ramabai and her colleagues followed the same principles of faith she had followed in buying the farm. Although, as we have seen, she wrote a great deal about the need and about the work in articles and letters that made their way around the world, she never held a fundraising drive or sent a direct appeal for funds or did anything other than ask God to supply the needs of Mukti. When the first famine began in 1896, there had been no extra money beyond what was needed for the running of the mission with its forty students, but as the desperate women flooded into Mukti, the money too flooded in as answer to prayers from around the world. In 1897 alone, eighty-five thousand dollars from all around the world arrived to meet the ever-growing needs of the famine refugees and the new buildings required to house them—not to mention the workmen (usually between eighty and one hundred and twenty) who would build those buildings and who

---

53   Ibid. 22.

would expect to be paid. The farm was increasingly self-supporting in good times, but famine, drought, and epidemic attacked the Mukti Mission just as they attacked the rest of India, withering crops and drying wells. The second great famine was an entirely different test of faith for Ramabai and her coworkers, because this time the famine and drought affected the region in which Mukti was located. Instead of traveling by train or cart to other districts to bring back famine refugees, Ramabai now found herself surrounded by dry wells and shriveled fruit trees. She had grown used, in this ministry of faith, to not knowing where the money for the next day would come from. Again and again there had been no money to buy food for the following day or the following week, with new famine victims still pouring in. Again and again God had supplied the money in answer to prayer. A check would come in the mail, a visitor would arrive with a donation—once Ramabai was at a train station, knowing there was no money for the urgent needs facing Mukti, and she had felt compelled to miss the train she had planned to take and wait for the next one. When it pulled in, a woman getting off the train hurried over to her and thrust a large sum of money into her hands.

During the second famine, Ramabai and her close circle of Christian friends and coworkers faced an entirely new test of their faith—not knowing where even the water for the next day was to come from, and going to bed with the image in mind of the bottoms of the wells, clearly visible below just inches of remaining water, praying for God to send water. They experienced desperate women begging for paid work when they had no money, and for food when they did not have enough for themselves. The Mukti prayer circle would gather and pray earnestly for God to meet the need. And again and again, He did.

"I am spared trouble and care, casting my burdens upon the Lord," Ramabai wrote. "We are happy, getting our daily bread directly from the hand of our Heavenly Father . . . having no bank account anywhere, no endowment or income from any earthly source, but depending altogether upon our Father God, we have nothing to fear from anybody, nothing to lose, and nothing to regret. The Lord is our Inexhaustible Treasure."[54]

Much like George Mueller, whose testimony had inspired Ramabai to trust God for the initial purchase of Mukti and to seek to give India a testimony of God's faithfulness like the one Mueller had given England, Ramabai was by no means careless or reckless with money. Instead, she was intimately involved in every aspect of the economy of the Mukti mission, and it was conducted without waste and with remarkable efficiency and

---

54   Ibid. 75–76.

resourcefulness. But like Mueller, Pandita Ramabai preferred to give away the money saved through such careful administration, rather than to save it up for a possible future need. She believed that it was important for her and her fellow believers at Mukti to be generous givers, not simply receivers, and during the second great famine, she led the way by giving away a tenth of all the money that came into the mission. Many Christian young women at Mukti followed suit, sending money to relief efforts in China, sponsoring needy orphans in Armenia, sending money to the needy in neighboring villages and around the world. One group of Mukti residents went without one meal a week, regularly, and collected the money that would have paid for the meal to give. "Our girls are learning lessons in prayer and faith," Manorambai, Pandita Ramabai's daughter, would write. "God does not send us money for a whole year in advance, nor for a month, nor for even a week . . . Our bookkeepers have learned to calculate just how much is needed day by day. They are trusted not to talk about the accounts to any who are not in their class, but we sometimes hear such remarks as this, "What shall we do for tomorrow?'" Often, Manorambai recorded, the response would be for a small group of young women from the bookkeeping and accounting departments to kneel together in prayer, asking God for what would be needed the next morning.[55]

Of course, money and provisions were not the only new challenges presented by the arrival of waves of famine refugees. Instead of the handful of comparatively privileged women, seeking an education, that had been the earliest members of Ramabai's home for widows, among this vast influx of new residents were many who were completely illiterate, and many who had no interest in Christianity whatsoever. Some of these were devout Hindus, while others were thieves and prostitutes. Many who were rescued died, already being too weak from starvation to recover—just as Ramabai's own mother had once died despite her daughter's urging her to eat the food for which she had, at last, begged, breaking her promise to her father. Some brought with them the terrible epidemic diseases of famine. But many survived, and Ramabai soon found she was reaching a far wider swathe of Indian women, far more quickly than she could ever have imagined would be possible. During the second famine, the wave of new arrivals for whom a place, a purpose, and a future at Mukti must be found included one hundred and fifty girls under the age of seven, five hundred between seven and fourteen, and six hundred between fourteen and twenty! None of them had received any education whatsoever.

55 Miller 106.

And so the ministry of Mukti expanded, and its different departments multiplied. There was a school for boys at a separate nearby location. There would be another school in another district, run by Ramabai's daughter. There would be a school especially for lower caste children, and a school that welcomed the children of the neighboring village. A program was added for the blind, many of whom faced an almost certain future of begging or prostitution, and who at Mukti learned to read and write Braille and to practice handcrafts and other marketable skills. Vocational training for young women was added, as was special training for the "Bible women" who would be prepared to travel from village to village, teaching the Bible to Indian women. The miracle of Mukti was that, like the five loaves and fishes of the Gospels or the generosity of the widow of Zarapheth to Elijah, Ramabai and her colleagues faced the huge need of others with no resources to share, but shared anyway. And God multiplied their generosity, causing each new challenge, each new crisis the mission faced to give birth to a whole new facet of the ministry.

The influence of the mission spilled over onto the surrounding community. In return for a promise that no liquor licenses would be granted in the surrounding area, Ramabai agreed that the mission would help run a weekly bazaar where the mission and the local residents could meet to buy and sell fruit, vegetable, cloth, and other goods. The workmen who came to build the mission's buildings, dig its wells, and labor in its fields were considered important to the mission's work, as well, and the Christians of Mukti took seriously the chance they had to both show and speak the love of Christ to these men.

The property would come to include 230 acres, growing vegetables, fruits, and grains, and supporting about one hundred each of sheep and cattle.[56] In addition, "The many industries she developed for women in her Mukti 'home' included vegetable oil presses, brick kilns, weaving hundreds . . . and a printing press."[57] Cloth was woven, dyed, and sewn into clothes at Mukti.[58] There were usually between 800 and 2000 residents, as well as a constant stream of visitors.

Ramabai's own story is only one of many heroic stories of generosity and faithfulness behind the Mukti Mission. As one biographer notes, "Her Mission was at that time unique in being interdenominational and international," and she had around twenty-five missionaries from countries all over the world serving with her.[59] But in accordance

56 Dongre 26.
57 Testimony Preface.
58 Miller 104–105.
59 Dongre 25.

with her desire to see leaders arise from among the women of India, there were also native-born Indian leaders with stories as extraordinary as her own. One special aspect of Ramabai's ministry was that, despite the international flavor of Mukti and her own gratitude to the Church of England which had first introduced her to Christ, she preserved and welcomed the cultural expressions of Indian Christians in a way many churches and missionaries of the time failed to do. She put many Christian hymns and psalms into traditional Indian chants.

The mission also became known for the "Mukti Revival," a tremendous rekindling of spiritual fervor and prayer that led to hundreds of new conversions to Christianity, and an event that occurred at the same time as, and resembled in many ways, the famous Welsh revival of the early twentieth century. "We are now seeing the results of God's work in transfigured lives marked by intercessory prayer, Bible study, and more preaching . . ." wrote a Reverend Franklin who visited Mukti during this time. Four hundred residents of Mukti committed themselves to pray regularly for others around the country. "Some friends have doubted as to how we are going to manage to pray for so many others . . ." Ramabai wrote. "When we were Hindus, we used to repeat one or two thousand names of gods daily and repeat several hundred verses from the so-called sacred books in order to gain merit . . . should we not as Christians be able to pray for many hundreds of people by name?"[60] In January of 1906, one biographer notes, the "prayer bands" of Mukti were praying among them, by name, for twenty-nine thousand Indian Christians, asking especially for God to empower them to witness for Christ. In addition, 750 believers from Mukti committed themselves to traveling into surrounding villages to share the gospel. "The Mukti revival was indeed a turning point in India's spiritual history," notes one writer.[61] The Mukti revival, like others occurring around the world in the same period of time, was sometimes criticized, doubtless with some justice, for excessive emotionalism and dramatic displays of miraculous or unusual experiences. But it left behind so much undoubted and lasting transformation of lives and communities that it remains an undeniably valuable facet of Mukti's legacy.

Bible Translation

The second of Ramabai's two great lifeworks, in addition to the founding of the Mukti mission, was the one that occupied the final fifteen years of her life: the translation and publication of a new Marathi Bible. Ramabai, who read fluently in so

---

60   Miller 89–90.
61   Ibid. 91.

many languages, and whose life had been transformed by the reading and studying of the Bible, understood as few could have done the value of a truly excellent translation that was both accurate and readable—one that made the Scriptures genuinely accessible to people in the language of their thoughts and their daily lives. The Marathi Bible then available was, she believed, so bad that it was almost a crime to offer it to people. Existing translations, she believed, "have many words which teach purely Hindu ideas of religion. There are some words which cannot be separated from idolatrous ideas. They make wrong impressions on non-Christian hearers, and if done knowingly it is dangerous and sinful to use them." She estimated that there were probably an average of five such misleading or mistranslated words or phrases in each chapter of the Bible, for an appalling total of 5,945 mistakes in the Marathi Bible. "Ought we to teach and to preach the Bible with so many mistakes?" she demanded rhetorically.[62] As a girl traveling with her parents, Ramabai had experienced the custom of reading aloud from the Puranas to people who did not understand a word of the language, but who hoped to gain merit simply by hearing them. Now, as a Christian, she understood that the Word of God was not an incantation or a mysterious ritual, but a living text that must be understood if it was to change lives and hearts.

For Ramabai, the answer was simple. A new translation of the Bible was needed, and no one could have more passion or more preparation for the task than she. The one obvious obstacle was that she read and spoke neither Hebrew nor Greek, and any translation made from English or Sanskrit or another language into Marathi would inevitably be poorer and less precise than one made directly from the original languages. But the little girl who had been so quick to learn the difficult Sanskrit her father taught her, who had found English almost too easy to learn, was now a woman who, at fifty, did not hesitate to set about teaching herself both Hebrew and Greek. She had always been an excellent scholar, and she was accustomed to studying different alphabets and radically different grammars. She studied the Biblical languages until she felt proficient enough in them both, and then she began to translate. For the remainder of her life, while continuing to supervise and fully participate in the running of the multiple locations of the Mukti mission and the life of the Mukti community, Ramabai would rise early to work on the translation, printing, and binding of the new Marathi Bible.

Up until very near the end of her life, Pandita Ramabai would rise at four or five every morning, and, after a time of prayer and Bible reading, work hard until ten at night. She

62   Ibid. 94.

devoted ten to twelve hours a day to work on the Bible translation, but she also continued supervising the work of the school, training the girls who would work on printing and binding and other aspects of the Bible publication, writing the newsletter that carried reports of the work at Mukti around the world, seeing visitors, and responding to countless other aspects of the work. Her administrative ability astonished those who visited Mukti, just as her linguistic and academic abilities had astonished the Brahmans of Calcutta decades before, and the genuine and enthusiastic interest she took in every aspect of Mukti, and her gentle patience with everyone who crossed her path, made a lasting impression on those who knew her or worked with her.

As usual, Ramabai and her colleagues and supporters relied on prayer and faith to fund the steady stream of Marathi Bibles and New Testaments that flowed out of Mukti and throughout India, all given away without charge as Ramabai believed it was wrong to profit from selling the Word of God so desperately needed by so many. There was, she said, a famine for the Word of God in India just as real as the famines that had taken so many lives, and just as she had given away all she could for famine relief, she would give away as many copies of the Bible as she could.

In 1919, two years before her death, Pandita Ramabai was awarded the rare and prestigious Kaisar-i-Hind medal, bestowed by the King of England, in his capacity as Emperor of India, on someone with outstanding achievements in uplifting the people of India.[63] But the achievement she would have celebrated far more is that, just as she had hoped and prayed, her work at Mukti outlived her—and still does. The final agonizing loss of Ramabai's life was the death of her beloved daughter, who had seemed the ideal successor for the mother whose work she had shared and helped her whole life, a few months before her own. After this devastating blow, Ramabai's own health deteriorated rapidly, and the loss of both these leaders so close together was one that might have shaken the work of Mukti to its foundations. But the many dedicated and faithful leaders who had grown up within Mukti and its network of supporters around the world ensured not only its survival but also its continued growth. Ramabai had longed and prayed to create something far bigger than herself, something that would reach far beyond herself in both space and time. She wanted to plant a seed that might grow into a tree that would grow and spread long after her own death, and that desire was granted. Today the website of Mukti Mission celebrates the fact that "Over 100,000 women and children have received hope, healing, and life at Pandita Ramabai Mukti Mission since 1889," and

---

63   Ibid. 112.

describes the many different ministries of today's Mukti Mission, carried out under a Board of Directors by committed staff at several different locations.

Pandita Ramabai died on April 5, 1922. Not only throughout Mukti but also throughout India, widows and children who had not been cared for or valued by anyone until their lives were touched by Ramabai wept for the woman who, like the Master she served, had looked with compassion on the outcast, the voiceless, and the unwanted. Even though her Christian friends celebrated her heavenly meeting with her Savior and her reunion with her beloved daughter, who had died less than a year earlier, countless tears were shed for Pandita Ramabai around the world. A constant stream of visitors poured into the Mukti church to pay their respects to a woman whose fearless generosity and faith in God had saved so many lives in times of famine.

Three years before Ramabai's death, in 1919, another famine had added to the miseries of India during a time of virtually global economic depression in the wake of World War I. For the third time, hundreds of people had besieged Mukti in search of refuge and relief, begging for work to earn the food that could keep them alive through the famine. One day, looking at the crowd of gaunt and desperate famine victims crowded around Mukti to wait for work or pay or food, a man observed "If Bai did not pay so much money to these people she could build a very big bungalow." Another bystander replied, in words that might have been Pandita Ramabai's epitaph, "Bai is building bungalows in heaven."[64]

---

64 Ibid. 111.

CHAPTER 10
Mary MacLeod Bethune
DEPART TO SERVE

She was stunned. The blood pounded in her ears as she felt the cruel disappointment, the bewildering injustice, the bitter irony, slam into her like a freight train. Seven years! For seven years she had been studying, training, praying, and preparing. For even longer than that, she had felt so certain she was on the right road.

The pictures flashed through her mind—everyone in her hometown crowded around the train station to wave her off, herself walking across the stage to receive her diploma, the long nights studying, praying, planning. Surely it could not all have been for nothing! The need was so great, and she had longed to fill it since she was a child. Surely it was impossible to imagine anyone better qualified. Yet now, after seven years of higher education, she had been rejected by the very church of which she was such a faithful and zealous longtime member. She was not, after all, qualified to serve as a missionary to Africa. Because she was black. There was no place, the board regretted to inform her, for a Negro missionary in Africa.

She was no stranger to the pervasive racism that was the defining characteristic of American life for every black man, woman, and child—even those who had not, like her, been born to former slaves in South Carolina. And she knew all too well that the church was no refuge from it. Still, it was a blow to learn that a young Christian black woman with a gifted mind and an astounding work ethic could be the only African American student graduating in a class of hundreds from a world-renowned Bible school—but could not be a Presbyterian missionary to Africa. It was the one thing she had longed and worked for since she was a little girl, and now it was not to be.

But she was no quitter, and she refused to waste any time or energy on anger, resentment, or self-pity. Her name was Mary MacLeod Bethune, and she recognized and accepted immediately what America would one day realize: her true calling was not to the children of Africa, but to the children of America. There were countless African American children born into nominal freedom, but also into desperate poverty, ignorance, oppression, and injustice. They were owed something better. Mary MacLeod Bethune turned away from the distant continent she had dreamed of, and looked toward the numberless black children of America. She never looked back.

Childhood and Family

Mary was the fifteenth of seventeen children, and the first born free to former slaves Samuel and Patsy MacLeod, who lived in a tiny log cabin in South Carolina. In a photograph of the cabin, the structure appears so small that it is hard to picture more than two people living there, let alone Mary's parents, grandmother, and so many siblings—especially since the MacLeods were known for their hospitality and often had visitors. Like so many nominally freed slaves who would end up trapped in the dead-end system of sharecropping, the MacLeods still worked for their former masters. But they were determined to own their own land. They worked and saved with relentless determination, and eventually were able to buy five acres of their own land, on which they built the cabin in which Mary was the first of their children to be born.[1] In later years, as the family grew and pooled its resources, they would be able to buy thirty more acres.

The MacLeods were natural leaders in the black community, and their home was a refuge and a center of gravity not only for their own large family but also for the community of freed slaves around them. Despite raising seventeen children on very little money in a tiny cabin, Patsy MacLeod was known for the cleanliness and order of her home, and both she and her husband taught their children the value of working hard, pursuing excellence, and serving others. The family arose at 5 AM and headed out to the cotton field to work—young Mary was the family's champion picker by the time she was nine, able to pick 250 pounds of cotton a day.[2] The MacLeods had a sense of destiny, of the importance of the moment in history they occupied as the first generation of black Americans after slavery. They were known for helping young mothers, and for serving as advocates for others as they could, even participating in the local justice system. As Beverly Johnson-Miller writes, "many people found the McLeod home a refuge filled with spiritual faith, integrity, compassion and human care."[3]

---

1   Colman, Penny. *Adventurous Women*. NY. Henry Holt. 2006. Page 86.
2   Ibid. 87.
3   Johnson-Miller, Beverly. "Mary MacLeod Bethune." Database: "Christian Educators of the Twentieth Century." Talbot School of Theology; Biola University. https://www.biola.edu/talbot/ce20/database/mary-mcleod-bethune.

The center of the MacLeods' life and home was their Christian faith. They were leaders and faithful members of the local Methodist church, and led their family in daily prayer. They welcomed circuit-riding ministers, and especially treasured the opportunity to hear the Bible read aloud by those who were literate. For the MacLeods, the fact that they had lived to see the end of slavery demonstrated the active care and faithfulness of God in their lives, and no matter how difficult their own circumstances, they believed in the very real presence and guidance of God.

Young Mary had a formative experience of her own as a young child, one that would become as foundational to her life as the end of slavery had been to her parents, and which would reinforce two beliefs that had already taken root in her mind as she listened to the occasional literate circuit rider reading from the Bible. One conviction was that the magical gift of reading and writing was one of the most precious known to man, and the other was that the God Who had delivered His people from Egypt and sent His Son to redeem those who believed in him still acted in response to the prayers of His people.

It happened when Mary had gone with her mother to the home of her employer, the white family who had once owned Mary's parents. While her mother worked, Mary and the family's white granddaughters went to play in a playhouse full of books. Mary was drawn to the books, but a white girl informed Mary, quite correctly, that she, Mary, could not read. The white girl directed her away from the books filled with mysterious words, and pointed her to the picture books instead. Mary MacLeod would never forget this moment. She began to pray that she might one day learn to read and write. As Beverly Johnson-Miller writes:

> This experience left Mary with life-altering self-awareness, a determination to read, and a drive to engage and unleash the power of God (Newsome, 1982, 47-49). Through this event, prayer became central to Mary's life as she prayed continuously for the opportunity to learn to read and write.[4]

Education

When Mary was ten years old, her prayers were answered. The Board of Mission for Freedmen of the Trinity Presbyterian Church opened a school for the children of freed slaves, headed by an enthusiastic young black woman who visited families in the area to recruit students. Mary would always remember the teacher's knock on the MacLeods' cabin door as a turning point in her life. She started school with joy, undaunted by

---

4   Ibid.

walking ten miles a day to get there and back, or by facing the harassment of white children along the way. As well as joy, however, she felt a weighty sense of responsibility. It could not be by chance that she had the opportunity to become the one educated person in her family—the one whose labor was spared from the cotton fields despite the family's unrelenting need for income. God had a unique purpose for her life.

Mary devoured the lessons in reading, writing, and basic math offered at the mission school, but her three years there also shaped her life in other ways. One of Mary's earliest Bible lessons, on John 3:16 and God's offer of redemption to anyone who believed in Christ, gave her a transforming vision of the equal value of all lives in the sight of God.[5] And the example of her beloved teacher, who had devoted her life to the service of God and of the most needy of her fellow human beings, fired Mary's imagination with the desire to find a similar missionary purpose for her own life.

Meanwhile, Mary saw almost immediately how God could use her new abilities to bless others. As she would later recall, "As soon as I understood something, I rushed back and taught it to others at home."[6] She could now read the Bible to her family each day, so that they didn't have to wait for the visits of literate ministers to hear it. Because she could now do basic arithmetic, she could sometimes protect them and others from the financial exploitation and fraud that many whites used routinely in their transactions with blacks—especially because it could be more than one's job, or even physical safety, were worth to speak up. On one memorable occasion, Mary accompanied her father to the cotton gin to sell cotton. The white man operating the scales announced that Mary's father had brought 280 pounds of cotton, but Mary could see that the scales actually read 480 pounds. She spoke up, pointing out what the scales read. Her father must have held his breath waiting for the white man's reaction; it was a bold and dangerous thing for any black person to point out a white man's mistake, much less to accuse him of cheating. But this time Mary's youth and gender protected her. The white man met her eyes for a long moment, then admitted that she was right and he had "made a mistake." Her father was paid a fair price for his cotton, perhaps for the first time ever. It was a moment Mary would always remember, and it strengthened her growing conviction that the way forward for her people was through education. Only if they, too, had the power to read, write, add, and subtract would they be able to build the kind of future that people like her parents were working so hard to give their children.

5　Ibid.
6　Colman 88.

During her years at the Presbyterian mission school, Mary attended the Presbyterian church instead of her family's Methodist congregation, and as a young teenager she officially joined it. She was occasionally invited to speak at Sunday School conventions and other events, and her latent talents for public speaking and debate began to emerge. Mary's sense of calling and stewardship grew, and she began to pray earnestly that God would show her His appointed direction for her life, and how He wanted to use the gifts He had entrusted to her.

When a visiting preacher issued an appeal for missionaries to carry the gospel to Africa, Mary believed her prayers had been answered. Every day in the MacLeod household had ended not only with hymn-singing and evening prayers but also with stories about life in Africa told by Granny Sophia, whose mother had known life in an African village before being sold into slavery. "The drums of Africa still beat in my heart," Mary would write one day.[7] Now everything in Mary's life and heart seemed to draw her toward the vast continent beyond the sea. She dedicated herself to a future sharing the gospel in Africa— not with a fleeting emotional impulse, but with a sense of purpose and conviction that would shape her life for the next seven years. She had no idea how she would get to Africa—she would require further education to prepare her for such a ministry, and there was no way her family could afford it. No way at all seemed open; her family had recently had to go into debt to buy a mule after the death of their old one, and there was not a penny to spare. Mary spent a year at home with her family, and the cotton fields seemed to close in around her. "I used to kneel in the cotton fields and pray that the door of opportunity should be opened to me once more," Mary would remember.[8]

Mary's prayers were answered again. A wealthy Quaker woman offered to fund a scholarship that would pay for the gifted young woman's education at Scotia Seminary in North Carolina. Despite its name, a seminary at this time was a private school, often for girls, and Scotia Seminary was a school especially for young black women.

Mary MacLeod seized with both hands the amazing opportunities offered in her new life. Reading great novels, participating in a debating society, singing in the choir, serving in every leadership role available to a student—whatever could be done by a student at Scotia, Mary did. She was determined to learn everything she possibly could, and during her years at Scotia the limits of her world expanded in all directions. The little girl who had grown up in a miniature log cabin now expected to spend her life on

7   Ibid. 87.
8   Ibid. 88.

a vast and distant continent, and she was hungry for knowledge of a wider world. Her time at Scotia also showed that she had a gift for leadership—a capacity to galvanize, organize, and inspire others. Even the teachers and staff of the school welcomed Mary's suggestions and input as she grew older, and incorporated some of her suggestions into the school's program. There were both black and white teachers, and the school seemed to Mary like an island of sanity and kindness in the sea of racial prejudice and oppression. Her teachers at Scotia, she said, "taught that the color of a person's skin has nothing to do with his brains, and that color, caste, or class discrimination are an evil thing."[9]

After graduating from Scotia, Mary completed a two-year course of study at the world-famous Moody Bible Institute in Chicago. She was the only black student in a student body of somewhere between six hundred and a thousand. But her experience at Moody was, for Mary, a transformative and strengthening glimpse of the possibility of racial harmony through the power of the gospel. The classes, the chapel services, the hands-on service and outreach in the community, the times of prayer, and the rich network of friendships—including a close one with D.L. Moody himself—gave Mary ever greater confidence that she was on the right track in preparing for missionary service. And the rare experience of acceptance and equality among at least a few white Christians confirmed for her that the truth of the gospel offered hope and freedom for men and women of all races. She drew a lifelong strength and hope from this experience, and she would need them.

"The Greatest Disappointment of My Life"

For it was after graduating from Moody Bible Institute and applying for missionary service with the mission board of her Presbyterian church that Mary suffered the most staggering disappointment of her life. Seemingly it had never occurred to her during the years of preparation that the very church which had opened the school where she had learned that John 3:16 meant that God valued the lives of all human beings, the very church that had welcomed her into membership, might consider her disqualified from serving the people of her ancestors in Africa simply because she was black. It was a bitter blow, and she would never forget the wounding rejection. "The greatest disappointment of my life," Mary would call it. "Those were cruel days."[10]

But the deep roots that had been planted by Mary's parents and nourished by her years of preparation and faith stood her in good stead now, and held her upright through

9   Ibid. 89.
10   Ibid. 90.

the storm. With the resilient faith and courage that would characterize her all her life, she swallowed her disappointment. She had seen God's hand shaping her life when the school opened in Mayesville, South Carolina, and when she had been offered five years at Scotia Seminary. She saw it now, even through the injustice and disappointment. She had thought God was preparing her for the children of Africa, but apparently He had been preparing her for the children of America—for children like her, the first generation of black Americans born into freedom, but neglected, impoverished, oppressed, and without the extraordinary support and opportunities she had been given. She knew there were many others praying in the cotton fields for opportunity, as she had done. Hers would be a missionary life—placed at the disposal of God for the service of others, undeterred by poverty, hard work, rejection, and persecution. But she would not be called a missionary. She would be called a teacher. She would give other children the life-changing gift of education that had been given to her.

Becoming a Teacher, a Wife, and a Mother

Mary MacLeod served as a teacher in schools opened specifically to serve poor black children, first in Augusta, Georgia (under a former enslaved woman who became a pivotal mentor) and then in Sumter, South Carolina. The former slave, Lucy Craft Laney, who was the founder of Mary's first school, gave Mary fresh inspiration and courage for the future. "From her I got a new vision: my life work lay not in Africa but in my own country," Mary would write.[11] It was characteristic of Mary that she wasted no time and none of her emotional energy on grieving her disappointment or resenting the injustice that had caused it. Instead, she threw herself into her new life. She poured her heart, her passion, and her energy into the mission of bringing hope and truth to the impoverished blacks of the rural South. Not only did Mary work hard teaching reading, writing, and math during the week, but she also spearheaded Sunday afternoon gatherings for Bible teaching and hymn-singing. Already, the holistic vision that would characterize her lifework—a vision for seeing the gospel transform and brighten every aspect of life for her students and their families—was emerging in the energetic young teacher. As Miller-Johnson writes, "[S]he continued her Sunday afternoon community ministry efforts working hard to ignite a passion for education, religion, and social advancement amongst the black population. Mary's continued sense of divine destiny could be seen in her missionary zeal and total submersion in her work."[12]

---

11   Ibid. 90.
12   Johnson-Miller.

Mary met Albertus Bethune in Sumter, South Carolina, and married him in May 1898. The couple moved to Savannah, Georgia for Albertus's job, and when Mary found she was pregnant she set aside her plans to find a new teaching post there. But when the young couple's son was nine months old, the Bethunes moved to Palatka, Florida, where both Albertus and Mary could work in a church and mission school. During their time there, Mary helped expand the school to reach a greater number and a wider age range of children and young people, as well as starting an outreach in the local jails. Like her parents before her, Bethune recognized the tremendous social injustice that ensnared African Americans, and knew that it must be attacked on many fronts at once if headway were to be made. But she continued to feel that, after the Christian gospel, it was education that was most important in securing a better future for black children. Always the innovator, she increasingly dreamed of starting her own school.

Starting a School

Five years after her family moved to Florida, Mary MacLeod Bethune moved to a desperately impoverished area of Daytona Beach to start a school there. She had one dollar and fifty cents to invest in the venture. Her husband would not join her for two years, meaning that she had full charge of her son as well as of the fledgling school. Threats, intimidation, and insults, as well as ridicule, greeted her plans. Her school opened with only six students besides her son. But Bethune was not surprised by setbacks and hardships; she had expected them. She knew this was only the beginning.

The early years of the Daytona Literary and Industrial School for Training Negro Girls tested every ounce of Bethune's fierce energy and relentless determination. She opened her first classroom in a rented building, and furnished it with discarded crates. She herself sat on an upturned barrel to teach. The end of the school day was only the beginning of a grueling task, as Bethune baked pies in the evening to sell, distributed leaflets advertising the school, and went from door to door raising money, as Michelle DeRusha writes, "nickel by nickel and dollar by dollar."[13]

"We burned logs and used the charred splinters as pencils, and mashed elderberries for ink," Bethune herself would remember. "I begged strangers for a broom, a lamp . . . I haunted the city dump and the trash piles behind hotels, retrieving discarded linen and kitchenware, cracked dishes, broken chairs, pieces of old lumber."[14]

---

13   DeRusha, Michelle. "Mary MacLeod Bethune: Enter to Learn, Depart to Serve." *50 Women Every Christian Should Know: Learning from Heroines of the Faith.* 252–258. Grand Rapids: MI. Baker. 2014. Page 254.
14   Colman 93.

The exhausting first two years paid off. The school grew from an enrollment of six at its opening to more than a hundred. Bethune also offered evening classes for adults, Bible studies, and "open house" events on the weekends. Not only black residents but also curious whites attended these events, and, characteristically, Bethune ignored Florida's strict segregation laws by encouraging people to sit wherever they liked instead of providing black and white seating. Not only did Bethune embrace a bold vision of racial equality but also on a more practical level, she knew that her school would need the support of both the black and white communities to succeed.

Albertus Bethune arrived in 1906 to join his wife and child, but their time together in Daytona was to be relatively short. Biographers disagree on the details, but it seems clear that Albertus was in poor health, perhaps requiring care Mary could not provide; it is also clear that Albertus (who worked as a taxi driver) did not fully share Mary's passion for the school, and that she may have irreparably damaged her marriage through her single-minded commitment to her task. Whatever combination of factors was the primary cause, Albertus ultimately returned to South Carolina, and in either 1918 or 1919, he died. Some sources suggest that he left his wife and son some ten to twelve years before his death; others believe he left only when forced by illness and died the following year. Whatever the truth of the matter—and whatever regrets Mary MacLeod Bethune might ever have come to feel—many decades of widowhood lay ahead of her.

Meanwhile, the Daytona school was outgrowing the rented building it used. Characteristically, Bethune saw the problem as an opportunity. She found a property on the edge of a black neighborhood, adjoining a garbage dump and known by the locals as "Hell's Hole." Despite its bleak location, the property was worth more than Bethune had, but the hard work she had invested in building credibility in the community paid off. The landlord accepted her meager down payment, "in small change wrapped in my handkerchief," and her promise that she could raise the rest.[15]

So Bethune built the school's future in two ways at once. She got the building started, and she also continued and expanded her efforts to build a coalition in the community who would value and support the school. Perhaps Bethune's gift for sharing her vision with others and building strong, diverse coalitions was her most unusual and important talent. She was not the kind of leader who wanted to create an institution in her own image; she wanted to be a bridge between the needs she saw and the strengths of others.

---

15 Colman 94.

Bethune succeeded in forming several advisory boards which—in a bold and unusual move—included both white and black members. Bethune did not attack the color barrier from its strongest side—black people trying to get into places and groups usually reserved for whites. Instead, she attacked its weak side—white people voluntarily attending places and events along with black. Bethune did not so much openly challenge as boldly ignore Florida's very strict segregation laws. She formed an advisory board of socially prominent white women, and another which, unusually, comprised both white and black men. The biggest name Bethune secured for her boards was James Gamble, of Proctor and Gamble. Gamble later confessed that when he received her initial letter he assumed she was white; it is likely he would never have answered had he realized she was a black woman. But when he and four guests visited her school in response to the letter, they were so impressed that all agreed to serve on the board.

With the backing and leadership of her advisory boards, Bethune succeeded in raising the money to complete the school's new building, christened "Faith Hall." At its official opening in October of 1907, the building still had a dirt floor, unplastered walls, no indoor plumbing, and very little furniture. But it was open, and it was big enough for the rapidly growing student body. The school's motto was inscribed over its doors: "Enter to Learn" over the front door, and "Depart to Serve" over the back. Bethune also founded a hospital on the same property, after visiting one of her students in the hospital after an emergency operation, and finding the girl in a corner of the porch behind the kitchen, kept away from white patients. "Even my toes clenched with rage," the usually patient Mary would recall, and with the help of two partners she started a two-bed hospital in a cottage behind the school.[16] Characteristically, Bethune believed that all aspects of her students' lives and communities must be built and healed together.

Politics and New Threats

The world outside Faith Hall was changing, and after women of all races received the right to vote in 1920, Bethune urged black men and women to vote, despite intense opposition. It cannot have been a surprise to Bethune when her success and her defiance of the segregated world around her attracted the hostile notice of a very dangerous enemy: the Ku Klux Klan. Bethune herself was absent from the school for the Klan's first

---

16 Colman 94.

visit, but she was there when they returned the night before election day. Bethune was at the school with the students and staff who lived there when darkness descended on the street. Supporters of the Klan had cut off the streetlights, and the torches of around eighty sinister hooded figures stood out against the darkness as they gathered in front of the school. They drove a cross into the ground and set it on fire, and as the flames leaped into the night the glow lit up the grounds. But the school had its own generator and Bethune had every light turned on, as if to answer the light of the torches. She stood silhouetted against her own lights and faced the Klansmen. "If you burn my buildings, I'll build them again. And if you burn them a second time, I'll build them again!" was all she said. Then Bethune, who had a rich, sweet voice, began to sing. Her terrified students joined in, and together the school sang the hymn "God will take care of us." At last the Klansmen wheeled and rode off into the night, silently.

The next morning, Bethune went to vote. From the intimidation of the night before, the opponents of the black vote shifted to delaying tactics, and Bethune and other black voters were forced to wait at the polls all day long before the poll workers ran out of excuses and had to let them vote. Both incidents were characteristic of Bethune. Always, her strength lay in perseverance—in believing that it didn't matter how long it took to do something, or how hard it was, or how many times you had to start over.

National and International Leadership

As the 1920s rolled by, Mary MacLeod Bethune became perhaps the best-known black woman in America—even in the world. In 1924 she became president of the National Association of Colored Women—the highest office open to a black woman at the time, and a valuable training ground for Bethune, who would ultimately found the eight hundred thousand strong National Council of Negro Women. Several presidents asked her for advice on issues related to black Americans, poverty, women, and education. Herbert Hoover and Franklin Delano Roosevelt appointed her to advisory positions on child welfare, home ownership, and other issues affecting the American poor and the future of African-Americans. She traveled the world, and was invited to meet the Pope, the Mayor of London, and other dignitaries. She even had the opportunity, at last, to visit Africa—a dream come true. From scavenging at the dump to baking pies to facing the Klan to advising US presidents, Bethune's perseverance and her holistic vision for her people led her step by step to an astonishing record of service and leadership.

Beverly Miller-Johnson describes Bethune's widening circle of activities:

Mary Bethune's influence extended far beyond the establishment of her school. In 1905, she organized a boy's club, in 1911, she established a hospital, in 1938, she acquired federal funds for a public housing project. Mary Bethune rallied for temperance, and made her college library available to the black community. She promoted spiritual and social transformation with her Sunday afternoon community meetings and was very active in Negro women's club work that was usually connected with churches and focused on assisting the sick, elderly, needy, and contributing to the church (Newsome, 1982, pp. 177-178).

Mary Bethune's participation in federal programs began in 1914 when she was recruited to assist the Red Cross. She managed the Florida chapter during the mid-1920s successfully organizing relief efforts following a destructive hurricane in 1928 (Newsome, 1982, pp. 189-190).

Mary Bethune promoted the development of a national coalition of organizations to work with federal agencies for the advancement of all blacks, particularly the cause of Negro womanhood by harnessing the power of women. Although she faced some criticism, at the first meeting in December of 1935, Mary Bethune persuaded these women leaders to vote in favor of a permanent organization, the National Council of Negro Women (NCNW), with Mary Bethune as the first president of the coalition (Hanson, 2003, pp. 164-172).[17]

The little girl from the South Carolina shack and the cotton fields did not always feel comfortable in the circles to which her achievements elevated her, and she grieved the harsh realities that made her the only black person in so many of the situations where she was able to make her voice heard. "I looked about me longingly for other dark faces," Bethune recalled of attendance at a meeting of the inauguration committee of Franklin Delano Roosevelt's second inauguration.

In all that great group I felt a sense of being quite alone.

Then I thought how vitally important it was that I be here, to help these others get used to seeing us in high places. And so, while I sip tea in the White House, my heart reaches out to the delta land and the bottom land. I know well why I

---

17   Johnson-Miller.

must be here, *must* go to tea at the White House. To remind them always that we belong here, we are a part of this America."[18]

Bethune faced criticism and rejection from many directions during most of her life—from those who thought her schools demeaning because they included vocational training for black students, and from those who thought them too ambitious because they included preparation for college. She was condemned from the right by those who mistrusted her alliances with left-leaning political groups, and from the left by those who condemned her willingness to work with white groups that excluded other blacks. "Love, not hate, has been the foundation of my fullness," Bethune wrote. "When hate has been projected toward me, I have known that the persons who extended it lack spiritual understanding . . . Faith and love have been the most glorious and victorious defense in this 'warfare' of life, and it has been my privilege to use them."[19]

Even during the desperate, grueling, door-to-door fundraising of her early years in Florida, the woman who had put a rejection by her own church behind her had refused to give bitterness even the smallest foothold. "If a prospect refused to make a contribution," she recalled years later, "I would say, Thank you for your time. No matter how deep my hurt, I always smiled. I refused to be discouraged, for neither God nor man can use a discouraged person."[20]

Final Years

Bethune spent the last years of her life as one of the most famous women in the world, visited by and corresponding with people of all walks of life from all over the United States. She looked across the decades with joy at the transformation of a garbage dump into the campus of a school and university, and at the progress made toward the still distant goal of racial equality. But success and prosperity always bring their own dangers, and, as her friend and biographer records, Bethune "remembered, faintly nostalgic, the less worldly attitudes of a more simple day, more selflessly consecrated to basic Christian principles." Looking at a new generation of well-dressed, confident young black women attending college, Bethune said wistfully, "you seldom see those heels now kneeling in a prayer."[21]

---

18   Holt, Rackham. *Mary McLeod Bethune*. Garden City, NG. Doubleday. 1964. Page 205.
19   DeRusha 257.
20   Marx, Jerry, and the National Park Service. "Bethune, Mary MacLeod." "Social Welfare History Project." Virginia Commonwealth University. https://socialwelfare.library.vcu.edu/eras/bethune-mary-mcleod.
21   Holt 279.

In her final decade, Bethune lived in a cottage fittingly called "The Retreat," surrounded by her son, grandson, six great-grandchildren, nieces, and friends—and by her beloved collection of elephant figurines, perhaps a nod to her undying love for Africa. She had been awarded an astonishing array of titles and honorary degrees, but she loved to be called "Mother Dear" by her growing family, and to think of herself as a mother to the black children of America she had spent her life serving.[22]

Bethune's friend and biographer wrote, "Her climb was always hopeful and she had no bitterness to shackle her." Even in her last illness, when she struggled to breathe and had frequent choking spells, she had only one answer when asked how she was. Once she could speak, she would say, "I'm wonderful."[23]

"At the end, Dr. Mary McLeod Bethune acknowledged that the work of her life was filled with divine guidance and a daily awareness of the presence of God," writes Kim Long.[24] Just five days before her death in May of 1955, the filing cabinets that had been ordered for the launch of her last great project, a foundation to fund scholarships for future students, were delivered. Shortly before her death, the students of the college she had founded gathered to sing her two favorite songs: the popular love song, "Let Me Call you Sweetheart," and her lifelong favorite hymn, "Leaning on the Everlasting Arms." And on the very day she died, Bethune sat in her favorite rocking chair on the front porch of her cottage.

She was buried on the grounds of the college she had founded, and flowers were planted on her grave. In bright, hopeful colors, they spelled out Bethune's favorite title—the word "Mother."

---

22   Holt 286.
23   Ibid. 284.
24   Long, Kim. "Dr. Mary MacLeod Bethune: A Life Devoted to Service." Forum on Public Policy. https://eric.ed.gov/?id=EJ969859.

Notes on William Tyndale

Born: c.1494

Ordained c.1521

Fled to Germany: 1524

Completed New Testament translation: 1525

Died: 1536

To Learn More:

The Hawk that Dare Not Hunt by Day by Scott O'Dell

God's Bestseller by Brian Moynahan

Tyndale: The Man Who Gave God an English Voice by David Teems

"God's Outlaw: The Story of William Tyndale." DVD. Director Tony Tew

Suggestions for Unit Studies:

Bible and Church History

Read about the extraordinary history of the Bible in English:

- http://www.greatsite.com/timeline-english-bible-history
- https://amazingbibletimeline.com/blog/q2_history_english_bible

See and read excerpts from Tyndale's New Testament:

- https://www.bl.uk/collection-items/william-tyndales-new-testament
- https://bible.org/article/william-tyndale-%E2%80%94-lasting-influence

Read about the debate between Tyndale and Thomas Moore:

- https://thomasmorestudies.org/tmstudies/DCH_Fabiny.pdf
- https://extra.shu.ac.uk/emls/moretyndale.pdf

History and Geography

Read about the history of religious wars and religious freedom in the Netherlands:

- https://www.museeprotestant.org/en/notice/protestantism-in-the-low-countries

Study the religious wars in Europe

- https://www.tomrichey.net/reformation.html

Read about student life and courses of study at
Oxford during Tyndale's student days:

- https://mtprof.msun.edu/Spr2000/MorgRev.html

Read about Henry VIII and the Reformation in England:

- http://www.bbc.co.uk/history/british/tudors/english_reformation_01.shtml
- https://www.pbslearningmedia.org/resource/5a4369fd-b9d7-4045-80dd-9c2947a17ddc/the-protestant-reformation-inside-the-court-of-henry-viii/#.WxPvHmCWxLM

Mathematics and Science

Make your own printing press:

- http://www.instructables.com/id/Desktop-Printing-Press

Social Sciences

Study the shifting economic and political trends of Tudor England:

- http://www.bbc.co.uk/history/british/tudors/poverty_01.shtml
- http://www.historyofparliamentonline.org/periods/tudors
- http://tudortimes.co.uk/politics-economy/economy

Study the wool trade between England and the Low Countries
that was vital to the economy of Tudor times:

- http://tudortimes.co.uk/politics-economy/the-english-wool-trade/economics-of-sheep-farming
- https://www.historic-uk.com/HistoryUK/HistoryofEngland/Wool-Trade
- https://midtudormanor.wordpress.com/the-wool-trade

Humanities

Study the "Northern Renaissance" art of the Low Countries:

- http://arthistoryteachingresources.org/lessons/northern-renaissance-art
- https://www.khanacademy.org/humanities/renaissance-reformation/northern-renaissance1/beginners-guide-northern-renaissance/a/an-introduction-to-the-northern-renaissance-in-the-fifteenth-century

Notes on Roger Williams

Born: c.1603

Arrived in New England: 1631

Founding of Rhode Island: 1636

Publication of "Bloody Tenent": 1644

Died: 1683

To Learn More:

Roger Williams and the Creation of the American Soul by John Barry

Finding Providence: The Story of Roger Williams by Avi

Roger Williams: Prophet of Liberty by Edwin Gaustad

God, War, and Providence by James Warren

Suggestions for Unit Studies:

Bible and Church History

Study the Protestant Reformation in England and the Puritan settlers of New England:

- https://www.museeprotestant.org/en/notice/protestantism-in-england-in-the-16th-century-separation-from-rome
- http://www.bbc.co.uk/history/british/tudors/english_reformation_01.shtml
- http://www.pbs.org/godinamerica/people/puritans.html
- https://public.wsu.edu/~campbelld/amlit/purdef.htm

History and Geography

Research the issues involved in the English Civil War and the Bloodless Revolution, and how those events affected the lives of Puritans and influenced the American Revolution. Try some of the interactive games available!

- https://www.nytimes.com/2010/07/04/opinion/04tinniswood.html
- https://historyofmassachusetts.org/how-did-glorious-revolution-affect-colonies
- http://www.bbc.co.uk/history/british/civil_war_revolution
- https://www.parliament.uk/about/living-heritage/evolutionofparliament/parliamentaryauthority/revolution
- http://www.englishcivilwar.org/p/interactive-maps.html
- http://www.bl.uk/learning/timeline/item104078.html
- http://ks3historygames.co.uk/the-english-civil-war-ks3-history

Study the perilous North Atlantic crossing on the sailing ships of Williams' day—navigation techniques, conditions on board, and weather encountered:

- https://www.penobscotmarinemuseum.org/pbho-1/history-of-navigation/navigation-18th-century
- http://bc.library.uu.nl/navigating-18th-century-sat-nav.html
- http://www.eyewitnesstohistory.com/passage.htm

Study the exploration and mapping of New England:

- http://www.google.com/url?sa=t&rct=j&q=&esrc=s&source=web&cd=12&ved=2ahUKEwjd18a

Notes on John Woolman

Born: 1720

Began first manuscript of his Journal: c. 1756

Philadelphia Yearly Meeting adopts, at Woolman's urging, formal minute urging all Quakers to free their slaves: 1758

Journey to England: 1772

Death: 1772

To Learn More:

John Woolman's Path to the Peaceable Kingdom: A Quaker in the British Empire by Geoffrey Plank

Beautiful Soul of John Woolman, Apostle of Abolition by Thomas Slaughter

The Journal and Major Essays of John Woolman, edited by Phillips P. Moulton

Suggestions for Unit Studies:

Bible and Church History

Study the life of George Fox, the founder of Quakerism:

- http://www.ushistory.org/penn/fox.htm
- https://www.georgefox.edu/about/history/quakers.html
- https://christianhistoryinstitute.org/study/module/george-fox

Study the beliefs and history of Quakerism:

- https://www.history.com/topics/immigration/history-of-quakerism
- http://www.religioustolerance.org/quaker1.htm
- https://www.racc.edu/sites/default/files/imported/StudentLife/Clubs/Legacy/vol_1/Quakers.html

History and Geography

Study the Native American tribes of the area that became
Pennsylvania, some of whom John Woolman visited:

- http://www.native-languages.org/pennsylvania.htm
- https://www.warpaths2peacepipes.com/history-of-native-americans/history-of-pennsylvania-indians.htm
- http://freepages.rootsweb.com/~florian/school-alumni/rockdoctor/vft/early-history/indian/natives.html

Study the immigration of Quakers to America, William
Penn, and the founding of Pennsylvania:

- http://www.quakersintheworld.org/quakers-in-action/282/Quakers-in-colonial-Pennsylvania
- https://www.ancestry.com/contextux/historicalinsights/quaker-life-1700s-united-states
- http://www.americaslibrary.gov/jb/colonial/jb_colonial_penn_1.html
- http://quaker.org/legacy/wmpenn.html
- http://www.ushistory.org/penn/bio.htm

Study the "French and Indian War" and its relationship to the
hemisphere-wide imperial conflict between France and England:

- https://www.youtube.com/watch?v=VJ31VuyTWB4
- https://www.eduplace.com/ss/socsci/books/content/ilessons/51/ils_gr5b_u4_c07_l1.pdf
- https://2001-2009.state.gov/r/pa/ho/time/cp/90614.htm

Study the relationship and conflict between Native Americans and
colonists in Pennsylvania, including the French and Indian War:

- https://explorepahistory.com/story.php?storyId=1-9-6
- https://hsp.org/education/unit-plans/the-french-and-indian-war-in-pennsylvania
- https://www.pennlive.com/life/2017/07/french_and_indian_war_sites.html

Mathematics and Science

Learn how to dye your own cloth eighteenth-century style:

- http://www.colonialsense.com/How-To_Guides/Crafts/Natural_Dyeing.php
- http://www.larsdatter.com/18c/dye.html

Study the textiles and dyeing industry and why it concerned Woolman:

- https://www.lib.umn.edu/bell/tradeproducts/indigo
- https://www.ancestry.com/contextux/historicalinsights/indigo-south-carolina
- https://liberalarts.utexas.edu/hemispheres/_files/pdf/eti/Indigo.pdf

Social Sciences

Study the global silver trade that troubled Woolman, and about the rise of a global trade-based economy:

- http://afe.easia.columbia.edu/neh/course7/activity4.html
- https://www.oxfordbibliographies.com/view/document/obo-9780199730414/obo-9780199730414-0084.xml
- http://users.pop.umn.edu/~rmccaa/colonial/hacienda/slides.htm
- https://15minutehistory.org/2016/04/13/episode-81-the-trans-pacific-silver-trade-and-early-modern-globalization
- https://ipfs.io/ipfs/QmXoypizjW3WknFiJnKLwHCnL72vedxjQkDDP1mXWo6uco/wiki/Global_silver_trade_from_the_16th_to_18th_centuries.html

Humanities

Study the music, dances, and characteristic beadwork of the Delaware, one of the major Native American Tribes of Pennsylvania:

- http://delawaretribe.org/blog/2013/06/26/social-dances
- https://nativeamericans.mrdonn.org/northeast/lenape.html

Read some of the writings of leading Quaker William Penn, founder of Pennsylvania:

- https://www.biblio.com/william-penn/author/42543

Notes on Richard Allen

Born: 1760

Free: 1793

Settled in Philadelphia: 1786

Founding of Free African Society: 1787

Publication of First Pamphlet: 1794

Dedication of Bethel Church: 1794

Creation of African Methodist Episcopal Church: 1816

Ordination: 1816

Death: 1831

To Learn More:

Freedom's Prophet: Bishop Richard Allen, the AME Church, and the Black Founding Fathers by Richard S. Newman

My Soul has Grown Deep: Classics of Early African-American Literature, ed. by Edgar Wideman

Suggestions for Unit Studies:

Bible and Church History

Study the Second Great Awakening, a revival during which Allen became a Christian and preached often:

- https://www.ushistory.org/us/22c.asp

Study Methodist circuit riders in colonial North America:

- www.gcah.org/history/circuit-riders
- https://christianhistoryinstitute.org/magazine/article/knock-em-down-preachers

Study the founding and history of the AME church:

- https://www.bethelame62901.org/history-of-the-african-methodist-episcopal-church.html
- https://www.learnreligions.com/ame-church-history-struggle-against-bigotry-699931

- https://www.ame-church.com/our-church/our-history

History and Geography

Study the history and importance of Philadelphia,
the first capital of the United States:

- https://www.history.com/topics/us-states/philadelphia-pennsylvania
- https://constitutioncenter.org/blog/how-philly-lost-the-nations-capital-to-washington

Use the interactive map of Philadelphia to learn
more about the city during Allen's time:

- https://teachingamericanhistory.org/resources/convention/map

Study Dr. Benjamin Rush, Allen's friend and the physician
involved in fighting the yellow fever epidemic:

- https://www.americanheritage.com/paradoxical-doctor-benjamin-rush
- https://www.npr.org/2018/09/02/643764214/rush-the-other-founding-father-from-philadelphia-named-benjamin
- https://www.cbsnews.com/news/benjamin-rush-the-founding-father-you-may-have-never-heard-of-2018-09-22

Study the history of slavery in the northern colonies:

- https://teachinghistory.org/history-content/ask-a-historian/25577
- https://courses.lumenlearning.com/boundless-ushistory/chapter/slavery-in-the-colonies

Study the Haitian revolution, which had a huge impact on the American
debate on race and slavery, and on Philadelphia in particular:

- https://www.blackpast.org/global-african-history/haitian-revolution-1791-1804
- https://history.state.gov/milestones/1784-1800/haitian-rev
- https://today.duke.edu/showcase/haitideclaration/haitiusa.html
- https://scholar.library.miami.edu/slaves/san_domingo_revolution/revolution.html
- https://www.history.com/news/louisiana-purchase-price-french-colonial-slave-rebellion

Study the War of 1812, an important event of Allen's lifetime:

- www.american-historama.org/1801-1828-evolution/facts-about-war-of-1812.htm
- https://www.khanacademy.org/humanities/us-history/the-early-republic/politics-society-early-19th-c/a/the-war-of-1812

Mathematics and Science

Study yellow fever and the eventual discovery of its cause and vaccine:

- https://www.historyofvaccines.org/timeline/yellow-fever
- https://www.healthline.com/health/worst-disease-outbreaks-history#3
- www.americaslibrary.gov/jb/progress/jb_progress_yellow_1.html
- https://news.virginia.edu/content/walter-reed-and-scourge-yellow-fever

Study long-staple and short-staple cotton:

- https://www.historynet.com/seeds-of-conflict.htm
- https://nature.berkeley.edu/departments/espm/env-hist/studyguide/chap7.htm
- tmsextendedresource.weebly.com/unit-3-slavery1.html

Social Sciences

Make your own working model of a cotton gin:

- https://jimsfortheloveofhistory.blogspot.com/2013/06/making-working-model-of-eli-whitneys.html
- https://www.scienceproject.com/projects/intro/elementary/EX038.asp
- https://classroom.synonym.com/build-model-cotton-gin-12046857.html

Humanities

Study the idea of the "republic of letters" and the importance of reading and rhetoric in colonial America and the early United States:

- https://www.neh.gov/humanities/2013/novemberdecember/feature/mapping-the-republic-letters
- https://www.iep.utm.edu/amer-enl
- https://www.constitutionfacts.com/founders-library/founders-reading-list

Study literacy and education in colonial America:

- https://dohistory.org/on_your_own/toolkit/writing.html
- https://www.umass.edu/umpress/title/learning-read-and-write-colonial-america

Study the Jewish historian Josephus, whose works Allen owned and studied:

- https://www.britannica.com/biography/Flavius-Josephus
- https://www.pbs.org/wgbh/pages/frontline/shows/religion/portrait/josephus.html

Notes on Hannah More

Born: 1745

Internationally successful play "Percy" published: 1777

Death of David Garrick: 1749

Wilberforce's visit to Cheddar Gorge: 1789

Blagdon Controversy: 1799-1802

Died: 1833

To Learn More:

Fierce Convictions: The Extraordinary Life of Hannah More, Poet, Reformer, Abolitionist by Karen Swallow Prior

Suggestions for Unit Studies:

Bible and Church History

Study the history of Methodism and evangelicalism in the Church of England:

- https://www.museeprotestant.org/en/notice/protestantism-in-england-in-the-xviiith-century
- https://www.christianity.com/church/church-history/timeline/1701-1800/evangelical-revival-in-england-11630228.html

Study the "Clapham Sect" of which More was a member:

- https://www.christianity.com/church/church-history/timeline/1701-1800/the-clapham-group-11630311.html
- https://www.thisisclapham.co.uk/sw4_local/the-clapham-sect
- https://themelios.thegospelcoalition.org/article/the-social-work-of-the-clapham-sect-an-assessment

History and Geography

Study the London of More's day:

- https://www.theguardian.com/books/2012/mar/25/london-eighteenth-century-jerry-white-review
- https://www.bl.uk/restoration-18th-century-literature/articles/the-rise-of-cities-in-the-18th-century

Study the Industrial Revolution in rural England:

- https://www.history.com/topics/industrial-revolution/industrial-revolution
- www.bbc.co.uk/history/british/victorians/speed_01.shtml

Study the French Revolution and its effect on British politics and culture:

- www.nationalarchives.gov.uk/pathways/citizenship/struggle_democracy/revolution.htm
- https://www.bl.uk/romantics-and-victorians/articles/the-impact-of-the-french-revolution-in-britain
- www.historyhome.co.uk/c-eight/france/impactfr.htm

Study the Abolitionist movement in England:

- www.bbc.co.uk/history/british/empire_seapower/antislavery_01.shtml
- https://www.nationalarchives.gov.uk/pathways/blackhistory/rights/abolition.htm

Study some of More's most famous friends:

- https://www.samueljohnson.com/briefbio.html
- https://www.bl.uk/people/samuel-johnson
- https://thegreatthinkers.org/burke/introduction
- https://www.thestage.co.uk/features/2018/david-garrick-theatres-first-star-brought-respectability-stage

Study the Bluestockings and their importance:

https://www.britannica.com/topic/Bluestocking-British-literary-society
https://artuk.org/discover/stories/who-were-the-bluestockings

Mathematics and Science

Study the mining and refining industries of England in the early Industrial Revolution:

- www.miningartifacts.org/English-Mines.html
- https://www.nationalarchives.gov.uk/education/victorianbritain/industrial

Study the science of thermodynamics and its roots in the Industrial Revolution:
- www.physics4kids.com/files/thermo_laws.html
- https://www.visionlearning.com/en/library/Physics/24/Thermodynamics-I/200

Social Sciences

Study the history of British education and the educational reforms and movements of More's time:
- https://www.schoolsmith.co.uk/history-of-education
- www.educationengland.org.uk/history/timeline.html
- www.umich.edu/~ece/student_projects/growing_up/titania-edu.html
- https://www.geriwalton.com/social-climbing-through-ladies-boarding-schools
- https://18thcenturyculture.wordpress.com/tag/sunday-school
- www.workhouses.org.uk/education/early.shtml
- https://www.parliament.uk/about/living-heritage/transformingsociety/livinglearning/school/overview/in19thcentury

Humanities

Study the theatre of More's time:
- https://www.bl.uk/restoration-18th-century-literature/articles/18th-century-british-theatre
- https://www.vam.ac.uk/articles/the-story-of-theatre

Study the fashions in clothes, hats, and hairstyles More considered so ridiculous:
- https://janeaustensworld.wordpress.com/2008/02/22/bonnets-caps-and-hats-a-regency-fashion-accessory-no-lady-can-do-without/
- https://www.fashion-era.com/regency_fashion.htm
- https://www.historic-uk.com/CultureUK/Georgian-Fashion
- www.vam.ac.uk/content/articles/h/history-of-fashion-1900-1970

Study the art and social criticism of William Hogarth, who captured the social and moral range of eighteenth-century England:
- https://www.nga.gov/collection/artist-info.4363.html
- https://www.britannica.com/biography/William-Hogarth

Notes on William Wilberforce

To Learn More:
"Amazing Grace," directed by Michael Apted (movie)
"The Better Hour: The Legacy of William Wilberforce" by TWC Films (documentary)
William Wilberforce: A Hero for Humanity by Kevin Belmonte.
Amazing Grace: William Wilberforce and the Heroic Campaign to End Slavery by Eric Metaxas

Suggestions for Unit Studies

Bible and Church History

Study the evangelical movement of eighteenth-century England
* https://www.museeprotestant.org/en/notice/protestantism-in-england-in-the-xviiith-century
* https://www.christianity.com/church/church-history/timeline/1701-1800/evangelical-revival-in-england-11630228.html

Study the Clapham Sect, a group of reformers
with whom Wilberforce was associated:
* https://www.christianity.com/church/church-history/timeline/1701-1800/the-clapham-group-11630311.html
* https://www.thisisclapham.co.uk/sw4_local/the-clapham-sect
* https://themelios.thegospelcoalition.org/article/the-social-work-of-the-clapham-sect-an-assessment

History and Geography

Study the British West Indies:
* https://www.britishempire.co.uk/maproom/caribbean.htm
* https://www.bl.uk/west-india-regiment/articles/an-introduction-to-the-caribbean-empire-and-slavery
* www.bbc.co.uk/history/british/empire_seapower/trade_empire_01.shtml

Science and Mathematics

Study the process of sugar refining and the global
sugar trade of the eighteenth century:

- https://www.brighthubeducation.com/history-homework-help/92096-slavery-and-the-sugar-trade-in-the-eighteenth-century
- https://eighteenthcenturylit.pbworks.com/w/page/102439633/Sugar
- https://www.bbc.co.uk/bitesize/guides/zjyqtfr/revision/3

Social Sciences

Study the education Wilberforce would have received as the son of a
wealthy eighteenth-century English family with political aspirations:

- https://victorian-era.org/georgian-era-facts/georgian-era-education.html
- https://sites.udel.edu/britlitwiki/classical-education-in-the-eighteenth-century
- https://www.historyextra.com/period/georgian/university-student-life-history-exams-curriculum-oxford-cambridge

Study the institutions and procedure of the parliamentary system
within which Wilberforce worked much of his life:

- https://www.history.com/topics/british-history/british-parliament
- https://www.bl.uk/georgian-britain/articles/popular-politics-in-the-18th-century
- https://www.english-heritage.org.uk/learn/story-of-england/georgians/power-and-politics
- https://thehistoryofparliament.wordpress.com/category/18th-century-history/page/1

Humanities

Study the public and cultural life of London in Wilberforce's time:

- https://www.bl.uk/georgian-britain/articles/georgian-entertainment-from-pleasure-gardens-to-blood-sports
- https://www.regencyhistory.net/2013/05/when-was-london-season.html

Notes on George Mueller

Born: 1805
Arrived in England: 1829
Moved to Bristol: 1832
Started first Orphanage: 1836

To Learn More:

George Mueller: Delighted in God by Roger Steer
Autobiography of George Mueller

Suggestions for Unit Studies:

Bible and Church History

Study the Lutheran Church into which Mueller was born.

- http://www.oxfordscholarship.com/view/10.1093/0198269943.001.0001/acprof-9780198269946
- https://www.firstthings.com/blogs/firstthoughts/2013/04/the-curious-case-of-the-german-church
- http://www.bible.ca/history/eubanks/history-eubanks-40.htm

Study the "Plymouth Brethen" movement to which Mueller belonged

- http://www.plymouthbrethrenchristianchurch.org/about
- https://www.christianitytoday.com/history/issues/issue-9/back-to-new-testament-plymouth-brethren.html
- http://www.victorianweb.org/religion/plymouth.html

History and Geography

Study the Industrial Revolution, and its creation
of and impact on cities such as Bristol

- https://www.bl.uk/romantics-and-victorians/articles/manchester-in-the-19th-century
- https://www.manchestereveningnews.co.uk/news/nostalgia/way-were-cotton-king-manchester-6085736
- http://revealinghistories.org.uk/how-did-money-from-slavery-help-develop-greater-manchester/articles/fuelling-the-industrial-revolution.html

Study the humanitarian efforts that were characteristic of
the Victorian response to the Industrial Revolution:

- http://www.britishmuseum.org/research/publications/online_research_catalogues/paper_money/paper_money_of_england__wales/the_industrial_revolution.aspx
- http://www.bbc.co.uk/history/british/victorians/reforming_acts_01.shtml
- http://www.parafrasando.it/TESINE/The-victorian-age.html
- https://eh.net/encyclopedia/child-labor-during-the-british-industrial-revolution/

Mathematics and Science

Study the system of currency used in Britain during Mueller's time:

- https://www.web40571.clarahost.co.uk/currency/PreDecimal/predecimal.htm
- logicmgmt.com/1876/living/money.htm
- www.victorian-era.org/victorian-british-currency.html
- https://www.oldbaileyonline.org/static/Coinage.jsp

Study the cholera epidemics of nineteenth
century European cities such as Bristol:

- www.branchcollective.org/?ps_articles=pamela-k-gilbert-on-cholera-in-nineteenth-century-england
- https://academic.oup.com/ije/article/31/5/920/745792
- https://www.thegazette.co.uk/all-notices/content/100519
- www.choleraandthethames.co.uk/cholera-in-london/cholera-in-westminster

Social Sciences

Study the problem of orphans and the lives
of children during Mueller's time:

- https://celestetmoc.weebly.com/industrial-revolution-childhoods.html
- https://www.bl.uk/romantics-and-victorians/articles/child-labour
- https://www.mtholyoke.edu/~hicks22a/classweb/Childlabor/WebsiteChildlabor/History.html

Humanities

Study the influential depiction of orphans and
poor children by Dickens and others:

- www.bildungsromanproject.com/industrial-revolution
- https://www.bbc.com/news/magazine-16184487
- https://owlcation.com/humanities/Charles-Dickens-and-Oliver-Twist-a-Social-History

Notes on Xi Shengmo

Born: 1835

Conversion to Christianity: 1880

Opening of "Hall of the Joyful Sound": 1881

Opening of first opium refuge in a larger city: 1884

Died: 1896

To Learn More:

Pastor His by Geraldine Taylor

Suggestions for Unit Studies:

Bible and Church History

Study the history and current reality of Christianity in China:

- https://www.ft.com/content/a6d2a690-6545-11e4-91b1-00144feabdc0
- https://www.christianitytoday.com/history/2017/october/chinese-christians-western-church-should-know.html
- www.bjreview.com.cn/nation/txt/2006-12/16/content_51347.htm

History and Geography

Use the interactive map to Study the provinces of China today:

- www.yourchildlearns.com/china-map.htm

Study the Opium Wars:

- https://www.khanacademy.org/humanities/world-history/1600s-1800s/imperialism/v/opium-wars-world-history-khan-academy
- https://asiapacificcurriculum.ca/learning-module/opium-wars-china

Study the Boxer Rebellion:

- https://www.history.com/topics/china/boxer-rebellion
- www.eyewitnesstohistory.com/boxer.htm

Science and Mathematics

Study the traditional mathematics and numbering systems of China:

- https://www.storyofmathematics.com/chinese.html

Social Sciences

Study the education system of nineteenth-century China:

- https://www.metmuseum.org/toah/hd/schg/hd_schg.htm
- https://www.chinaeducenter.com/en/chistory.php
- https://www.armstrong.edu/history-journal/history-journal-education-and-government-in-the-eyes-of-a-confucian-scholar

Humanities

Study the Chinese characters and their history:

- https://ltl-school.com/chinese-alphabet
- www.ancientscripts.com/chinese.html

Study traditional Chinese music:

- https://www.chinahighlights.com/travelguide/culture/traditional-music.htm
- https://www.chinaeducationaltours.com/guide/culture-chinese-music.htm

Notes on Pandita Ramabai

Born: 1858

First Book Published: 1882

Traveled to England: 1883

Return to India: 1889

Founding of Mukti Mission: 1897

Died: 1922

To Learn More:

Pandita Ramabai: India's Christian Pilgrim by Basil Miller

Pandita Ramabai: A Life of Faith and Prayer by R.K. Dongre and J.E. Patterson

Pandita Ramabai Through Her Own Words by Meera Kosambi

Suggestions for Unit Studies:

Bible and Church History

Study the history of the Sisters of Wantage with whom Ramabai stayed in England:

- https://csmv.co.uk/community-life/history

Study the Mukti Revival:

- https://romans1015.com/mukti

History and Geography

Use the interactive map to study the different states and regions of India:
- https://mapchart.net/india.html

Study the history of British India:
- www.bbc.co.uk/history/british/modern/independence1947_01.shtml

Study the famines of British India:

- www.environmentandsociety.org/exhibitions/famines-india

Mathematics and Science

Study Srinivasa Ramanujan, a great Indian mathematician who was Ramabai's rough contemporary:

- www.mathshistory.st-andrews.ac.uk/Biographies/Ramanujan.html
- https://www.usna.edu/Users/math/meh/ramanujan.html

Social Sciences

Study the history of the caste system and modern India's efforts to reverse its effects:

- https://www.thoughtco.com/history-of-indias-caste-system-195496
- https://www.ancient.eu/article/1152/caste-system-in-ancient-india
- https://www.bbc.com/news/world-asia-india-35650616

Humanities

Study the great epics of ancient India:

- https://ancientcivilizationsapwh.weebly.com/classical-indian-epics.html
- https://www.metrowestdailynews.com/news/20181012/two-great-epics-of-india

See the Sanskrit alphabet and script:

- https://www.omniglot.com/writing/sanskrit.htm

Notes on Mary MacLeod Bethune

Born: 1875

Opening of Daytona Literary and Industrial Training School for Negro Girls: 1904

Founding of National Council of Negro Women: 1935

Died: 1955

To Learn More:

Adventurous Women by Penny Colman, NY.

Women Every Christian Should Know: Learning from Heroines of the Faith by Michelle DeRusha

Mary McLeod Bethune by Rackham Holt. Garden City, NG. Doubleday. 1964

Suggestions for Unit Studies:

Bible and Church History

Study the history of the black Methodist church in America and its circuit-riding preachers:

- http://s3.amazonaws.com/gcah.org/United_Methodist_African_American_Timeline.pdf
- https://rdw.rowan.edu/cgi/viewcontent.cgi?article=3573&context=etd
- https://www.christianitytoday.com/history/people/denominationalfounders/richard-allen.html
- https://aaregistry.org/story/the-black-church-a-brief-history/
- http://www.umc.org/who-we-are/the-hard-road-of-a-methodist-circuit-rider
- https://christianhistoryinstitute.org/magazine/article/knock-em-down-preachers

History and Geography

Study the history of cotton and its relationship to the expansion of slavery:

- https://www.archives.gov/education/lessons/cotton-gin-patent
- https://www.pbs.org/wgbh/aia/part3/3narr6.html

Make a working model of the cotton gin:

- https://www.youtube.com/watch?v=QPPfFHF7nvg
- https://www.youtube.com/watch?v=0ozOJMCnaU0

Study the fight for black voting rights in the Jim Crow South:

- http://www.crf-usa.org/black-history-month/race-and-voting-in-the-segregated-south
- http://umich.edu/~lawrace/disenfranchise1.htm
- https://www.khanacademy.org/humanities/us-history/the-gilded-age/south-after-civil-war/v/jim-crow-part-2

Study the development of education for the children of freed slaves:

- https://ldhi.library.cofc.edu/exhibits/show/somebody_had_to_do_it/struggle_for_equal_ed/devloping_education
- https://www.pbs.org/wgbh/americanexperience/features/reconstruction-schools-and-education-during-reconstruction

Study the rise of the Ku Klux Klan:

- https://www.history.com/topics/reconstruction/ku-klux-klan
- https://www.pbs.org/wgbh/americanexperience/features/flood-klan
- https://www.splcenter.org/20110228/ku-klux-klan-history-racism
- http://americainclass.org/sources/becomingmodern/divisions/text1/text1.htm

Study and perhaps debate aspects of the New
Deal using the suggested activities:

- https://www.brighthubeducation.com/history-lessons-grades-9-12/127906-the-new-deal
- https://historyproject.uci.edu/files/2017/01/New_Deal_PartOne_Grade11.pdf
- https://scetv.pbslearningmedia.org/resource/pres10.socst.ush.dww.newdeal/fdr-new-deal-programs
- https://study.com/academy/popular/new-deal-lesson-plan.html

Study the nineteenth amendment and the granting of votes to women:

- http://teacher.scholastic.com/activities/suffrage/history2.htm

- https://www.history.com/topics/womens-history/19th-amendment-1
- https://www.khanacademy.org/humanities/us-history/rise-to-world-power/1920s-america/a/the-nineteenth-amendment

Mathematics and Science

Study the cotton industry and the process of growing and milling cotton:
- https://www.agclassroom.org/teacher/matrix/lessonplan.cfm?lpid=111
- https://www.cotton.org/pubs/cottoncounts/fieldtofabric/upload/Cotton-From-Field-to-Fabric-129k-PDF.pdf

Study the boll weevil and its transformation of Southern agriculture:
- http://www.americaslibrary.gov/jb/jazz/jb_jazz_weevil_1.html
- https://www.encyclopedia.com/history/encyclopedias-almanacs-transcripts-and-maps/boll-weevil-infestation
- https://extension2.missouri.edu/g4255

Social Sciences

Study the economics of the Great Depression:
- https://www.stlouisfed.org/the-great-depression/curriculum/lesson-plans
- https://www.uwp.edu/learn/departments/economics/upload/focus_ushistory_lesson30.pdf

Study the curriculum and teaching methods of the earliest schools for the children of freed slaves:
- http://www.heritageall.org/wp-content/uploads/2013/03/Americas-One-Room-Schools-of-the-1890s.pdf

Study the important debate about the future of black education, led by Booker T. Washington on one side and W.E.B. DuBois on the other:
- https://www.pbs.org/wgbh/frontline/article/debate-w-e-b-du-bois-and-booker-t-washington
- https://futuresinitiative.org/education16/2016/10/11/washington-vs-du-bois

Humanities

Study the musical traditions of African Americans in the South during Bethune's childhood:
- https://www.sc.edu/study/colleges_schools/music/community/csam.php

- https://www.si.edu/spotlight/african-american-music/roots-of-african-american-music
- https://www.loc.gov/item/ihas.200197495
- https://www.negrospirituals.com/history.htm
- https://www.youtube.com/watch?v=8zeshN_ummU
- http://www.google.com/url?sa=t&rct=j&q=&esrc=s&source=web&cd=22&ved=2ahUKEwi3tNavn6DiAhUBhuAKHcf2Ai8QFjAVegQIBxAB&url=http%3A%2F%2Fspirituals-database.com%2Fthe-negro-spiritual%2F&usg=AOvVaw1Nl0ceefFhFuW7jM1CDEVU

Study the importance of storytelling traditions among African Americans like Bethune's beloved grandmother:

- http://theconversation.com/how-african-american-folklore-saved-the-cultural-memory-and-history-of-slaves-98427
- https://www.nypl.org/blog/2017/02/01/10-african-and-african-american-folktales-celebrate-black-history-month

List of Images

Author Unknown. *William Tyndale*. Lithography. In *Foxe's Book of Martyrs*. England, John Day. 1563. Taken from Wikimedia Commons. Accessed December 2, 2022. https://commons.wikimedia.org/wiki/File:William_Tyndale.jpg.

The Miriam and Ira D. Wallach Division of Art, Prints and Photographs: Print Collection, The New York Public Library. *Roger Williams*. New York Public Library Digital Collections. Accessed January 8, 2023. https://digitalcollections.nypl.org/items/510d47da-f21c-a3d9-e040-e00a18064a99.

Robert Smith III. *Portrait of John Woolman*. In *The Journal and Essays of John Woolman*. New York, Macmillan Company. 1922. Page 1. Taken from Wikimedia Commons. Accessed December 2, 2022. https://commons.wikimedia.org/wiki/File:John_Woolman.jpg.

Author Unknown. *Richard Allen*. Photograph. In *History of the African Methodist Episcopal Church*. Publishing house of the A.M.E. Sunday-school Union. 1891. Frontispiece. Taken from Wikimedia Commons. Accessed December 2, 2022. https://commons.wikimedia.org/wiki/File:Richard_Allen.JPG.

Author Unknown. *Engraved portrait of Hannah More (1745-1833)*. Engraving. Photograph. In *Bristol Past and Present*. Arrowsmith, 1882. Page Unknown. Taken from Wikimedia Commons. Accessed December 2, 2022. https://commons.wikimedia.org/wiki/File:Hannah_More_1882_engraving.jpg.

H. Rousseau. William Wilberforce. Lithography. Wikimedia Commons. Accessed December 2, 2022. https://commons.wikimedia.org/wiki/File:William_Wilberforce_Rousseau.jpg.

Unknown Author. *A Portrait of George Müller.* In *Men and Women of Deep Piety.* Syracuse, N.Y. Wesleyan Publishing Association. 1920. Taken from Wikimedia Commons. Accessed December 2, 2022. https://commons.wikimedia.org/wiki/File:George_Muller_portrait.jpg.

Author Unknown. *Pastor Xi.* In *After Thirty Years.* Toronto, China Inland Mission. 1895. Taken from Wikimedia Commons. Accessed December 2, 2022. https://commons.wikimedia.org/wiki/File:Pastor_Xi.jpg.

Ramabai Sarasvati. *Portrait of Pandita Ramabai Sarasvati 1858-1922.* In *The High-caste Hindu Woman.* Philadelphia: Press of the J. B. Rodgers Printing Co. 1887. Taken from Wikimedia Commons. Accessed December 2, 2022. https://commons.wikimedia.org/wiki/File:Pandita_Ramabai_Sarasvati_1858-1922_front-page-portrait.jpg.

Author Unknown. *Mary McLeod Bethune (1875-1955).* In *Women of Achievement*: Chicago, Woman's American Baptist Home Mission Society. 1919. Taken from Wikimedia Commons. Accessed December 2, 2022. https://commons.wikimedia.org/wiki/File:Mary_McLeod_Bethune_portrait.jpg.

More from Ambassador International . . .

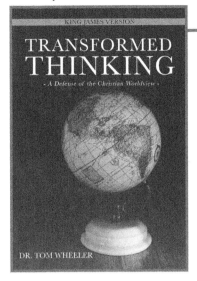

In today's world of varying religions, it's becoming more important for a Christian to know what they believe and why they believe it. In *Transformed Thinking*, Tom Wheeler clearly lays out the most fundamental beliefs of Christianity and compares them to other worldviews, providing arguments to support his beliefs. Even though this book is purposed for the classroom setting, it would be a beneficial read for any believer who wants to have a firm foundation on which to share their beliefs with unbelievers. From the beginning of the world to the inerrancy of Scripture, *Transformed Thinking* will provide you with solid answers for your faith. Available in both KJV and ESV versions.

From their earliest arrival in America 350 years ago, the Scots-Irish left a lasting legacy. The history of the United States is interwoven with outstanding personalities from the Scots-Irish diaspora and the distinctive characteristics of a people who pushed the frontiers to new horizons. This comprehensive study of the Scots-Irish in America by Northern Ireland author Billy Kennedy has created a much greater awareness of the accomplishments and the durability of the hardy settlers and their families who moved to the New World during the eighteenth century and created a civilization out of a wilderness.

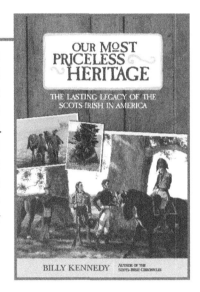

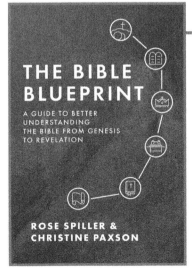

Have you ever wanted to read the Bible, but found it intimidating? Does it seem like there are contradictions in the Bible? Does the Old Testament even matter to Christians today? How do the sixty-six books of the Bible fit together? If you have asked yourself any of these questions, or others, you are not alone. *The Bible Blueprint* divides the entire Bible chronologically into six easy to read parts. It provides a basic understanding of Scripture as a complete story that links all the various books together. It gives an overview of each book, touching on highlights and some of the amazing and significant events in each, without the reader getting bogged down in the more difficult sections.

Made in United States
North Haven, CT
24 November 2023

44504060R00174